C000101711

'Finish Off w

A MISCE

Tony Lurcock grew up in Kent and studied English at University College, Oxford. He became lecturer at Helsinki University and subsequently at Åbo Akademi. Returning to Oxford, he completed a D.Phil. thesis and taught there, and in America, until his retirement. He has published numerous review articles, mainly on eighteenth-century literature and on biography.

Finish Off with Finland completes a series of books by Tony Lurcock presenting extracts from work by British observers of Finland with linking commentaries. The series was acclaimed in the *Times Literary Supplement* as 'a fascinating prism through which to view modern Finland'. Previous titles are:

Not So Barren or Uncultivated:
British Travellers in Finland 1760–1830 (CBe, 2010)

No ParticularHurry:
British Travellers in Finland 1830–1917 (CBe, 2013)

A Life of Extremes:
The British discover modern Finland 1917–1941 (CBe, 2015)

Cartoon created in response to a debate about mixed bathing,
late nineteenth centry (Raseborgs Museum, Ekenäs)

'Finish Off with Finland'

A MISCELLANY

Tony Lurcock

'She has been everywhere you can think of, and she's going to finish off with Finland. You can't go any further than that, can you?'
Henry James, *Confidence* (1879)

First published in 2021
by CB editions
146 Percy Road London W12 9QL
www.cbeditions.com

Front cover: Albert Edelfelt,
The Nyländska Jaktklubben Harbour in Helsinki, 1899

Printed in England by Imprint Digital, Exeter EX5 5HY

ISBN 978-1-909585-44-7

Contents

Acknowledgements   vii
Map of Finland   viii
Preface   x
Introduction   1

I FINNS IN ENGLAND

Mannerheim and Britain   9
Sibelius in England   30
Tancred Borenius   45
Finns in Kent: Provender   58

II TRAVELLERS IN FINLAND

William Allen   65
William Rae Wilson   77
Viipuri and the Saimaa Canal   92
Crossing the Russian Border   106

III POST-WAR VISITORS

John Grundy and the British Council   122
Diana Ashcroft   131
Walter Bacon   144
John Sykes   154
Kate Clanchy   166

IV BRITISH EXPERIENCES AND RESPONSES

The Kalevala in English   169
John Bowring and Early Finnish Poetry   184
British Sauna Experiences   194
'They can all read!'   208

V BRITISH NOVELS SET IN FINLAND

    'Paul Waineman' (Sylvia MacDougall),
        A Heroine from Finland   219
    Catherine Gavin, *The Fortress*   226
    Helen Dunmore, *House of Orphans*   237

VI POEMS IN ENGLISH ABOUT FINLAND   246

    Books, Etc. Cited   267

A detailed map of Finland can be found at Kartapaikka.

Acknowledgements

My principal debt has been to my son, Pontus, who has edited most of the chapters (the few which he did not may be self-evident). I am indebted to Patrick Salmon, Chief Historian at the Foreign and Commonwealth Office, for giving me both the opportunity and confidence to give the lecture on Mannerheim at the major symposium held in Helsinki to mark his 150th anniversary in 2017. I have had generous help from Diana Kaley, especially concerning the Borgström family, Diana Webster has given me both encouragement and advice, Pertti Hakala at the Finnish National Archives in Helsinki has been supportive and helpful, Professor Henrik Meinander gave me some revealing details about Mannerheim, and Gunnar Nyström identified people in 1820s Turku. Julia Hammett, Sandra Haill, and several other teachers from the early years of EFL in Finland kindly contributed details. Jonathan Clark has again helped with digitizing requirements.

Attempts to trace possible copyright issues of several books from extinct publishers have failed; in several instances I have provided current publishers or their agents with details about my application and its intended use, but have heard no more. Some of these failures are undoubtedly the result of Lockdown, which has entailed many of the relevant staff working from home. It has been especially difficult to discover the copyright holders of some of the poems reprinted here, several of which I snipped out of periodicals over the years, while others were passed on to me by friends, with no thought of further transmission. The publisher will rectify at the earliest opportunity any omissions or errors brought to his notice.

I am especially grateful to Kate Clanchy for allowing me to include her short memoir, as well as two poems. Extracts from John Greening's *The Silence* (2019) are reproduced by kind permission of Carcanet Press Ltd, Manchester; poems by Donald Adamson, published by Indigo Dreams, are included by kind permission of the author, and Hugo Williams gave personal permission to include 'Desire'. Extracts from *Direction North* by John Sykes, published by Hutchinson, are reproduced by permission of The Random House Group Ltd.

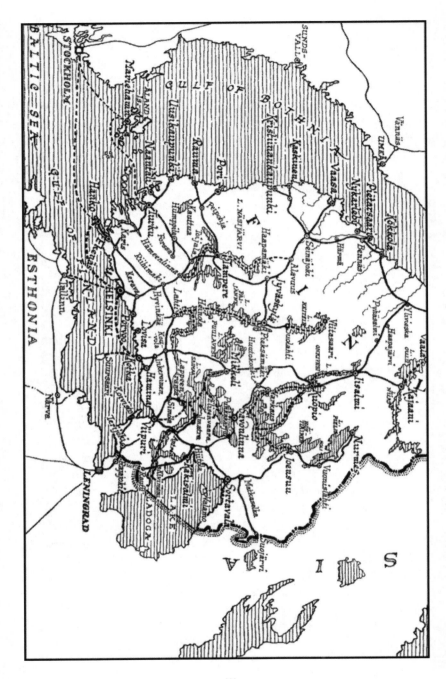

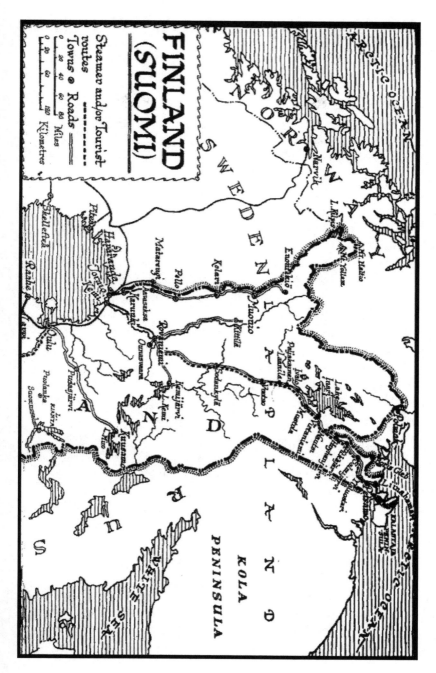

Map *c*.1930 with place names in Finnish

Preface

The varied contents of this volume come from the the mid-eighteenth century to the present day. I have retained the spelling of the earlier extracts, as well as the place names. Until the late 1930s British writers almost invariably used the Swedish rather than the Finnish place names – Helsingfors, Åbo and Tammerfors for example, instead of Helsinki, Turku and Tampere – and I have retained them in quoted passages. In my own text I have used the Finnish names, which with a couple of exceptions are now used almost universally. Ekenäs is also known by its Finnish name, Tammisaari. I have annotated with square brackets any places where there might be confusion. Vyborg, as it is now called in English, was very variously spelt by early travellers, and occasionally recent writers have used the Finnish name, Viipuri.

Several of the chapters contain material which might seem distantly familiar to one or two readers who have read any of my earlier Finland books. Some of the sauna experiences, for example, have appeared before, but here contribute to a focused presentation of how the British experience and response to the sauna have developed over two centuries. The same goes for 'Crossing the Russian Border', and for some of the observations on Finnish education.

The title of this volume is a barely-disguised statement of intent: it is the last book I shall write about Finland, and calling it a miscellany acknowledges that it does not have the coherence of the earlier volumes. The Contents page shows how I have arranged the material into some semblance of order.

All books and other authorities cited are listed. A * next to a name indicates a figure who is described in more detail in another chapter.

Introduction

This book is the sequel and conclusion to what I have termed *The Finland Trilogy*. This consists of *Not so Barren or Uncultivated* (2010), *No Particular Hurry* (2013), and *A Life of Extremes* (2015), which chronicle the discovery of Finland by the British in the eighteenth, nineteenth, and twentieth centuries, concluding in 1941.

Unlike its predecessors, this fourth volume is thematic rather than chronological. I had already been heading this way in Volume 3, expanding the theme of the first two volumes from 'British Travellers in Finland' to 'The British discover Modern Finland'. Here the pattern has been modified and considerably expanded. In the first section the arrangement of the earlier volumes is actually reversed, presenting Finnish experiences of England. Opening the book with a long essay on 'Mannerheim and Britain' immediately establishes the change.

Section 2 first reverts to the territory of the first volume of the Trilogy with two early travellers who had eluded me ten years ago; they both deserve being rescued from oblivion. They are followed by two accounts of British experiences in eastern Finland over the last two centuries.

A Life of Extremes, which was based largely on travellers' accounts, concluded in 1941. The British visitors in Section 3 also travelled in Finland, but were principally settled in one place. This gives them very different responses and much better insights than had been possible for most of the earlier travellers, ever on the move.

The starting point of Section 4 is the present day, looking back at the history and developments of some of the aspects of Finland which have been particularly noticed in Britain in recent years – the Kalevala and early Finnish literature, the sauna, and education.

I have come across more than a dozen English novels set in Finland, and have read several of them to the end. They are no better or worse, I suppose, than any random selection of novels. I have chosen three which present very different faces of Finland in style, content, and period. The poems are a selection from the large number which I have found over the years, and am still finding.

Slowly, after the war, the British presence in Finland had revived, thanks partly to the arrival of English teachers; German was losing its position as Finland's first foreign language. The Olympic Games in Helsinki in 1952 formed a turning point, putting Finland back on the map, as it were. Visitor accommodation had to be contrived for the occasion; it remained in use as tourists began to return, but the opulent style of travel writing which had been prolific since the 1890s did not revive. British writing about travel in Finland appeared not so much in dedicated volumes as in books with wider views of Finland, and in magazine articles.

Earlier accounts of Finland by the British, especially those described in *No Particular Hurry,* were written principally by tourists; the cover picture, Victor Westerholm's 'A View at Ruissalo' – ladies in white muslin out boating, with an elaborate summer villa reflected in the water beside them – hints at the contents of the volume. The contact which these travellers had with the ordinary life of Finns was very limited, and for many of them non-existent. During the inter-war period only two British writers described experiences of everyday life in Finland: Jim Ingram lived hand-to-mouth, and was more likely to have slept in a hayrick than at an inn, while Bernard Newman on his bicycle travelled on a budget of five shillings a week.

All the post-war writers in the present volume who record their time in Finland show, in different ways, some of the conditions in which Finns actually lived; Diana Ashcroft* lodged at the doctor's house in Kaajani, where her room doubled as the patients' waiting room. In Ivalo Walter Bacon* was fully involved with the work of his wife, the only dentist in the whole commune; he undertook the developing of the dental X-rays, which had to be done in the bathroom. These temporary British residents often describe happenings which are important parts of daily life, distinctively Finnish but not in any way grand or remarkable. For these reasons they have been missed, or have simply passed under the radar of earlier travellers. Mayday, or 'Vappu', with its singing and attendant student antics, is one. Ashcroft alone, among the unnumbered British travellers whose books I have read over the years, describes a Finnish family Christmas. She and John Sykes* each describe the all-engrossing traditional ceremony of student graduation from High School; the huge contrast between the austerity of 1948 and the prosperity of 1965 is sobering. Both Ashcroft and John Grundy* took part in midsummer festivals. Sykes's portrayal of the middle-class family with whom he lodged in Tampere shows his skills as a novelist; the account of his experience as a passenger in an incident of competitive Finnish driving is, quite simply, hair-raising. Many such first-hand experiences appear in these post-war accounts, with the writers now partakers rather than observers of Finnish life.

Julian Evans, reviewing *A Life of Extremes* in the *Times Literary Supplement* (27 May 2016), wrote that 'to describe the 1930s as 'little short of triumphant' [my term in the Epilogue] is to overplay a decade that had vicious undercurrents of nationalism and score-settling dating back to the Civil War of 1918.' I could certainly have made it clearer that 'triumphant' was not my own opinion, but that of the many writers whose accounts were the subject of my book. They were very far from discovering everything: none of these authors wrote of undercurrents, or would even have known what they were. That in itself reveals – exposes, one might say – something about British travellers: their lack of curiosity was one of their limitations. In writing all three books I had been aware of the superficiality of many of their observations, and on occasion, usually parenthetically, gave my own 'take' on an issue, termed by the *Vasabladet* reviewer as 'satirical asides'.

Earlier generations of travel writers had not followed any tradition of investigative journalism; readers who wanted objective information about Finland could turn elsewhere. A number of the 'non-travel books' about Finland published between the wars did provide, or purported to provide, such information. These books included few or no first-hand experiences, but provided a history of Finland, describing its institutions, economy, and politics. While some of these writers certainly did take the trouble to put themselves in the picture of Finland's wider interests and concerns, these rarely took them very far, or very deep: none of them gives any idea at all of the extent of poverty, urban slums, and tuberculosis. Neither Frank Fox in *Finland Today* (1926) nor Kay Gilmour in her excellent *Finland* (1931) has anything to say about these conditions. Fox, a journalist and former war correspondent, actually has a whole chapter on 'Finland's Social Conditions', but the nearest he comes to describing them – and it is not very near – is one sentence: 'Co-operation helps Finland considerably to a happy social life, both in keeping down prices for consumers and in helping producers to market their goods profitably.' T. W. Atchley was for several years Lecturer in English at Helsinki University; one would expect that his *Finland* (1931) would see, or even look, below the surface of the life around him. He gives a whole page to Kallio, but only to describe the church, adding simply that the area is 'inhabited chiefly by poor people'. The University is a short walk from Kallio, but if he ever walked around there and saw the slums, and how the poor people actually lived, he either did not register the experience, or else thought it unsuitable as material for his book. A year earlier Harry A. Franck, in *A Scandinavian Summer*, had stated boldly: 'There are no slums in the Scandinavian lands, no easily approachable poor'. The travel writers on Finland were not alone in wearing blinkers.

British knowledge of the Nordic nations has both increased and improved in recent decades. Beyond the illustrated brochures and weekend travel supplements, perceptions have been brought sharply up to date by the gritty realism of some of the television dramas; 'Nordic Noir' has become a brand name. Starting with *Wallander* and *The Killing* we have, thanks to BBC4 on Saturday evenings, seen a good deal of the less attractive sides of Sweden, then of Denmark, Norway, and Iceland. The political and social issues which underlie many of these series – crime, poverty, drugs and immigrants – get little coverage in the British press, and none at all in the travel pages. Awareness of these aspects of modern Finland had come mainly from the cinema, especially the films of Aki Kaurismäki. Only in 2021 did *All the Sins (Kaikki synnit)* and *Man is Room 301 (Huone 301)* arrive on BBC4, but subscription networks had already moved in on the Nordic market with two highly acclaimed Finnish crime series, *Deadwind (Karppi)* and *Bordertown (Sorjonen)*.

I have given quite detailed presentations of Finnish education in 'They can all read!'. It has been a particular interest in Britain for thirty years, but in more recent times has been rather displaced by the 'discovery' that Finland is one of the most equitable countries in the world. Not unconnected with this was 'The World Happiness Report', released by the United Nations in 2018 and confirmed in 2019 and 2020, where Finland was named the happiest country in the world. (This met with some surprise, even in Finland. A British TV reporter in Helsinki, seeking the reactions of people in the street, had this response from one incredulous interviewee: 'You mean there are places worse than this?')

It was in 2017 that Danny Dorling, Professor of Geography at Oxford University, and Annika Koljonen, a Cambridge postgraduate, met in Cambridge during a course of lectures organised by an affiliate of the Equality Trust. The following year they began their attempts 'to understand why statistics about Finland's education, healthcare, and political system were beginning to be mentioned so frequently in discussions about equality'. They decided to 'take a detailed look at one of the world's equitable countries, and along the way to work out how its people had created it and how they benefited from it.' This led, in September 2020, to the publication of *Finntopia. What we can learn from the World's happiest Country*. 'Of course,' they concede in the Preface, 'Finland is not Utopia – but its people have worked to build a better world with far more rigour and determination than any other nation on the planet.'

The first pages of this book gave me a sense of déjà vu; I felt that I had been here before when writing about British travellers in Finland in the 1930s. There the homogeneity of society was widely noted and admired: F. J. North, for example, remarked on the 'comparatively slight differences to be seen between the standards of living attained by various sections of the community'. Halliday Sutherland agreed, adding 'class distinctions are further reduced by the children of all classes meeting in secondary schools and at the universities.' The dust jacket of Sydney A. Clark's *Finland on Ten Pounds* reads in part:

> A great curiosity has been awakened concerning the post-war republic of Finland. How does Finland do it? What is her formula for success? With a population half that of London in an area three times that of England, with a language of mysterious origin and great difficulty, she has quickly set her mark on civilisation.

Clark wrote 'I hope sincerely that my praise of Finland has not exalted her to a pedestal of tedious perfection.' *Finntopia*, unlike these largely impressionistic accounts of Finland, is a rigorous, yet very readable, academic study, bristling with 'a huge range of statistics and sources'; in an Appendix it lists more than a hundred of the areas in which Finland is 'deemed to excel', provided by 'Statistics Finland'.

The reviewer of *Finland on Ten Pounds* in *The Spectator* wrote wistfully, 'It is a mixed pleasure for us who live further south to read this book.' I think that British readers of *Finntopia* will probably feel the same.

I

FINNS IN ENGLAND

Mannerheim and Britain

[Revision of a lecture given at *Mannerheim 150*, an international symposium held over two days in Helsinki in 2017]

On 16 May 1918 Mannerheim made his triumphant entry into Helsinki on horseback, at the head of sixteen thousand men. Military bands struck up, white flowers were thrown in his path, the guns of Suomenlinna fired a salute, and the crowds were cheering. Six months later he arrived, seasick and unrecognised, in a gloomy Aberdeen. It was 11 November – Armistice Day. With his secretary Michael Gripenberg he lunched at the Palace Hotel, and took the East Coast Express to London, arriving at King's Cross the following morning at about 8 a.m.

The Armistice celebrations were all around them as they scoured London for a hotel room, eventually finding one at Claridge's. Mannerheim, observed Tancred Borenius*, would have viewed the celebrations with very mixed feelings: they 'cheered the heart of the northern visitor, who had himself fought his hardest on the Eastern front to achieve an Allied victory', but his mission now was to persuade the Allies to recognise Finnish independence, which had been declared nearly a year earlier. With no official accreditation, and coming from a small and largely unknown country which had had no direct part in the victory, he knew that he had a difficult task ahead.

Although Finland's independence had been given *de facto* acknowledgement by Britain in January 1918, the reluctance to recognize it *de jure* reflected the understandable concern of the Allies about the stability of a state which had marked its independence with a civil war, and which had moved decisively into the German sphere of influence.

It was in response to this move that in May 1918 Mannerheim had brusquely resigned as army commander-in-chief, and sailed for Stockholm, distancing himself from the Finnish government both geographically and politically. It was the prelude to his new career as an international statesman. On 9 October the Finnish Senate offered the crown of Finland to Prince Frederick Charles of Hesse, brother-in-law of the Kaiser. A month later Germany collapsed, leaving Finland in crisis. 'The victorious Allies,' wrote John Screen 'would determine territorial questions at the peace conference, and they alone controlled the food supplies urgently needed in Finland.' In other words, both Finland's immediate and long-term futures were uncertain.

Mannerheim was recalled to Finland by the Regent, Svinhufvud, and authorised to travel to London and Paris in a private capacity, not as a government representative. He would rely on his own reputation, his carefully cultivated connections, and his personality to attempt to extricate Finland from the quagmire in which the government had landed it. He could do this with clean hands, but would have his work cut out.

After essential shopping for clothes, he and Gripenberg met Rudolf Holsti, the Finnish representative in London, for dinner. The next day they had a meeting with James Young Simpson, a Cambridge professor called by Gripenberg 'the Finland expert'.

Despite the obstacles, there was much in Mannerheim's favour. In the first place he was indubitably the man for the job. In the diplomatic world Finland was the new kid on the block, its difficulties compounded by what Jägerskiöld termed "the Finns' political naivety": Finland had never had an independent foreign policy. Mannerheim, though, was a cosmopolitan: a striking figure, aristocratic, speaking fluent English and perfect French, he could sit comfortably at tables with foreign diplomats with centuries of political culture behind them, and could talk on an equal footing with Sirs and Lords. He had prepared himself for this mission in several ways. During his self-imposed exile in Stockholm he developed contacts with the diplomatic corps, especially the Allied Ministers, discussing with them his idea of visiting London and Paris. He formed a lasting friendship with the British Minister, Esmé Howard, who minuted to the Foreign Office 'It is clear that he is our friend, and his influence in Finland will probably revive in time.' Only a few months later they were dining together in London. Back in St Petersburg many years before he had got to know several British diplomats, notably the Ambassador, Lord Hardinge, who was now back in London at the Foreign Office.

People noticed Mannerheim. Admiral Cowan described him as 'the handsomest foreigner I have ever met, very tall, gracefully built, with beautifully made clothes.' For Colonel Paul Rodzianko 'A more perfect envoy to Great Britain would have been hard to find. He had all the traits which the English like most. He was calm, serious, and a gentleman. Besides, any man who was such an excellent judge of a horse must be a good fellow.' Patrick Donner wrote that 'In the course of a long life, I never met anyone in the world with so impressive an appearance. To this the court of the Tsar had added a *royal* manner.' At a reception in Mannerheim's honour, he continued, 'every woman guest, peeresses of the realm included, instinctively curtsied, as if he were royalty.' To Francis Shepherd, the British Minister in Finland from 1944 he was still 'an impressive figure' who gave 'an impression of royalty'.

His acquaintance with England had begun early. There was a distinct English theme in his childhood home Louhisaari: his father was ideologically a liberal, who looked to Britain and France as political models, while his mother, Hélène von Julin, was from an Anglophile family, which had had connections – commercial, cultural, and political – with England since early in the century. Enrolled in the Chevalier Guards,

Mannerheim became technically a member of the Imperial Household; when Tsar Nicholas II married Princess Alix of Hesse, a granddaughter of Queen Victoria, English was the common language of the couple. In about 1907 John Dover Wilson, lektor in English at Helsinki University, visited him, he wrote, 'for a series of conversation lessons, just to polish up the English of which he already had a pretty good command.'

Mannerheim soon found that before the subject of recognition could be discussed, he would need to dispel the British belief that Finland was a 'kind of German protectorate'. On 15 November he and Holsti met a senior Cabinet Minister, Lord Robert Cecil, at the Foreign Office. Mannerheim stressed Finland's desperate need for food supplies; this was noted and acted upon, but he was given to understand that the recognition of Finland's independence would depend upon decisions made at the peace conference. One thing was made clear to him: 'For the good of your country you should not insist on the prince.' Sir Esmé Howard concurred.

Mannerheim was elected Regent on 12 December. 'As supreme Head of State,' he wrote 'I could now continue the discussions with greater authority.' Lord Curzon wrote to Balfour, the Foreign Secretary, stressing that he 'remains the best guarantee against Bolshevism, and it is in our interest that he remains in power.'

The Secretary of Finland's independence delegation in Western Europe, Tancred Borenius*, was a fellow-countryman; a lecturer in fine art at University College, he had lived in London for some ten years, and was able to provide Mannerheim with many useful contacts. His political mission did not absorb all of his time in London; Elizabeth Carnavon hosted a dinner to celebrate his election as Regent, and he consorted with, among others, Borenius and another Finn, Edvard Westermarck, Professor of Sociology in London, and active in the Finnish cause since the dark days of Russification. On 18 November Mannerheim gave the small Finnish community a rousing talk – hardly a sermon – at the Finnish Church. This was largely a patriotic update to cheer on the faithful with the reminder 'that we, a handful of people, with bad equipment and even worse hopes, were able to take on the reds and their Russian cronies.' He continued modestly

> Here too the Finnish colony in London has its own under-takings, and has my good wishes. This country, for which I have always had strong sympathies, I have not had occa-sion to visit for many years; if I am able to some extent to contribute to a closer relationship between this country and our own and thus also 'add a straw to the pile' it would make me more than happy.

Gripenberg recorded a breakfast given by Lady Muriel Paget, who had met Mannerheim at the Anglo-Russian Hospital in St Petersburg in 1916, and again as Red Cross represent-ative in Odessa. In London Lady Muriel was now parading her skills as a hostess, and showing off a prize exhibit. She had assembled what Gripenberg termed *högdjur* ('big shots') 'for whom Mannerheim was obliged to perform'.

In his official report of a meeting with Mannerheim, Balfour wrote 'no-one could wish that the boundaries should be the same as before; for instance, Finland could not be included within them. Finland had been much ill-used by Russia in the past, and though the Allies had little reason to be satisfied with the conduct of Finland in the last year, it could not be our policy to deliver Finland to her former yoke.'

Mannerheim's mission had been more successful than was at first apparent: he realised that, as far as Britain was concerned, Finland was on probation, but he had made Fin-land, and Finland's position, known among statesmen who mattered. Some of them would be restructuring the world at Versailles. The Finnish government now knew what the Allies expected of them. After the king-elect Frederick renounced the throne on 14 December, Mannerheim himself seemed to be in little doubt that recognition by Britain was only a matter of time. At the Stockholm Embassy he badgered Sir Henry Clive, the Chargé d'affaires, who reported twice to London that 'the General was very disappointed' by the lack of progress. His grumpy interviews with the British Consul General in Finland, Henry McGrady Bell, revealed his impatience:

> 'Herr Consul, do you bring me good news today?
> I blushed and stammered.
> 'I regret, Your Excellency . . .'
> 'Herr Consul,' he interrupted imperiously, 'if you so not soon bring me good news – that Britain had recognised the independence of Finland – your visits will no longer be welcome. Good-day.'

Eventually Mannerheim's optimism was justified: on 6 May 1919, Bell, received from Balfour the following telegram:

PLEASE CONVEY FOLLOWING STOP HIS BRITANNIC MAJESTY'S GOVERNMENT ACKNOWLEDGE THE INDEPENDENCE OF FINLAND AND ITS GOVERNMENT

Just three days later he was in Sweden, where the head of the British squadron, Admiral Sir Walter Cowan, gave a ball in his honour. Later he and Cowan were present at a lunch with General Sir Hubert Gough, Chief of the Allied Military Mission to the Baltic and his associates. Mannerheim's prolonged contacts with the British and French military missions show that for him the recognition of Finland's independence was the beginning, not the end of the task which he had undertaken. It is a reminder that he was first and foremost a soldier, and was, especially in England, held in rather higher regard by military chiefs than by politicians. That he headed abroad so soon after 6 May showed clearly his own recognition that the promotion of Finland as an independent state could not at that moment be done in Finland. Later in the year he would be in London again.

Mannerheim had to stand down as Regent after the presidential election in July, when he was decisively defeated by Ståhlberg. He left Finland on 17th of September. Travelling on the same boat to Stockholm was was Augustus Agar, fresh from his exploits at Kronstadt, and returning to England to receive the Victoria Cross. His is an unusually intimate picture of Mannerheim:

> He looked a sad yet impressive figure standing at the stern of the small steamer with his gaze fixed towards the receding shore as we wound our way in and out of the islands and past the impressive battlements of the fortress of Sveaborg . . . Not for a moment did that figure standing in the stern of the ship take his eyes off this exquisite panorama which to him was his native land. He watched until the coast faded away into a thin black line, and finally out of sight altogether.
>
> Then, as the twilight disappeared, he gravely removed his hat and bending his head, stood motionless for a few moments – it seemed to me that he was saying a prayer – after which he walked straight down below to his cabin.

He arrived in London on 25 September to find the country paralysed by a rail strike. He wrote at length to his sister about this experience, which gave him an insight into how an established government responded to 'industrial action', as it is now termed. He had said at the Finnish Church that he had 'always had strong sympathies' with Britain; his feelings about the strike clearly mark a political dimension of those sympathies. He reports the threatening appearance of the striking workers parading with their red flags, and describes with evident admiration the firmness of the government. As Screen remarked, 'A deep mistrust of organised labour pervaded his comments.' Another letter was more explicit: he was 'glad to see that the government has not allowed itself to be frightened.' He suspected that the strike had been inspired, if not actually provoked, by Moscow: Britain showed what should be done with Bolsheviks. He even suspected Lord Acton, the first British ambassador to Finland, of socialist leanings, warning him 'that one of these days it will be necessary for the Legation to obtain the protection of the members of the White Guard.'

Mannerheim was now a private citizen, but one with status of a former head of state. Sir Coleridge Kennard, who succeeded Bell as chargé d'affaires in Finland in June, did not fully share Bell's confidence in him: 'in any dealings which we may have with General Mannerheim,' he wrote 'honest though I believe him to be, we should proceed with extreme caution and reserve.' Nonetheless, he advised the Foreign Office that he 'continues undoubtedly to be the centre figure in the present situation in Finland.' For Ossian Donner, the newly appointed Finnish minister in London, he was certainly the centre figure: the formal reception held for him on his next visit to England, according to Donner's daughter, had the character of 'an official dinner for royalty'. Donner had hinted to the Foreign Office that they might recognise Mannerheim's visit, and Lord Curzon agreed, suggesting in a memo 'I think we might give him a small private dinner of twelve or fourteen.' Lord Hardinge responded, 'He is a person of importance that it would be well to keep in with.' [sic]

An important reason for Britain 'to keep in' with Mannerheim was that he offered a focus for anti-Bolshevik unease. With Finland now recognised in the west, Mannerheim's urgent concern now was in the east. With the threat from the Bolsheviks increasing, and a British squadron under Admiral Cowan based at Björkö Sound, it was important for Finland to know what the British intentions in the Baltic were. Mannerheim's personal position was not a secret: at a meeting with Kennard on 6 September, fully reported to Curzon at the Foreign Office, he 'left no doubt as to the subject with which he wishes to deal and started to speak immediately of his plans for a Finnish advance on Petrograd.' Mannerheim stressed to

Lord Hardinge that British policy in the Baltic was a legitimate concern of Finland's, and warned him that if Finland fell to the Bolsheviks all of Scandinavia would be in danger. There is unfortunately no contemporary record of the meeting between Mannerheim and Winston Churchill, Secretary of State for War, another former cavalry officer. A link more potent than horses was their mutual detestation of the Bolsheviks. 'In the intervals of listening,' wrote Oliver Warner 'Mannerheim was able to put Churchill in the picture – a lurid one – of events in the north since the advent of the Soviet regime.' According to Jonathan Clements 'Mannerheim gave Churchill a lurid account of life in Russia under the Soviet regime, nimbly linking it with the Finnish Civil War.' Churchill, wrote Mannerheim in his *Memoirs*, 'shared my fears for the future of a Europe in the event of the Bolsheviks being allowed to consolidate their position in Russia.' It would be interesting to know if they discussed the rail strike: Churchill had a record as a strike-breaker. Perhaps they talked about cigars.

Another significant meeting in 1919 was with the press baron, Viscount Northcliffe, owner of *The Times*. Borenius accompanied Mannerheim, and recorded some details:

> From the moment conversation began, Gustav Mannerheim captivated the attention of the host completely; the latter listened with the utmost intentness to the exposition, which went into some detail, of Finland's struggle and Finland's case in the international controversies then pending. At the end Lord Northcliffe said: 'General Mannerheim, in one hour you have given me a completely new perception of what Finland stands for. My whole influence is henceforth unreservedly at your disposal.

After this interview *The Times* became supportive of Finnish intervention in Russia. Mannerheim was given a column where he was able to summarise his foreign policy:

I have worked for a free and independent Finland, in close relationship with the great Western Powers, seeking agreement also with Scandinavian countries, and striving to secure foundations for good and fertile relations with the Russia of the future.

The 'liberation' of Petrograd, he wrote, would 'permit the establishment of a stable and healthy-minded Russian [ie White] Government, and thus remove from our frontiers the peril of Bolshevism.' It could, he wrote, 'render to this country [Britain], to civilisation, and to the Russia of the future the signal services which Finland alone can render at this hour.'

Some of the language in this article, and Mannerheim's positioning of Finland as the bulwark against Red Terror anticipates Churchill's speech in January 1940, during the Winter War:

Only Finland – superb, nay, sublime – in the jaws of peril – Finland shows what free men can do. The service rendered by Finland to mankind is magnificent. If the light of freedom which still burns so brightly in the frozen north should be finally quenched it might well herald a return to the Dark Ages when every vestige of human progress during two thousand years would be engulfed.

One can only guess whether Churchill's mind was reverting to that discussion with Mannerheim twenty years earlier.

One of the staff at the Mannerheim Museum told me that Mannerheim 'was Franco inside, and Anglo outside'. His dress, like his whole appearance, was impeccable: his suits came from Savile Row, and his shirts from Jermyn Street. His military greatcoat was a Burberry trench-coat, made to measure by a London tailor. The two shotguns he bought in London in 1924 were by William Powell and Son, and his double-barrelled sporting rifle by James Purdy and Sons. His tropical kit was, naturally, from the Army and Navy Stores, where he spent nearly £1000 equipping himself for his hunting trip to India in 1937. Henrik Meinander described to me an incident during Princess Anne's visit to the Mannerheim Museum. She was terminally bored, but showed a spark of interest in some of the Marshal's riding equipment; examining a saddle, she noted that it had been made in England.

The Mannerheim materials in the National Archives in Helsinki, as Pertti Hakala wrote to me, 'are vast, but at the same time disappointingly meagre'. I certainly found them so, and was disappointed to discover that his many private visits to England will have to remain largely private. Between the wars, according to Jägerskiöld, Mannerheim took at least one trip a year to continental Europe, and these usually included England. He visited leading political and military leaders 'to make himself known and to adjust his own opinion of the situation in the world.' His daughter Stasie lived in England from 1914, for many years in a convent. Nadine MacDougall told Jägerskiöld that Mannerheim's 'devotion to his daughters was one we shall never forget'. Stasie ended her days in Kent, at Provender*, and is buried in the local churchyard. Mannerheim sometimes visited Provender, and had a close friendship with Nadine, lasting until his death.

In 1923 Mannerheim spent a week in London, once again at Claridge's Hotel. There is no record of his ever staying anywhere else in London; indeed, had Claridge's offered a loyalty card between the wars he would have earned several free nights. In the heart of Mayfair, its long-standing connections with royalty have led to it sometimes being called an 'annexe to Buckingham Palace'. The famously luxurious beds must have been a great contrast to the austere narrow camp bed in his Helsinki home, now the Mannerheim Museum.

In 1931 he was appointed Chairman of Finland's Defence Council. He was now a significant figure commercially, as well as politically: Finland was arming, and in May 1934 British military leaders invited him to what Jägerskiöld termed 'an orientation of the war industry's product range'. He was taken to the annual military air show at Hendon; although his military experience was extensive it had not extended to war in the air, and he returned to Finland full of enthusiasm for what he had seen.

George V died on 20 January 1936. His funeral would be one of the last occasions when the British Empire was seen in its full glory. Svinhufvud – at Ambassador Georg Achates Gripenberg's suggestion – sent Mannerheim as his personal representative. Gripenberg managed to establish for him political contacts more important than his actual position or rank entitled him to; this was part of Svinhufvud's political agenda. He arrived in London on 26 January, and that evening attended a reception held by the new King, Edward VIII, for the foreign representatives. Gripenberg recorded the occasion in his diary:

> Mannerheim was immediately surrounded by acquaintances. The German Foreign Minister Neurath was one of the first who spoke with him. Then the King of Denmark, who talked with him at length.

Mannerheim was, in modern terms, networking. Even among these notables he stood out; had he met the king on this occasion some of those present might perhaps have wondered who it was talking with Mannerheim.

Gripenberg's greatest coup was undoubtedly to get him an audience with the king at Buckingham Palace. Mannerheim wrote that he 'appeared extremely simple and natural without losing any of his royal dignity, and I left the audience with the feeling that I had met a monarch of independent views and knowledge of European conditions.' He found that the king shared his concerns about the continuing danger of Communism in the western world. 'The king led the conversation to Germany,' he wrote 'and asked me if I had been there recently and what my opinion was about the political developments. I expressed the personal opinion that whatever one might think of the Nazi movement, it could not be denied that that it has put an end to communism in Germany to the advantage of Western civilisation. The King said that he was of the same opinion.' Warner writes that 'of all the distinguished visitors from abroad who came to pay their respects to the memory of his father, Edward found Mannerheim the most impressive.' Quite possibly Mannerheim, familiar with life at the royal court in St Petersburg, was instinctively putting the new king at his ease.

The funeral itself was possibly the grandest occasion which Mannerheim had attended since the coronation of Nicholas II; 'his martial figure,' wrote the admiring Borenius 'attract[ed] general attention in the striking uniform with the white fur cap as he walked in the procession which slowly moved through London amid the vast and silent crowds.'

A few days after the funeral Ossian Donner, now a British citizen, arranged a dinner with Churchill, where they talked until long after midnight. The only detail Donner records is that Mannerheim cut short a Churchillian oration about the international security afforded by the League of Nations with the comment 'to come back to reality . . .' Mannerheim believed that the League would be of no help to small nations; only three years later he would be proved right. Churchill wrote to Mannerheim after the dinner 'we shall meet again, and be united in our endeavours to prevent the whole world being ruined and afterwards Bolshevised by another hideous war.'

He returned to England in September for an 'Official Visit', which took on some of the trappings of a *state* visit (one accorded only to a head of state.) The British legation in Helsinki put together some notes to prepare the British hosts for their guest:

Mannerheim is over 65 but looks much younger. He is a tall, strongly built vigorous man, still in the prime of his

forces, a hard worker, a good shot and a keen horseman
. . . he is fond of golf, although he would not claim to be
an accomplished golfer . . . But the Marshal is more than
a keen sportsman and a distinguished soldier . . . He is
also an enthusiastic social worker . . . The Marshal who is
an accomplished linguist . . . is a great lover of music and
in Finland is known as an eloquent speaker. He also has
several literary accomplishments to his credit.

A separate note, written perhaps by someone else, adds 'He is
proud of his noble birth and his military achievements, and is
somewhat susceptible to flattery.' In an earlier document the
legation had noted 'He is accustomed to be treated with exces-
sive deference, and is vain (this is a weak side of is character)'.

The Illustrated London News, 19 September 1936, pictured
Mannerheim arriving at Croydon Airport to stay in England
'as the guest of the British Government.' The two-week programme arranged for him emphasised strongly the intention
to show British *military* developments on land, on water, and
in the air. In the course of two weeks he saw more of England
than he had ever seen before. He stayed, of course, at Claridge's Hotel, where on the first Tuesday the Finnish Ambassador Georg Achates Gripenberg, gave a dinner in his honour
('Evening dress; decorations will be worn'). The previous day
he had observed tank exercises on Salisbury Plain with Sir
Walter Kirke, and later in the week he toured RAF Halton
in the Chilterns, and Sandhurst. On the Saturday it was a
race meeting at Windsor. The next week took him north to,
among other destinations, Newcastle, where he had tea in the
Deanery, and Barrow-in-Furness to visit Vickers Armstrong, a
major naval shipyard. The latter part of the week was spent at
the Bristol Aeroplane Company Works, and Woolwich Arse-
nal. His visit was concluded with another day at the races, this
time at Newbury. An official of Vickers took him to the Lake
District, and Gripenberg introduced him to Scotland.

The protocol for an Official Visit states that 'No luncheon or dinner is required', but the Government pushed the boat well out with their 'Dinner for Field-Marshal Baron Mannerheim', held at Lancaster House, St. James, on Wednesday 23 September.' Here the seven course dinner was accompanied with spectacularly fine wines. The host, the War Secretary Duff Cooper, made three speeches, the third being the toast to 'Our Guest'. The Guest replied with assured care, beginning with a reference to the race meetings, the leisure part of his visit, where he seems not to have backed any winners. He confessed that his chauffeur, provided by Scotland Yard, 'proved himself a much greater and more successful authority on horses than I, an old cavalry officer with some fifty years service behind me.' 'What I have seen,' he continued 'has only increased the admiration I have had, ever since my young days, felt for England . . . We in the north look to this country for leadership and inspiration, because here, perhaps more than anywhere else, we find that spirit of tolerance and understanding, of ordered freedom and peace, which we honour and appreciate more than anything else.'

A *Daily Mail* correspondent in Helsinki in 1939 called Mannerheim 'the uncrowned king of Finland'. Lady Diana Cooper described him as 'half-Godhead, half-royal'; many similar epithets can be found in in the writings of British visitors to Finland. Not all British responses to Mannerheim were enthusiastic, though; the personal feelings of politicians and officials were muted by diplomatic cotton wool – Coleridge Kennard's reservations are an example already cited. It is only among left-wingers that we come across public opprobrium. The *Daily Worker* had headlined his arrival in Britain 'Fascist Chief on Arms Works Tour Here.' I have come across no accounts of public demonstrations against him, even on his official visits; the epithet 'Butcher' was occasionally seen, but not heard. The outspoken critic was D. N. Pritt, Labour MP, and Soviet apologist. His book *Must the War Spread,* published in January 1940, identifies Finland as 'a client state' of Britain. The subtitles of his chapter on 'Finland's Recent History' indicate the tendency: FINLAND FREED BY SOCIAL-ISTS./ ENTER BARON MANNERHEIM./ GERMANY HELPS MANNERHEIM./ FINNISH WORKERS MASSACRED./ CLASS WAR IN FINLAND./ MANNEHEIM'S WAR ON SOVIET/ . . . THE BARON DINES IN LONDON.

Two years after the Lancaster House Dinner, Duff Cooper, now First Lord of the Admiralty, paid a courtesy visit to Helsinki on his official yacht *The Enchantress*. He gives the occasion only one sentence in his memoirs, but Lady Diana devotes several pages of her published journal to the visit. Thomas Snow, the British Ambassador, gave a dinner where she met Mannerheim. She wrote 'He's an old Russian Imperialist (that I find irresistible), and says in French *'Pardon'*. I had never heard of him...' It seems to me very odd that Duff Cooper had not even mentioned Mannerheim to his wife, either after the Grand Dinner, or in Finland. Lady Diana describes the Finns she met, including the Prime Minister and several members of the cabinet, with amused and patronising condescension, but she was actually overawed by Mannerheim when he returned Duff Cooper's London hospitality. She calls it his 'blow-out': 'Wonderful house, marvellous food and wines, all of which he arranges, the right flowers, china objects and the right lighting, and after dinner a first-class budding she-pianist. She played everything I liked best and so beautifully that I gave her a handsome jewel off my person.' (Diana Kaley has identified her as Merete Söderhjelm). By contrast, the dinner on board *The Enchantress* the next evening she describes as 'rock-bottom': 'the food tasted to me filthy because of Mannerheim's epicureanism.' Twenty years on this was still the Mannerheim to whom, in Patrick Donner's words, 'peeresses of the realm instinctively curtsied.'

At the end of the year 480 people attended the Anglo-Finnish Society Independence Day Dinner, held at Grosvenor House in

Park Lane. *The Tatler* magazine featured a whole page of photographs, reporting that 'In the chair Sir George MacDonogh proposed the toast to Finland, and it was responded to by Field-Marshal Baron Mannerheim, the celebrated military leader.' *The Morning Post* lists the other speakers, and well over a hundred of the more distinguished guests.

Mannerheim was in London on his way to India: on 10 December he boarded the SS *Mooltan* bound for Bombay. This was his second trip to India, and to see the origins of his interest one must backtrack to his friendship with Sir Walter Kirke. Like many of Mannerheim's British friendships – with Lord Howard, Muriel Padget, and Sir Walter Cowan, to name only a few – this had its origin abroad. They first met in January 1924, when Kirke was appointed Head of the British Military Mission to Finland. At Finland's request he returned in early October, and his friendship with Mannerheim developed. Their paths crossed repeatedly. They met again in 1927 during his first trip to India, where Kirke had become Deputy Chief of the General Staff. He was introduced to the Viceroy, Lord Irwin, with whom – as Lord Halifax – he was to have important discussions in London eleven years later. Back in England in 1936 he met Kirke during his funeral visit, and later in the year at the Salisbury Plain manoeuvres. The following year Kirke issued a glowing seventieth birthday tribute 'from one who is justly proud of including him among his many friends.'

Less then a year ago it was my privilege to accompany the Field Marshal during part of his tour in the United Kingdom, where his fine appearance, soldierly manner, perfect courtesy and acute intelligence made a ready appeal to all my countrymen with whom he came into contact.

Their last meeting was in Helsinki in June 1939. Few of Mannerheim's British friendships were revived after the war, but Kirke was a lifelong correspondent. 'During the time he was in Finland,' he wrote in his *Memoirs*, 'this gentleman and soldier won general regard and made many friends, and until his death in 1949 he remained a warm friend of Finland.'

Mannerheim's last visit to England, in November 1938, was purely political and strategic, full of worries about British rearming, and war preparations. Gripenberg arranged and hosted meetings with Collier and Hore-Belisha (Defence Minister). Lord Halifax, now Foreign Minister, held a lunch for him. India was not on the agenda now; Mannerheim's overwhelming concern in their discussion was Britain's apparent unawareness of the situation in the Baltic area.

Among Mannerheim's vanities was a love of medals and decorations; at his funeral they were carried on cushions by seven bearers. The British decided in April 1938 to appoint Mannerheim an honorary Knight Grand Cross of the Order of the British Empire (Civil Division) 'In recognition of the valuable services which he has rendered to British cultural and other interests.' There were prolonged deliberations at the Foreign Office, since no-one could find that Mannerheim had made any contribution at all to British culture. In a four page letter to Eden, Ambassador Snow eventually came up with something: Mannerheim's occasional attendance at lectures promoted by the British Council. His 'presence at such a lecture is in itself enough in the eyes of the Finnish public to confer the highest possibly distinction upon the proceedings.' This seemed to be enough, and he received the insignia formally from Snow on 3 May. Although only recently instituted, it looked like a relic of an Order of Chivalry, and as such would have had a special appeal for Mannerheim: the royal connection was certainly an added attraction, and he 'expressed his extreme gratification at the honour which had been conferred upon him'. Sadly, he did not hold it for long, since the British declaration of war against Finland at the end of 1941 meant that the honour was automatically withdrawn. It was restored, at least on paper, after the war, but no replacement insignia is known to exist.

It is a sad irony that Mannerheim's name became widely

known in England only during the Winter War when, as Evelyn Waugh put it, he 'held the place in English hearts won in 1914 by King Albert of the Belgians.' He became the subject of numerous articles and reports, and Borenius published a full-length biography in 1940. Although reporters swarmed to Finland, very few of them got as far as Mannerheim's headquarters – indeed, some of them got no further than the Kämp Hotel. Sir Walter Citrine was the only one who published an account of a meeting, but several emissaries from the British Government did get through, and returned to report back. Among them were Brigadier Christopher Ling, who twice visited Mannerheim at the front, and the Military Attaché, Lt.-Col. J. A. Magill, who reported on 4th March that he had seen much of him, and had never seen him so depressed. Immediately after the Winter War, Lord Balfour of Burleigh flew to Finland and held a number of conversations with Mannerheim and with President Ryti. This would have been one of the last official contacts between Mannerheim and Britain. At about this time he inscribed a photo of himself, now in the Finnish Embassy.'With sincere thanks to the English men, women, and organisations who during our war 1939–40 gave their sympathy and valuable support.'

After the Winter War Finland was no longer front page news. Fifteen months later the Continuation War began, and shortly after that the Anglo-Soviet Agreement was agreed. Churchill's personal letter to Mannerheim, dated 29 November 1941, sought to avoid putting Finland in the enemy camp. It shows clearly that although their personal relationship had hardly blossomed, it had been indelible:

Letter from Prime Minister Churchill to Field-Marshal Mannerheim
Personal, secret and private
   I am deeply grieved at what I see coming, namely, that we shall be forced in a few days, out of loyalty to our ally

Russia, to declare war upon Finland. If we do this, we shall make war also as opportunity serves... My recollections of our pleasant talks and correspondence about the last war lead me to send this purely personal and private message for your consideration before it is too late.

Mannerheim's reply concluded

it would deeply sadden me if England felt herself forced to declare war on Finland. It was very good of you to send me a personal message in these critical days, and I appreciate it fully.

On 6 December war was declared, and Mannerheim and England, effectively, parted company. As the British Legation prepared to leave, Magill wrote a letter, marked 'strictly personal':

My dear Field Marshal,
    before I leave this country I want to thank you for all [your] kindness and consideration . . . I shall always look back with pleasure and gratitude at these past 18 months, sad though I am at the manner of their ending, and shall count it a privilege to have been able to see something of you and your gallant army during your great fight of 1939–40.

Mannerheim never visited Britain again; Finland's association with Hitler had soured public opinion, and he faded out of British consciousness. In August 1944 President Ryti resigned, and Parliament declared Mannerheim, now aged 77, President. He saw through the conclusion of the Continuation War and, in increasingly poor health worked with the Allied Control Commission. He resigned in 1946, having done all that he had been elected to carry out. He retired to the Valmont Sanatorium in Switzerland, where he died in 1951. His obituary appeared in *The Times*, but the account of his funeral is sombre. Even the Finnish Government, fearing the Soviet response to any patriotic occasion, sent only two ministers. *The Times* reported:

> The Kings of Sweden and Denmark and the Federal President of Switzerland were represented by their ministers in Helsinki and sent wreaths. Also represented were the governments of Sweden, Denmark, Iceland, Switzerland, Greece, and Canada. All the foreign missions participated in the floral tributes of the diplomatic corps except the Soviet *bloc* and Norway.

The British Embassy, it would appear, sent a wreath.

It would be a pity to end on this note. Let Mannerheim's oldest and most faithful English friend have the last words. Sir Walter Kirke wrote to Mannerheim in 1949, just a few months before his own death:

> I have met most of the world's leaders during the last 30 years, but there is no-one I rate so high as yourself, and to me, you will always be the beau ideal of soldier, diplomat, and gentleman.

Sibelius in England

One's immediate response to the name Sibelius is a picture of
Humpty Dumpty. That image – the massive domed head and
furrows between his eyebrows (one for each of the symphonies, it was said) – has been made familiar from generations
of record covers. But he was once young, and had hair: the
Sibelius who transformed early twentieth century music cut a
very different figure from Humpty. Rosa Newmarch described
how 'with his hair the colour of oats in sunshine, his ice-blue
eyes, his well set-up figure, neat and admirably tailored, he
presented a complete contrast to the unkempt musikant with
whom one associated the apparition of a "new genius"'.

'[T]he English world is more than ever "Sibelius mad",'
wrote Walter Legge in a letter to Sibelius in 1934. '[Y]our music
is now the sensation of London and . . . your symphonies are
being frequently performed in all the important provincial cities.' Legge was supervising the recordings being made for the
Sibelius Society, recently founded by Robert Kajanus. Three
years later twenty-eight of his works, including all of the symphonies, were played at the Promenade Concerts in London,
and in the following year Thomas Beecham organised a full-
scale Sibelius Festival in London.

There seems to have been no suggestion that Sibelius himself
might attend, let along conduct, any of these concerts. His last
trip to England had been in 1921, and although he was now
only just over seventy, with another twenty years still ahead of
him, he was staying put, despite numerous enticements from
English orchestras and impresarios. As I showed in *No Particular Hurry*, anyone who wished to meet him after that date
had to travel to Finland.

Harry Bell, Britain's first consul in Finland after independence, describes in his Finland memoir *Land of Lakes* a party
given by Jacob von Julin at Hotel Kämp in Helsinki in July

1934 'just after the Finnish National Orchestra [according to Legge, the Finnish National *Radio* Orchestra] had given triumphant performances of Sibelius's music in England'. Bell gives his admittedly 'poor translation' of a long 'laudatory poem' recited on this occasion, beginning

> So Finland's voice was heard
> On Albion's happy strand;
> Sibelius tones on wings of genius furled
> Forced stalwarts' love to never dying beauty's world.

Legge had congratulated Sibelius 'on the success of the concerts of the Finnish Orchestra'. Elsewhere in his book Bell writes that Sibelius 'is . . . a great admirer of this country, which he delights to refer to as Old Albion'. (There is a sort of parallel here in Granville Bantock's habit of addressing Sibelius as 'Dear *Väinämöinen'.)*

Bantock, along with Newmarch and Henry Wood, had been an admirer of Sibelius's music since the beginning of the century. The latter, founder of the Promenade Concerts which still bear his name, conducted the King Christian II Suite in October 1901, and the First Symphony two years later; in the same season he included Mahler's First and Bruckner's Seventh. In March 1905 Hans Richter conducted the Second Symphony with the Hallé Orchestra in Manchester, and in the same month Bantock, himself a composer, and permanent conductor of the Liverpool Orchestral Society, invited Sibelius 'to conduct his own music' in Liverpool. Sibelius accepted the invitation, but postponed at the last minute, so Bantock conducted *Finlandia* and the First Symphony himself.

Sibelius's arrival later in the year at Dover was hardly a welcoming introduction to Old Albion. H. M. Customs and Immigration subjected him to a body search, and fined him more than two pounds for trying to smuggle some cigars in his luggage. On their railway journey from Euston Bantock had to endure 'the pungent odour of those enormous black cigars

which Sibelius . . . smoked incessantly'. This first visit must
have been bewildering – decanted into Liverpool, an English
November, and an unfamiliar language – had Bantock not
taken care of him, shepherding him everywhere, and usually
picking up the tab. Sibelius told John Grundy*, the first post-
war British Council Representative in Finland, that he had
never needed to become 'acquainted with the English coin-
age'. Philip Bullock has written that Sibelius's first visit 'may
have been brief, yet it was decisive in dispelling something of
the ignorance that necessarily surrounded perceptions of his
music at that time.'

In Liverpool Sibelius reacquainted the audience with *Finlandia* and the First Symphony. Ernest Newman's review in
The Manchester Guardian can be regarded as a seminal document in the record of Sibelius's reputation in England. 'The
impression it makes on one,' he wrote 'is the same as that
made by the Second Symphony – that here we have a man
really saying things that have never been said in music before'.
He continued:

> For my own part, I have never listened to any music that
> took me away so completely from our usual Western life
> and it transported me into a quite new civilisation. Every
> page of it breathes of another manner of thought, another
> way of living, even another landscape and seascape than
> ours. For some of us it has an extraordinary fascination
> on this account, but we can quite realise that to others it is
> like a poem recited in a language they do not understand.

'For this very reason,' he concluded 'it probably fails to take
hold at once of a good many normal English listeners . . . I can
quite understand this Finnish music of Sibelius knocking in
vain at the gate of many normal English ears.'

This was an astute judgement; although Sibelius's music certainly did achieve some popularity at this time, it left many
listeners both curious and perplexed. In 1906 Henry Wood

conducted *En Saga* – 'a haunting work' he wrote – and *Finlandia*: 'what a furore *that* created! . . . It was a revelation to London'. He gave the first performance of *Pelleas and Mélisande*, but conceded that 'Karelia' 'never quite caught on with London concert-goers'. Newmarch shared Bantock's sense of excitement about the complete originality of Sibelius's music: the first two symphonies, she wrote, 'bear no indication of any literary basis; they are not fettered to the expression of any particular sentiment, heroic, pathetic, pastoral, or even domestic'. Twenty years later Cecil Gray, in *Survey of Contemporary Music* concurred: 'His finest work is supremely original, owing nothing to any other composer, past or present'. It was, perhaps, for reasons such as these that it was a full thirty years before England became 'Sibelius mad'.

It was Bantock who introduced Sibelius to Rosa Newmarch. She was an early champion of Russian and Slav music, and, some years later, of the music of Sibelius; their friendship developed quickly, and ended only with her death in 1940. Sibelius called her 'la femme incroyable'. She provided English translations (*via* German) for many of his songs; her own poetry is only now being discovered and valued. No-one in England promoted his work for as long or as faithfully as she did; her *Jean Sibelius: a Finnish Composer* was published in 1906, and her brief memoir of their friendship in 1939. She recorded their first meeting, at Bantock's house in 1905:

> I was put next to him at dinner with a vague idea that, as nobody knew the language he spoke, a little Russian might come in handy. I had been long enough in Russia and over the Finnish borders to know that the Finns were not too keen to speak the language of their big neighbour, but we soon effected a compromise: a sort of sandwich between French and German, to which, looking over our correspondence, which has lasted thirty years, I found to my amusement we always adhered.

She explained that 'I had begun to realise that it was not merely a large packet of new music, but a new country and the representative of an unfamiliar culture I had undertaken to interpret'. By introducing Sibelius in these terms she established the direction that was to inform the whole approach to his music in Britain for a generation: he was a composer whose music 'seemed more and more to sum up and express the spirit of an ancient race lately reborn among the nations'.

Early in 1908 Sibelius was back in England, making his London début under the auspices of the Royal Philharmonic Society. His two symphonies had a growing reputation, and his violin concerto had been played a year earlier at the Proms, so there were great expectations of the British première of his Third Symphony, which he conducted at the Queen's Hall. It met with a 'polite reception' from the critics – Newmarch records that the three-movement structure 'laid itself open to reproach from the more straight-laced critics as lacking in form and balance', but Sibelius wrote to his wife Aino of its success: 'the orchestra applauded me after the performance, and the public was in ecstasies'. The symphony was dedicated to Bantock; Sibelius never forgot what he owed to him.

'London music lovers were thrilled at the first appearance of Sibelius on February 13, 1909,' wrote Wood. He conducted *En Saga* and *Finlandia* at the Queen's Hall, a performance which he considered 'a great success', writing to Aino:

> After the Saga I was called back to the podium seven times, and after *Finlandia* many more times. The orchestra is altogether perfect. They all stood up as I made my entrance, which is the greatest honour I have ever been paid! The hall was sold out.

This was the start of his third and longest visit to England, which again was London-based. His music had been played at the Proms, and he was getting known in a larger and wider musical community. He decided that London could give him an agreeable working environment, so he moved out of the Langham Hotel (today's rates: from £340 per night) and Newmarch found him rooms at 15 Gloucester Walk, Holland Park, 'where he could stay and work undisturbed'. It was here that he composed his string quartet 'Voces Intimae'. In 1995 English Heritage set up a blue plaque at this address, with the inscription *JEAN SIBELIUS 1865–1957 Composer lived here in 1909*. 'He certainly worked hard in London,' wrote Newmarch. 'Often he would concentrate all day on his compositions, and come out among friends in the evening.'

He usually had a full evening programme. 'I received much kindness from my English friends,' he wrote 'and was invited to a great number of dinners which I enjoyed'. According to one biographer he was pampered by 'London's social elite'. He attended concerts and recitals; among the music he heard was Elgar's First Symphony. On medical advice he had given up wine and cigars, and 'found that the new regime benefited my composing'. (The regime was temporary: he soon resumed, and continued with both for the rest of his long life.) The following year Newmarch spent several weeks in Finland, much of the time with Sibelius, and formed a firm friendship with Aino.

In September 1912 he arrived in England to conduct the British première of his Fourth Symphony at the Birmingham Festival – Bantock had four years earlier succeeded Elgar as Peyton Professor of Music at the University of Birmingham. Newmarch travelled with him; much of their time, she recorded, was 'spent at rehearsals and performances in the Town Hall'. At the final rehearsal of the Fourth Symphony she sat next to Delius, who was 'fully appreciative of the Finnish composer's forcible originality. "Damn it, this is not conventional music" he drawled at intervals in his soft rather nasal voice.' 'I like Sibelius,' he continued, 'he is a splendid fellow.' Another listener was Philip Heseltine, just eighteen years old, who 'called it a work of great beauty; absolutely original and genuine Nature music'. Alan Fearon has kindly supplied me with this anecdote, from a slightly later period, which indicates a different sort of reception of the symphony:

> Neville Cardus was in the Free Trade Hall listening to the Hallé rehearsing Sibelius 4th Symphony (conductor – almost certainly Beecham) when he noticed a man in a cloth cap listening intently a few rows away. He couldn't resist approaching the man during a break in the rehearsal and asking him what he thought of the music. 'Can't say as I understand much of it' came the reply. 'Where does this Sibelius come from?' asked the man. 'Finland' said Cardus. 'Well that explains it,' came the reply. 'I'm from Bradford.'

'One can hardly say,' Newmarch wrote 'that the Fourth Symphony was received with public enthusiasm at its first performance', but, as had happened with the Third, Sibelius's impression was rather different. In a letter after returning to Finland he wrote 'Many artists, including Busoni, have spoken enthusiastically about the Fourth Symphony'. To the surprise of several commentators, it turned out, in time, to be his most widely admired work. The symphony nurtured, as Byron Adams has written, 'a new sort of appreciation as Sibelius was transformed in the eyes of the British from a piquant nationalist of exotic origin into a modernist master'. Critics and commentators continued to praise the originality of his music, discerning no influences on it. By contrast, his influence on other composers is now widely recognised. The musicologist J. P. E. Harper-Scott has called Sibelius 'the influence of choice' among British symphonists in the years between the two World Wars, citing Walton's first symphony, all seven of Bax's, and the first five of Havergal Brian, as well as Vaughan-Williams's fifth. Bullock writes that 'Sibelius's music found a ready home in Britain because it seemed to offer answers to the very questions which critics and composers were asking about the nature and development of British music in the early twentieth century, particularly with respect to nationalism and modernism.'

Sibelius 'had several times expressed to me a wish to see the Shakespeare country' wrote Newmarch. She was now able to take him to Stratford-upon-Avon, to visit Shakespeare's birthplace. They set off early by train to Leamington, and continued by carriage with 'a pair of sound horses'. This was Sibelius's first close view of the English countryside, and he admired the 'the beauty and rich foliage of the trees', relics of the Forest of Arden. They stayed at the Shakespeare Hotel, from where he wrote to Aino 'Here I am where S. was born and lived. Great memories.' They returned to London again by way of Leamington, and the next day his busy schedule resumed.

A further mark of his favourable adoption into the British musical scene was an invitation to write a choral work for the Three Choirs Festival in 1913, but he wrote to Newmarch 'I cannot go to Gloucester because I have no new choral work to offer'. Nonetheless, as the Three Choirs website records, 'The soprano Aïno Ackté travelled from Finland to sing in the Verdi Requiem, the first performance of *Luonnatar*, Op.70, by Sibelius, and the hair-raising closing scene from Richard Strauss's opera *Salome*.' The concert took place not in the cathedral but at the Gloucestershire Hall in Westgate Street, designed with an impressive façade in the Greek Revival style and then, as now, the headquarters of Gloucestershire County Council. The reviewer of *Luonnatar* in a local paper was lukewarm, but also puzzled, writing 'in this strange elemental music the breath and colouring of the wild northern wastes are pictured'. It was clearly rather out of place in the Cotswolds.

Soon after the war Sibelius wrote to Newmarch, in his only letter to her in English, 'I wish I had very soon the pleasure and honour of pressing your hand'. It was more than a year later that, on behalf of the concert manager Robert Newman, she wrote to ask if he 'felt disposed to accept an engagement at Queen's Hall.' He replied that he 'would very much like to conduct his new symphony [No. 5] or any other of his new compositions which would occupy forty or fifty minutes'. There was no body-search for Sibelius on his arrival on 6th February 1921 – the immigration officer actually knew who he was: 'it felt so good to be recognised and welcomed' he wrote. His income had been greatly diminished by the war, so in order to augment his fee Newman 'arranged for four appearances at the Queen's Hall', and after this, tiring enough in itself, an exhausting tour of provincial concert halls. Although Sibelius was worried that the London public, unlike the immigration officer, would not remember him, his visit coincided with Finland's interest in promoting the country's independence, which had been recognised by Britain only in 1919. The Finnish Minister, Ossian Donner, was anxious to make the British public more aware of Finland, and Sibelius could obviously have a part in this. Rather oddly neither Sibelius nor his music had been involved in the movement in Britain which from the turn of the century had championed Finland against the increasing Russification under Tsar Nicholas II. *The Nation*, from 1907, had included graphic accounts of the Russian assault on Finnish rights. In June 1910, for example, under the heading 'The Murder of a Nation', it lamented 'the wilful murder of a singularly noble and attractive nationality'.

Crawford's translation of the Kalevala* had come out in 1889, and Kirby's in 1907, readily accessible in Everyman's Library. In Finland it was closely connected with the rise of nationalism; its popularity was enhanced by Sibelius's Lemminkäinen Suite (first called the 'Four Legends'), written in the 1890s, but this was not included in any of the concerts in England; the only movement played was The Swan of Tuonela. Finlandia was always well-received, but still the interest in Sibelius's music was musical, not political, Even Rosalind Travers, the most engaged British member of the anti-Russification movement, makes no mention of Sibelius in her *Letters from Finland*.

Newmarch organised a reception for Sibelius at Claridge's, one of the most exclusive London hotels, and Mannerheim's invariable choice. Donner and his wife were present, and the occasion, reported in the *Morning Post,* was one of many reminders to the public that an independent Finland had arrived. Listed among the guests was 'Dr. von Williams'; Sibelius realised only at the last moment who this was, and but there was no time for them to do more than exchange some words in halting French, and wish each other well. In 1943 Vaughan Williams completed his Fifth Symphony, 'Dedicated without permission and with the sincerest flattery to Jean Sibelius, whose great example is worthy of all imitation.' Sibelius wrote to Adrian Boult 'the dedication made me feel proud and grateful . . . I wonder if Dr. Williams has any idea of the pleasure he has given me?'

The following day he spent at the Queen's Hall rehearsing for his first concert. When he walked onto the rostrum the audience, he wrote, 'received me with prolonged applause'. After conducting the British première of his Fifth Symphony '[t]he orchestra applauded and the audience gave me an ovation. I took five bows'. This afternoon concert was followed by a dinner party at the Donners, for 'about 50 people, Finns.' 'Donner made a very good speech in my honour and I answered in my well-known fashion,' Sibelius wrote, continuing 'The newspapers have had long articles on me'.

The next day he was invited to lunch at the Royal College of Music by the Director, Sir Hugh Allen, and the students 'played *En Saga* under my baton'. Then off again the next day, this time to the coast, to conduct the Bournemouth Municipal Orchestra, whose conductor Sir Dan Godfrey was a Sibelius admirer; fifty years later Paavo Berglund became permanent conductor in Bournemouth. In 1934 the orchestra performed the Sixth Symphony; the *Radio Times* provided a brief and insightful introduction:

it is more like the fourth than the fifth, and has not, perhaps for that reason, quite the same appeal to the average listener. We are beginning, however, as we know Sibelius better, to appreciate a temperament which speaks its own mind without reference to the susceptibilities of an audience whose tastes are studied more usually with perhaps a better discretion but with less honesty.

The following days are tiring even to read about: from Bournemouth he returned to London for a day of rehearsals for a concert with the New Queen's College Hall Orchestra, then to Birmingham to conduct in a packed-out Theatre Royal, and from there back to London for another concert. He had a day and a half of rehearsals for two 'ballad concerts', and 3pm and 7pm, so it must have been a very late train that he took to Birmingham, where Bantock had prepared a heavy programme for him to rehearse. He stayed with the Bantocks, where he felt at home. It was a traditional English experience, one which many visiting Finns have endured incredulously in England in winter: 'cold English houses . . . it's freezing cold,' he wrote to Aino 'And you can see everyone's breath in the air'. Before leaving for Oxford he was given a reception at Birmingham University.

The Oxford visit was by invitation of Allen, who combined his role at the Royal College with his post as Professor of Music at Oxford; Newmarch accompanied Sibelius from Birmingham. In Allen's rooms at New College they 'spent the afternoon among a small circle of representative musical people'.

Sibelius was entirely fascinated by the architectural beauties of the Oxford buildings. It was a moonlight evening, and we went for a short walk with Sir Hugh Allen as our guide to catch a glimpse of the exterior of New College and Magdalen Tower in the lovely light. Sibelius dined in the hall, an honour for which I was not naturally eligible, but a pleasant, though solitary, meal was served to me in Sir Hugh's college rooms. The next day was spent in sightseeing, and we returned at the end of the week for his second Symphony Concert at Queen's Hall.

Lewis Stevens, in his biography of Newmarch, gives the following detail:

> Sibelius expressed the wish to hear the organ in New College Chapel. The organist, Sir William Harris, took him to the organ loft where he played a Bach Chorale . . . Sir William was somewhat disturbed that Sibelius continued smoking 'the irresistible cigar' during the visit to the organ loft.

Sibelius's biographer, Erik Tawaststjerna, quotes him writing to Aino 'The University . . . are speaking of a doctorate, and are keen that I should return every year.' I have failed to discover any record in Oxford of either of these suggestions.

Back in London he conducted his Fourth Symphony, sharing the concert with Busoni, who played Mozart's piano concerto, No.23. Thirty two years earlier Busoni had spent a brief period as piano instructor at the Institute of Music in Helsinki, where Sibelius was a student. They had become drinking companions in a group known as the Leskovites (named after Busoni's huge dog Lesko), meeting the Hotel Kämp or Erikson's café. Although Newmarch had Sibelius properly organised, Wood wrote how he dreaded the two of them getting together: 'they would forget the time of a concert at which they were to appear . . .They were like a couple of irresponsible schoolboys'. Sibelius consorted also with Eugene Goossens, who rather vaguely recalled how 'a few of us – Bax, Bliss, Ireland, and myself' met him on a visit to London at a luncheon given in his honour at Pagani's Restaurant.

After another Sunday of 'ballad concerts', it was off to Manchester, where he conducted before a capacity audience in the Free Trade Hall, followed by a concert in Bradford. His farewell concert was held on Sunday 6th March in the Queen's Hall, and the following Wednesday he left England, for the last time as it turned out. Newmarch, quite as much as Bantock, had made this tour successful. The tone of a note she wrote to Aino tells a good deal about the nature of the care she took of Sibelius: 'I grumble at him for smoking and for not taking care of his health, but for the most part he has been very sensible during this trip. Wherever he goes he makes friends'. Her care extended to drafting all his letters of thanks, having them typed by the Legation, and leaving him only to sign them. She never saw him again: plans to meet in Paris and Karlsbad came to nothing; he was not a prolific letter writer, and, as Newmarch explained, 'the disabilities of advancing years' allowed them to drift apart.

A section in *The Silence*, John Greening's long poem about Sibelius's later decades, imagines his mood in Georgian London.

> Good Morning, England. The mirror replies, a courteous host
> whose silver is wearing thin, whose views incline to emphasise
> Port and pudding. He weighs up which of the various different ties
> will match his swan-white suit, and now descends, the Guest,
>
> to Georgian London, royalty, oysters, Rosa and Sir Henry Wood.
> They press his weak hand. They snatch at his coat. How people love
> his work here – and love to copy it, though he can hardly disapprove
> except when they make of it some gilt-edged drifting cloud
>
> and moonshine nonsense, as if the very highest art were varnish.
> English artists, much as he loves them, lack a vital spark,
> internal compulsion to bring out their enigma from the back
> of all those sideboards they inherited. It's not about the finish.

Among the friends which Sibelius made in London was Harriet Cohen, a piano student at the Royal Academy of Music. She amazed Sibelius with her intelligent knowledge of his music, playing *En Saga* from memory for him, and showing close technical understanding of the Fifth Symphony. 'You are undoubtedly one of the half-dozen people who understand my Fifth symphony' he told her. She became a favourite of his, although after 1921 they met only in Finland, for the last time when he was over ninety; for the rest of his life she sent him an annual gift of cigars. In London she noted that 'he mixed happily among writers, and got on especially well with the painters, Paul and John Nash'. Cohen was involved with many famous and some improbable lovers, but most permanently with Arnold Bax, an English composer who Sibelius especially admired. In 1955, two years before his death, Sibelius was asked to become the first President of the Bax Society and replied 'I give my consent gratefully and whole-heartedly'.

It was be more than a decade after his final visit before England became 'Sibelius mad', but not even this could tempt him to return. It was not for lack of invitations. He had conducted his first five symphonies in England, and the sixth and seventh were performed in 1923 and 1924, but what really aroused curiosity was the eighth. Walter Legge wrote in January 1934 asking for 'score and parts of the Eighth Symphony, but received only the enigmatic reply "I cannot say anything about Symphony No.8."' After one of Sibelius's epic lunches in Helsinki Cohen was asked 'What did he tell you about the Eighth symphony? Has he written it?' she replied 'My secret with composers is in knowing what *not* to talk about.' Whatever his reasons, Sibelius declined all invitations to return to England; it is hard not to suspect that what Newmarch regarded as insensitive bullying was one of them.

The frustration and disappointment concerning the Eighth Symphony can be readily understood in the light of the English musical world being 'Sibelius mad'. At the very time that Legge coined the phrase the composer Constant Lambert published *Music ho! A Study of Music in Decline*. He positions Sibelius as a prominent force against this decline – 'It is only recently indeed that he has been estimated at anything like his true worth'. The huge popularity of *Finlandia*, he felt, had led to a damaging popularity: 'the pleasantly Nordic nationalism of his work has led many people into believing Sibelius to be no more than a local petit maître, a Finnish Grieg'. Proclaiming him as 'the greatest orchestral innovator of our time', he concluded

> not only is Sibelius the most important symphonic writer since Beethoven, but he may even be described as a the only writer since Beethoven who has definitely advanced what, after all, is the most complete formal expression of the musical spirit.

Although he never visited England again, Sibelius kept in contact in many ways for the rest of his life, most obviously through the many and varied visitors, usually to Ainola, but sometimes in Helsinki. (See *A Life of Extremes*, pp.130-144). He followed the performances of his music in Britain with close and enthusiastic attention, listening to recordings, especially those of the Sibelius Society. He told Legge 'Beecham's performances have come to me by wireless, and they are superb'. The day before he died he talked on the telephone with Malcolm Sargent, who was in Finland to conduct the Helsinki Philharmonic Orchestra; Sibelius died the next evening, very shortly after the broadcast performance of his Fifth Symphony.

Tancred Borenius

In July 1885 Emperor Alexander III made a grand state visit to Vyborg, regarded then as Finland's third city, after Helsinki and Turku. There is a fine photographic record from that time which gives a detailed picture of the city where, just six weeks later, Tancred Borenius was born. His father, a businessman and politician, was wealthy, cultivated, and generous. He often went to St Petersburg on business trips, and as a child Tancred sometimes went with him, spending time at the Hermitage. The family travelled extensively in Europe, where his strong artistic interests became apparent. Kerstin Lindman-Strafford, in *Tancred Borenius – europé och viborgare*, cites letters written when he was twelve, describing visits to the Louvre, and to other art galleries. The family spoke Swedish but his mother, who had lived for two years in Switzerland, spoke French with the children, and the family would have spoken Finnish with the servants. Young Borenius was a European in the making.

The 1890s saw the beginning the Russification of Finland under Tsar Nicholas II, a proceeding which was meeting strong opposition throughout the country. Borenius was well aware of this movement from an early age; his elder brother Einar was a close friend of Eugen Schauman, who in 1904 assassinated the Russian governor of Finland, Count Bobrikoff.

In the autumn of 1902 Borenius enrolled at Helsinki University, where he studied art history under Professor J. J. Tikkanen. The following year in Berlin he attended seminars on medieval Italian art. He graduated in 1905, with Laudatur in Art History, and other levels of attainment in aesthetics and modern literature, in Finnish, Russian and Nordic History, and in 'Roman literature'. In Rome he attended the Prussian Historical Institute; it was probably there that he met the English painter and art critic Roger Fry, initiating a friendship which was to have a major effect on his life and career. The following year saw him in London, working in the British Museum Reading Room, and visiting some private art collections. All this, and another trip to Italy, led to the the completion of his doctoral thesis, which was published in English by Chatto and Windus in 1909 as *The Painters of Vicenza, 1480–1550*. The Bodleian Library has a printing of this book in paper covers with the following note attached to the title page:

> To be presented with the permission of the Philosophical Faculty of the University of Finland, for public criticism in the History and Philosophy Section on September 29, 1909, at 10 o'clock *a.m.*

It seems that the book constituted his doctorate, a most unusual arrangement. Well-received, and praised by Fry, it launched Borenius on his career: almost immediately the publisher John Murray engaged him to complete a revised edition of Crowe's and Cavalcaselle's *History of Painting in North Italy*. He was engaged to Anne-Marie Runeberg, who he had met at university, and now felt that he was in a position to marry; the couple settled in an unpretentious house in Bloomsbury.

As his artistic career developed, Borenius was also becoming involved in politics. Although the Tsar's manifesto of 1904, coming after the general strike in Finland, had rowed back on many of the repressive measures, and confirmed the *status quo ante* Bobrikov, the oppression of Finland was resumed a few years later by Stolypin, Minister of Internal Affairs of the Russian Empire from 1906 until his own assassination in 1911. As Professor Bill Mead has written, 'From 1899 onwards there was a mobilisation of British opinion on behalf of Finland. Members of the Fabian Society and the Labour Party were especially responsive to Finns who came to London to call attention to the situation in their homeland.' Edvard Westermarck (from 1907 until 1931 Professor of Sociology at the London School of Economics and Political Science), along with two English professors, Westlake and Pollock, was a leading figure in the Committee which arranged an international conference in London to publicise the resumption of the repression of Finland under Stolypin. Westermarck was a founder member of the Anglo-Finnish Society in 1911, which, Mead wrote, 'came into being as one of the consequences of Finland's time of troubles.' Borenius became the contact in England for Julio Reuter, Professor of Sanskrit and Indo-European Linguistics at Helsinki University, and Secretary of Kagaali, a clandestine organisation which had organized passive resistance at the turn of the century, and had been bringing Finland's struggle before the public in Europe and America. Borenius introduced Fry to the circle of eminent figures who supported the Finnish cause. The Committee kept up the pressure, but finally it was the Bolshevik Revolution which shifted the log-jam and enabled Finland to free itself from Russia.

Finland's declaration of independence on 6 December 1917 was the end of one struggle, but the beginning of another: it was of limited benefit without international recognition. A first step was taken by Mannerheim*, who travelled to England with the permission of Svinhufvud, the president of the Senate. Arriving in London on 12 November 1918, a day after Armistice Day, he was able to see prominent ministers, some of whom he knew from his time in Russia and in Sweden, but these contacts, Borenius later wrote, 'quickly brought it home to him what an uphill task he had undertaken'. 'At all times,' he continued, 'there was personal courtesy towards the distinguished visitor; but officially there was great reserve'. As a long-term resident in London, Borenius was of great use to Mannerheim, and they developed a lasting friendship; Mannerheim visited the Borenius family at home, and Borenius later had intermittent contact with Mannerheim's daughter Stasie, who made her life in England.

The official approach to the British Government came in January 1919, with the arrival of a Finnish diplomatic mission, sent to seek recognition of Finnish independence abroad. Borenius was immediately appointed as its Secretary, and took the petition to the Foreign Secretary, Arthur Balfour, whose 'attitude throughout the interview,' he wrote in his biography of Mannerheim, 'was one of the utmost friendliness. [He] explained that the British government fully understood Finland's striving after independence, and in this connection expressed a sharp disapproval of the Czarist oppression which for years had been taking place in Finland', but as 'an ally of Russia' Great Britain would have to wait for it to 'define its attitude'. He assured Borenius that it was 'his firm conviction that Finland would soon take her place among the sovereign nations of the world.' Borenius became Finland's temporary diplomatic representative in London, and for various reasons, principally perhaps that Finland was now dismantling its ties with Germany, was more immediately successful than Mannerheim had been in bending political ears. He had, after all, been in England for ten years, and had developed a good sense of the British temperament. On Mannerheim's next visit to England, in 1919, Borenius accompanied him to a meeting which he had arranged with the press baron, Viscount Northcliffe, owner of *The Times*, and kept notes of the meeting during which 'Mannerheim captivated the attention of the host completely'.

Denis Farr, in his article in the *ODNB* (*Oxford Dictionary of National Biography*), describes how Borenius

flourished when the professional art historian was an exotic rarity in England; he brought a European breadth to the subject (he admired the cultural historian Jacob Burckhardt), ranging widely over medieval to eighteenth-century art. He also admired French nineteenth-century artists as diverse as Ingres and Cézanne, and took an informed interest in the contemporary artists of his adopted country.

In 1910 Roger Fry had become editor of the *Burlington Magazine,* a leading monthly publication devoted to the fine and decorative arts. He quickly involved Borenius, who assisted also in the setting up of the famous Post-Impressionist Exhibition in London in 1910.

His abilities were recognised not only by Fry and by publishers, but also in the academic world: in 1914 he succeeded Fry as lecturer in fine art at University College, London. 'He appeared to be a popular teacher among his students, a personality, whose Finnish flair was a part of his reputation,' wrote Johanna Lindfors. Among his acquaintances were characters from the literary world: Max Beerbohm, the Poet Laureate Robert Bridges, and the Sitwell family. Although he was now fully established in England, and rarely left the country, he kept his Finnish citizenship. This may have impaired his chances of becoming Director of the National Gallery.

Caricature of Borenius by Max Beerbohm, 1922

The Art Museum of the Ateneum in Helsinki benefitted from his expertise; he was able to help in the procuring of valuable works of art for Finland, corresponding with Yrjö Hirn, Professor of Aesthetics and Literature at Helsinki University, and advising him on purchases. One of his first significant recommendation was Cézanne's *The Viaduct at L'Estaque*, which he stressed was particularly recommended by Roger Fry, who was directly involved in the selection of further acquisitions, including Alfred William Finch's *Rainy Weather at Hampton Court*.

After the war, and the British recognition of Finnish independence in May 1919, Borenius could devote himself more fully to London life, social as well as academic. He was involved in founding the art magazine *Apollo* in 1925, becoming one of its most active contributors. He joined the consulting committee of *The Burlington Magazine*, and was managing editor during the Second World War. In Oxford he collaborated with the Keeper of the Ashmolean Museum in cataloguing the pictures in Christ Church gallery. He was now becoming part of the smart London scene, including the Sitwell family, prominent members of London's cultural aristocracy. While he was busy with club visits, cocktail parties, and after-theatre suppers, Anne-Marie was usually at home with their two small children. In 1922 he became the first Durning-Lawrence Professor of the History of Art at UCL; this appointment crystallised the two major aspects of his life (family life seems not to have made a third). In the same year he was caricatured by Max Beerbohm. In an article in *Apollo* in 2017 Robert O'Byrne wrote 'Contemporary accounts make it clear his extra-curricular hours were equally busy: [Denys] Sutton called him "both cosmopolitan and erudite", and one was as likely to encounter him at one of aesthete Stephen Tennant's weekend house parties as at the opera in Covent Garden.' The artist Adrian Daintrey recalled:

I was surprised and delighted when Dr. Tancred Borenius whose inaudible lectures in his own brand of foreigner's English and whose solemn appearance I remembered from the Slade days, swam into my ken again in this circle. Now he was, it appeared, the most gallant social butterfly imaginable; rotund, a little stertorous, and infinitely good-natured, he was usually escorting the delightfully funny, and charming Dolly Wilde – niece of Oscar Wilde. Tancred not only adored pretty ladies, but company generally; for the purpose of enjoying as much as possible of it, at one period, one day a week at lunch-time he held open house at a table in Prince's Restaurant in Piccadilly. Any of his friends who were passing were welcome. I only attended one, with Dorothy Warred, but so many people were thronging round the table with prior claims to ours that we thought it best to make an excuse and retire.

One of the most notable British art historians of the century was John Rothenstein, whose *Modern English Painters* (3 vols., 1952–74) earned him the title of 'The Vasari of British Art'; he was Director of the Tate Gallery (now Tate Britain) from 1938 to 1964. He owed a significant debt to Borenius, as he recounts in his autobiography *Summer's Lease*. He wrote how, in 1929,

I enrolled as a student at University College, London, with the intention of obtaining a doctorate in the History of Art, but at once encountered an unexpected difficulty. Professor Tonks, Head of the Slade, objected to the proposed subject of the thesis, and when pressed by Tancred Borenius, the versatile and prolific Finn who was Professor of Art History, declared that he saw no reason why degrees in the History of Art should be granted at all. Borenius persisted – 'don't worry', he said to me at a difficult moment in negotiations, a wide grin on his wily cherub's face, 'Ve unhook a degree for you – only you must be patient', and thanks to his benevolent persistence my subject, 'the interaction of Classicism and Romanticism in Nineteenth Century Painting' (or something of the sort), was accepted, and in the fullness of time my thesis, was accepted, defended in a viva, and I became in 1939 a Doctor of Philosophy.

Borenius's extraordinarily convoluted English accent was described or, as with Rothenstein, parodied, by many of those who met him or heard his lectures; 'his heavy accent left students struggling to understand what was being said,' wrote Robert O'Byrne. Lindman-Strafford wrote that his English was 'hopplöst oengelsk ' ['hopelessly unenglish], and punctuated with grunts – yet he was reputed to be fluent in nine languages. The spoken English of Swedish-speaking Finns is often near pitch-perfect; that Borenius's accent should still have induced comment after so many years in England is puzzling.

During this period he was establishing himself at Sotheby's as their foremost expert in early painting, and this in turn meant that he was often in demand as advisor (for a fee) by private collectors who sought his judgement. He also joined Sotheby's Old Master's Paintings Department in 1923, where, according to their official historian, he was considered 'commercially adept', well worth his 1929 salary of £600. Academics and researchers in England frowned at anyone benefitting financially from their expertise, and considered it incompatible with academic integrity. This disapproval of the art establishment did not, however, carry much weight in the cultural and aristocratic circles in which Borenius principally moved; the way of life that he had chosen could not be conducted on an academic salary. There was a price to be paid, though: in 1934 the post of Surveyor of the King's Pictures became vacant, and Borenius, despite his friendship with the Princess Royal, was not appointed because, wrote Robert O'Byrne, he was felt to be 'tainted by a too-close involvement with the art trade'.

Borenius's close friendship with Lord Harewood, who was married to Mary the Princess Royal, only daughter of King George V, made him a frequent guest at Harewood House in Yorkshire. He wrote *Catalogue of the Pictures and Drawings at Harewood House and elsewhere in the Collection of the Earl* (published privately by OUP), and advised his Lordship on the paintings by masters of the Italian Renaissance which are still on display there. Harewood wrote to him: 'you have taken so much interest in the pictures . . . Every one, in fact, has been bought on your advice'. One of the paintings was Titian's *The Death of Actaeon*, bought for £60,000; it was sold by Harwood's son in 1971 for £1,680,000, and is now in the National Gallery. The Princess Royal came to value Borenius's company as much as her husband did – and so did her mother: Lindman-Strafford wrote that 'For many years he was a stimulating companion for Queen Mary. Every week he was he was invited to drink tea [with her] at Buckingham Palace and discussed art, 'objets d'art', history, genealogy . . .'

In Yorkshire in the summer he became a favourite 'uncle' of the Harewood children. During the late 1930s he on occasion accompanied the widowed Queen on her holidays to visit her daughter at Harewood House. John Harris mentions reports in local Yorkshire papers of Queen Mary embarking on antique-buying trips, typically accompanied by Borenius. He was close enough to the royal family to be invited to the coronation of George VI in 1937. For the occasion he was made a member of the order of St Gregory, which entitled him to wear a fancy uniform with decorations.

Kenneth Clark, twenty years younger than Borenius, became director of the National Gallery in 1933. His twelve years there saw the gallery transformed, and made accessible and attractive to a wider public. He became, in some senses, an adversary of Borenius, whom he regarded as a 'typically Germanic pedant, lacking imaginative range'. Three years earlier he had organised an exhibition of Italian art in London, and had, perhaps rather pointedly, not asked for any contribution from Borenius, who in turn aimed at some sort of retaliation when, in 1937, Clark purchased for the Gallery paintings which he exhibited as the work of Giorgione. As Clark later explained, they were funded by the National Art-Collection Fund, on condition that they they 'should be labelled "Giorgione", not "school of" or "manner of". 'In a moment of unforgivable weakness I agreed,' he wrote. Borenius was quick to publicise this misattribution, and proceeded to what Clark termed a vendetta:

> I had plenty of time to repent of my mistake. A massive attack was mounted and organised by my old friend Tancred Borenius. It was directed not so much against the charming little pictures, as against me, and was intended to force my resignation. Tancred would give a summary of my shortcomings, and end by saying 'Think of all that and scales will fall from your eyes.' He was indefatigable, persuading the most unlikely people to write letters of indignation to the *Daily Telegraph*.

During the 1920s Borenius developed an interest in English Medieval Art, and wrote in collaboration with Professor E. W. Tristram *English Medieval Painting* (1927), described as 'one of the most comprehensive surveys of its day'; he also edited a series of monographs on English medieval art, and in 1932 published *St Thomas Becket in Art*, described by Farr as 'a major survey of the iconography of that saint.' The Borenius family had taken a country cottage near Salisbury, and he become involved in examining the nearby ruins of Clarendon Palace, which had been a royal residence in the middle ages. It was completely overgrown, and more under ground than above. Together with a young archaeologist, John Charlton, he oversaw the excavation of the ruins during summer camps. Here Anne-Marie seems to have emerged from the shade, becoming an expert on medieval tiles; she was even given her own desk for research at the British Museum. The outbreak of war put an end to all this; after 1945 Borenius was in poor health, and the grass and bushes returned to cover the ruins.

Mannerheim was a regular visitor to England, always staying at Claridge's Hotel, and often meeting Borenius. In 1936 he was invited by the Government for what was virtually a State Visit and Borenius was a guest at the 'Dinner for Field-Marshal Baron Mannerheim', held at Lancaster House, St. James. Less than four years after this, in April 1940, he published *Field-Marshal Mannerheim,* a full-length biography. The dust-jacket explains that

> Dr. Tancred Borenius, the authority on art and Professor of London University, is a fellow-countryman of the Field-Marshal's, and has known him for many years: also, under the Field-Marshal's Regency, he was for a while Finland's Diplomatic Representative in England.

The book was published just weeks after the end of the Winter War, when Finland had been in the international news as never before or since. Borenius was at the centre of the British effort to support Finland in its David and Goliath struggle against the Soviet invasion. Twenty years after the mobilisation of British opinion on behalf of Finland against the Stolypin regime, Britain again came out in support of the Finnish cause – a revival of the activity of those days – with Finns resident in London especially active. Borenius and Westermarck, with their many international contacts, were again at the forefront of the propaganda, and of some of the more practical details of aid to Finland.

In 1939 Borenius became Chair of the Polish Relief Fund, which sent aid and assisted Polish refugees in Britain. He collaborated with the BBC during the early months of the Continuation War, but after the Anglo-Soviet treaty of 1941 his position in Britain became uncomfortable, although he and his family were permitted to remain in the country. Despite the problems posed by the war, he continued throughout to write for and to edit *The Burlington Magazine*.

There are inconsistent accounts of his last years and death. The UCL website records that he 'remained professor until his death in 1947', while Lindman-Strafford wrote that his nerves never recovered after a breakdown in 1945, and he died of a heart attack at Coombe Bissett. 'He became more reclusive in the 1940s,' wrote Farr, 'seeking solace in his library of 30,000 books at his home in Kensington Gate, London. He retired to Stockbridge Cottage, Coombe Bissett, near Salisbury, Wiltshire, and died in a nursing home, Laverstock House, near Salisbury, after a long illness on 2 September 1948.' None of these accounts is compatible with that of John Harris, who gives a very different, documented version of events, writing that Borenius was

> sectioned under the 1890 Lunacy Act. Initially, he was admitted into St Andrews, Northampton, in early 1947 and was subsequently transferred to Laverstock House, near Salisbury, in March 1948, where he died on 2 September, aged 63.

Laverstock House was in fact a private lunatic asylum, once highly regarded, but then already heading for bankruptcy and closure.

In 2015 Phaidon Press reissued his *Rembrant* as a 'Phaidon Classic'. The publisher's jaunty advertisement sets out to boost Borenius:

> Today, we're focussing on Tancred Borenius, the Finnish professor, entrepreneur, diplomat and author of our Rembrandt book (originally published in 1942) who socialised with the Bloomsbury Group; worked as a consultant at Sotheby's; spoke nine languages fluently; served as an art advisor to the Earl of Harewood as well as members of Oscar Wilde's family; was a leading expert on Italian art

during the early Renaissance; and even have [*sic*] worked as a spy for the British government, helping the Allied Forces win World War II. Some going, we think you'll agree!

The exposure of Borenius as a 'spy' had come before the British public in *The Daily Telegraph* on 25 Oct 2010:

> The reason for Hitler's deputy [Rudolf Hess] making his solo flight to Scotland in May 1941 has kept conspiracy theorists busy for decades. He was arrested in Renfrewshire and spent the rest of his life in prison. Nearly 70 years on, a fresh theory has emerged. Author John Harris claims that Hess was lured to Britain in an MI6 plot led by Tancred Borenius, a Finnish art historian who was working as an agent for the British secret service. Borenius travelled to Geneva in January 1941 and convinced Hess that members of the Royal Family were willing to broker a peace deal with Germany, according to Harris. 'Tancred was key in giving Hitler hope that Britain was interested in joining an alliance,' he said. Harris claims that Borenius's son, Lars, gave him the information shortly before he died.

Harris's book *Rudolf Hess: The British Conspiracy* had actually been published in 1999, purporting to explain 'the most bizarre and inexplicable episode of the Second World War.' A complex, confusing, and unconvincing account concludes that 'A royal coup led by the King and Queen, aided and abetted by Borenius as messenger, might seem quite credible, if told convincingly.' No such telling has appeared, and Harris's ideas have been ignored rather than rejected by historians.

Borenius's name lives on. In 2017 the Anglo-Finnish Society promoted a blue plaque, which was unveiled by the Finnish Ambassador at the house on Kensington Gate where he had lived. This was followed by a seminar at the Ambassador's Residence in nearby Kensington Palace Gardens.

Finns in Kent: Provender

In East Kent, few miles south of Faversham and near the village and church of Norton, stands Provender. Dating from 1342, when it was built as a hunting lodge of the Black Prince, the house as seen today embodies some six centuries of architectural history. It has been restored over the last twenty years or so, and is now open for tours on selected days.

Owned by Edward Knatchbull-Hugessen, the first Lord Brabourne, it was rented in 1890 by Constance Borgström, a widow from Finland with four children – Léonie, Sylvia, Henrik and Emmeline (known as Aline). Constance was a Paterson, descendant of William Paterson, founder of the Bank of England in 1694, while her husband Emil was the son of Henrik Borgström, an eminent banker and businessman. They could afford to live in style.

'Our arrival at Provender,' wrote Sylvia in her Memoirs, 'was something like a sensation, not only in the village but for miles around'. In Faversham shopkeepers and their customers rushed out to see them when they drove by. 'My mother,' she explained 'always drove in a barouche with a pair of high-stepping horses and two immaculate liveried men on the box.'

That part of Kent still retains several large estates; in the 1890s there was no shortage of fashionable society.

The County called. They did more than call, they rushed! – judging by the rows of visiting cards laid out on the hall table by the butler when we returned to Provender after our afternoon's drive. I never looked at the cards, but at the laden tea-tables waiting also for our return in the hall. It was a fine large hall with massive oak beams, a red tiled Tudor floor and a great open fireplace, down which every draught imaginable came soaring . . . [A]ll the county came to the Provender dinner parties. They were set ceremonious affairs, never under twenty-four covers, with ten courses, besides ices, dessert, and many wines.

Lord and Lady Harris from Belmont were among the most frequent guests and hosts. Lord Harris had captained England and Kent at cricket (and played in his last match at the age of 77). Provender was one of the few great houses in the area which did not have a private cricket ground; the best-known now are Torry Hill, home of the Leigh-Pembertons, and Otterden Place, but it would have been at Belmont or at Canterbury that Sylvia watched cricket. This provides a scene in her novel *A Heroine in Finland* (1902)* where the Russian princess describes 'the national amusement of the English'. The author shows scant understanding of the game, unless she was trying to make the princess sound amusing:

> . . . an enormous concourse of people – thousands! surrounding a large circle of grass, breathlessly gazing all at the same object, – in silence. One fixed rule is never to speak, even to whisper is a crime!... Sometimes, not very often, there is a break – the ball seems to run away and then a poor man (Mon Dieu, I was so sorry for him! – he was a fat man). Well! he runs up and down between two small sticks . . . Someone throws the ball back, and – voila tout! C'est fini. At least that coup is – otherwise it continues for hours at a time.

But cricket was for summer days. The winter, especially in this exposed area of Kent, meant that the house was assailed by 'every draught imaginable'. The Borgströms discovered, like many Finns who move to England, that in winter you feel colder indoors than you did in Finland outdoors. This could have been one reason that the family, with a selection of their domestic staff, 'migrated every year in October to our villa at Cimiez near Nice, where we spent the winter months.'

With this arrangement they must have missed much of the

hunting season. Sylvia wrote lyrically how 'At the sound of John Peel's horn, men left their ploughs, women their work, children their lessons, to rush and obtain the best view, however far away, of hounds in full cry with horses and their riders in pink galloping after them.' Provender was, and is, adjacent to the kennels of the famous Tickham Hunt (Now the Ashford Valley Tickham Hunt), and the Master of the Hounds 'brought his hounds and hunt servants to be photographed at Provender'. Sylvia bought Provender and part of the estate at auction in 1912 (with Borgström money that she had had telegraphed to the post office in Faversham), and the hunt continued to ride there.

One winter at least, in 1904, was certainly spent in England. Märta Arppe had come from Finland to spend the autumn in London with Constance's niece Lisi Borgström, and was invited down to Provender for Christmas. More than fifty years later, in a Swedish magazine article, she recollected the visit. The house was decorated with holly and mistletoe, but the Christmas Eve dinner was 'in the Finnish fashion'. The English mood was enhanced by four guests, monocled majors from a local regiment, dressed in fashionable English tailcoats. We do not learn whether they dined on ham or on turkey. After breakfast on Christmas Day the family all went to church, which, like the house, was tastefully decorated with holly and mistletoe.

> The choirboys sang. The old, gray-haired priest preached really well . . . After the service we went on a long walk . . . On Boxing Day Aline and her husband took Lisi and me on a drive to see what an English fox-hunt looks like. We saw riders galloping on the route on their fine steeds, in hot pursuit of the hounds. The red coats looked brilliant . . . but we did not see any foxes.

What with all their English Christmas decorations, hunting, and dining and dancing with the grandees of Kent, they

never lost sight of Finland. Sylvia's grand-daughter Diana
Kaley recalls that 'my mother always told me how as a child
she remembered her mother decorating the whole of Provender
with laurel garlands, blue & white flowers and Finnish flags
every time Paavo Nurmi won a race.' Nurmi was one of the
'Flying Finns' who carried all before them in the Olympics in
the 1920s. In Paris in 1924 he made history by becoming the
first athlete ever to win five gold medals at a single Olympic
Games.

'It's possible that Jane Austen would have visited Provender
from her brother's home nearby in Godmersham,' claims the
Provender website. It is indeed very possible: there certainly is
a significant Austen connection. In a letter to her sister Cas-
sandra she had written (26 June, 1808) of a 'very agreeable
visit' to Canterbury adding 'Mr Knatchbull from Provender
was at the W[hite] Friars when we arrived & staid dinner'. In
1820 he (now Edward Knatchbull-Hugessen) married Austen's
favourite niece, Fanny Knight, and they lived at Provender.
Their son, later Lord Brabourne, found 'in a box at Provender'
a manuscript of her short novel *Lady Susan*, and letters which
he was able to include in the first edition of *Letters of Jane
Austen* in 1884.

There is an amusing Austen echo at Provender. With three
unmarried daughters in the house, the arrival of an eligible
gentleman in the area is reminiscent of the opening of *Pride
and Prejudice*. Sylvia describes the occasion in 1906 when
there was a last-minute drop-out for a dinner party; her sister
remarked 'There is a Captain , a bachelor, who has just taken
Colonel Tyler's place, Loyerton. Why not ask him? I know
nothing about him, he may be eighty or eighteen; he is a cavalry man, Third Hussars.' When Colonel Herbert McDougall
arrived Sylvia saw that 'he was not eighty', so she switched
place cards in order to sit next to him. Two weeks later he
proposed; they eloped, and two weeks after that 'got married
by special licence'. She had already at this time published sev-

eral of her five novels – all set in Finland – and published *A Summer Tour in Finland** in 1908, all under the pseudonym Paul Waineman.

Sylvia's younger sister, Aline, also married a soldier posted locally: General George Macdonogh, who became head of Military Intelligence in World War I. They lived at Nouds House, about a mile from Provender. Looking closely at a large-scale map one can see that there was a very loose Finnish network developing, with Provender at the centre. After their marriage the McDougalls lived very close to Nouds, at Loyterton Farm, where Nadine, their first child, was born in 1908. In the next generation the local network expanded; Pamela, their second daughter married George Mills-Lade, heir to Earl Sondes of Lees Court, called 'the finest estate in Kent', which had been in the Sondes family for the past 700 years. After the wedding they moved to live in grand style in Nash Court, at Boughton-under-Blean, just south of Faversham. Within a couple of years Lord Sondes died, and they moved to Lees Court, which is about seven miles from Provender. A further Nordic connection, 'Swedish houses' in Lynsted caught my eye on the map but I discovered that these were 'pe-fab' houses, imported from Sweden at the end of WW2.

Nadine become a close friend of Field-=Marshal Mannerheim*, still regarded in Finland as 'the greatest Finn of all time'. He was a visitor to Provender between the wars, and developed a close – even flirtatious – relationship with Nadine, which lasted to the end of his life. He gave her a silver mascot of a wolf, a radiator cap for her car, to which he had attached a card with these words: 'A gift for you so the old grey wolf will always canter in front of you.' It was at Provender that his elder daughter Anastasie (Stasie), who lived in England, came when she needed nursing. She died in hospital in Faversham in 1978, and is buried at Norton, alongside many Borgströms. After the war, not many miles away, at Woodside Green, there lived Anna Sinikka Paasikivi, granddaughter of another Finnish President.

It is unlikely that the arrival of the Borgströms in Kent put Finland on the map, in any sense of the term. Locally they were, understandably, often spoken of as Russians. It is amusing to consider what a very misleading impression of Finland and of Finns the locals must have formed, whether they belonged to the 'county' set, or were lookers-on in the nearby lanes and the streets of Faversham. Shortly before the coronation in 1937 Sylvia and her twin sister (married to Count Aminoff) were presented to HRH Princess Louise, the King's sister. The description is Sylvia's:

> When Lady Grosvenor presented us, the Princess turned to our hostess and exclaimed 'How very interesting, I have never met anyone from Finland before, and Baroness Aminoff and her sister look exactly like ourselves'.
>
> I suppose that Princess Louise had imagined that the inhabitants of Finland were akin to Laplanders, and that we ought to have been dressed reindeer skins, with tallow candles in our hands. Our civilisation apparently surprised her as greatly as her remark surprised me.

There had been a similar misassumption when Edvard Westermarck, the Professor of Sociology at the University of London, was invited to a society dinner in London and was given a high chair, to spare him any embarrassment.

The Finnish connection was kept energetically alive by George Macdonogh. Retiring in 1925 with the rank of Lieutenant-General, he became President of the Anglo-Finnish Society. The highlight of his presidency was the Society dinner in 1938 (see pp. 24–5).

During the first months of 1940 Nadine organised a branch of the Red Cross Hospital Supply Depot at Provender, with a team of helpers filling wooden cases to be sent to the Finnish Red Cross, as part of the effort to support the Finnish troops fighting the Soviet invasion during the Winter War. The whole operation was co-ordinated by Macdonogh as Vice-President of the Finland Fund, and a member of the Finnish Aid Bureau.

Sylvia gave Provender to Nadine as a wedding gift in 1942, keeping the use of two rooms for herself, and lived there until her death in 1962. Nadine had done more than just *meet* royalty: in 1942 she married Prince Andrew of Russia, the eldest nephew of Tsar Nicholas II. The wedding – 'a full fanfare of pomp and circumstance' – was at Norton church, conducted by the Archbishop of Canterbury. It must have been a tight squeeze for the four hundred guests. It was followed immediately by the Russian Orthodox ceremony at Sheldwich church.

Provender had by then been requisitioned by the army; during the rest of the war and the time that Sylvia and her daughter Flora took – well over a year – to make the house habitable after the army had left, the Romanoffs lived at 'Lynsted Lodge'. This was probably Lynsted Court, a Grade 1 listed house a few miles from Provender, a residence which would not have disgraced royalty. Sylvia lived at this time at Wormshill, further widening the Finnish sphere in east Kent. Prince Andrew died in 1981 and Nadine in 2000. According to *Faversham Life* she was 'still a legend in these parts' in 2017.

Provender was inherited by Nadine's daughter, Princess Olga Romanoff, who now lives there and has overseen the restoration of the house from a near-ruinous state to a one bordering on the magnificent. Although its Finnish history is not very easy to detect today behind the Romanov portraits, Provender is actually a relic of the great *Finnish* family, the Borgströms, whose presence in East Kent spread in several directions over several decades.

II

TRAVELLERS IN FINLAND

William Allen

Quakers have made periodic appearances in the story of the British Discovery of Finland. After the Crimean War, for example, Thomas Sturge and Thomas Harvey travelled to Turku on a fact-finding mission to investigate British incursions into Finnish ports in 1854–5. As a result of their findings, a committee was set up and a subscription raised back in England which produced £9000 for the relief of farmers and fishermen who had suffered from the British raids. Some of this money was used in the following years for famine relief. Further and more substantial famine relief was provided during the 'great hunger' years in the later 1860s. In 1939–40 British Quakers served as firemen, ambulance drivers, and helpers during the Winter War. One of them, John Sykes*, a member of the Finnish Company of the Friends Ambulance Unit, reappears in the current book, describing his return to Finland twenty-five years later. The first Quaker relief mission arrived in Rovaniemi in 1945, and subsequently moved south to help with the resettlement of Karelian refugees. In Kajaani in 1948 Diana Ashcroft* met a member of the Quaker Relief Unit in Lapland, which was aiming 'to re-open the schools in Lapland and to see that the children who attended were fed there.'

William Allen's Quaker parents were proprietors of a prosperous silk-manufacturing business in London. Born in 1770, he showed an early aptitude for science, and in 1792 joined the Plough Court pharmacy, run by another Quaker, Joseph Bevan. Pharmacies in those days did more than dispense and advise: they also researched and developed new medicines. Here he prospered, and was able to follow and further his

scientific interests. He became a fellow of both the Linnean
Society and of the Royal Society, and was appointed lecturer
at Guy's Hospital in 1802. His interests developed to embrace
philanthropy, and he became an active campaigner against the
slave trade, following this through by monitoring the condition of former slaves. His concern for the relief of poverty, at
home and abroad, developed into a life-long involvement. He
met Tsar Alexander I during his visit to London in 1814; the
Tsar became very interested in Quaker ideas, including their
promotion of agricultural techniques, and particularly in their
promotion of mass education in basic skills.

Four years later, with a another famous Quaker, Stephen
Grellet, he travelled to St Petersburg to visit the Tsar, passing
through Sweden and Finland (and returning by way of Moscow, Constantinople, and Italy). He left Stockholm in late
October in

> a vessel which is well fitted up as a packet, but no bedding
> was provided, so we borrowed two beds of our landlady,
> who was to receive them again by the return of the ves-
> sel . . . They do not furnish provisions on board, so we
> brought ours with us.

He enjoyed the 'beautiful weather', and

> was engaged, most of the morning, writing, and look-
> ing through my telescope. In the evening our little party
> amused themselves on deck, admiring the stars and mak-
> ing out the constellations . . . It was near twelve o'clock
> before we retired to rest, and we arrived at Abo about
> four in the morning, after a most extraordinary passage
> (for the time of the year) of only forty hours.

> The officers came on board to inspect, but gave us no
> trouble; we came to the 'Society's Inn', a very large house,
> where they only speak their native language, so it was
> some time before our breakfast was ready.

He found no further problems with language: 'Almost all well-educated persons here speak French' he wrote.

Allen's interests were almost exclusively with society, and with facts and figures; what little description he gives is brief and perfunctory:

> The houses at Abo are low, they are built of wood, and are generally painted red. A river runs through it, which is only navigable about a mile farther, on account of a fall. The streets are rather narrow, and paved in the same way as at Stockholm [presumably cobbles], which makes it very uncomfortable in walking. After passing the bridge, some of the houses are plaistered. The poor live on peas, potatoes, bread, and fish.

He soon got to work:

> One of the merchants, to whom we had a letter of intro-duction, kindly provided us with a servant, who has a good character, and has been fifteen times to Petersburg. In the afternoon we delivered several of our letters, and have become acquainted with some highly interesting characters, principally in the philanthropic line, but we feel it all as a part of the great work. Dr. Haartman's appearance indicated a fine open-hearted young man. I found that, in the year 1815, he had been in London, and visited the Borough Road school. He went with us to the Governor General Steinhielt, a very interesting person, who gave us much information about schools and pris-ons; he says, crime increased very much, in consequence of the war, and the use of ardent spirits. I find he is a mineralogist, and has a beautiful collection of minerals; he invited us to see it; we took tea with him, and felt quite at home. We were glad to learn that, in some of the public institutions, the work of reformation is beginning. From hence we went to visit J. Julian, who has a large, neat,

apothecary's shop; he is a sensible, intelligent man, and has a scientific turn also; we found him very busy, preparing to draw fine platina [platinum] wire for the new lamp, without flame, invented by Davy; I was quite pleased at becoming acquainted with him. We laid our plans of operation for to-morrow, and returned to the inn, where we found our fellow traveller, M. Dunn, who could not set off for Petersburg until to-morrow; after supper we had a good deal of interesting conversation on our religious principles and discipline.

'J. Julian' was evidently Johan Julin, a naturalist and chemist, and also a member Svenska Vetenskapsakademien (The Royal Swedish Academy of Sciences) in Stockholm. A few years later his son John Jakob Julin, also a licensed chemist, bought Fiskars Ironworks, today one of the oldest businesses in the western world, and famous for its orange-handled scissors. Dr. Haartman must be Carl Daniel von Haartman (1792–1877); the Haartman connection with medicine is writ large in modern Helsinki, giving its name to both an institute and a hospital. He acted as Allen's guide and mentor during his time in Turku.

The next morning they made a early visit to the Archbishop, Jacob Tengström, who received them 'very kindly'. 'We then went to Julian's to breakfast, where Dr. Haartman met us, and there was a very pleasant party – great openness and kindness prevailed.' Two missionaries who were in Turku at around this time, Robert Pinkerton and John Paterson, were members of Bible Societies, but their concerns were principally with the distribution of bibles. Although Allen did distribute some Quaker literature, his mission was to collect facts: poverty relief, schooling, and prisons were what occupied him. Breakfast was followed by a tour of the city.

We first called on a clergyman, who is secretary to the committee for the poor; there are two parishes, one

Swedish and one Finnish, and the clergyman of each parish is always a member of the committee. We visited several schools, the poorhouse, and a place where poor women are supplied with flax for spinning; this, as far as it goes, is an excellent establishment.

He is, I think, the first of uncounted British writers to describe education in Finland:

> With regard to schools, a more extended system of instruction is obviously needed; the education of girls in general is greatly neglected, and yet the parents are so anxious that their children should learn to read, that they most frequently contrive to teach them, or have them taught. In the country the poor seem to be distributed among the farmers, who are responsible also for their education . . .

He gives accounts of places and scenes, some of them unsavoury, which are not mentioned by any other nineteenth-century British travellers:

> The poor-house contains almost wholly those who from age, or infirmity, from weakness of intellect or insanity, are unable to provide for themselves; many parts of it were in a very dirty state.
>
> We now went to the house of correction, containing about ninety prisoners. In one room were six or seven gipsy women, confined merely for being what their mode of life makes them, that is vagrants. These poor creatures seem to be held in supreme contempt, being in a state of total ignorance. In the whole of this prison, the only thing wanting seems to be a good system of classification, and the attention of such a committee as E. J. Fry has established at Newgate. The women were all employed.

The mention of Elizabeth Fry in this context is an interesting one: a century later Mathilda Wrede, a pioneer prison reformer became known as 'the Elizabeth Fry of Finland'. Fry, of course, was a Quaker.

Haartman kept Allen busy. A working breakfast at his hotel with visitors was followed by a round of visits which was punctuated by dining with a large party at Haartman's own house. 'He and Julian were very earnest to hear from me the history of the School Society, and I gave them a full account of it; they are quite disposed to adopt the system here'. Friends (Quaker) Schools in England date back to 1699, and Allen himself had attended one in Rochester.

> Several of the party accompanied us to the castle, where the prisoners for [sic] all the province, containing a population of two hundred thousand, are confined after sentence, though there were some untried. The number is about sixty.
>
> The details of this prison are of an affecting nature; some persons confined for murder, under very aggravated circumstances, were loaded with manacles, chains, collars, &c.; many of the prisoners were heavily ironed, and one man had an iron hoop over his head, from which a bell was suspended.

Both here and at other dinners customs similar to Quaker practice were observed:

> After dinner we all rose from the table as usual, but made a pause standing, before we withdrew. I observed there was also a pause before dinner, though no one uttered a word. We retired into the next room to take coffee. I like this practice very much.

Dr. Haartman accompanied him to dinner with the archbishop, and again Allen was pleased that the whole mood and disposition again seemed again similar to Quaker practice:

Before we sat down, they all made a solemn pause, standing, no one uttering a word. On rising after dinner, there was another pause, when Stephen advanced a step or two, and in a very delicate and suitable manner, sweetly addressed them in a few words, which seemed to be well accepted; a good feeling prevailed throughout, and after retiring to the next room to take coffee, the Archbishop seemed to be more and more interested in the conversation. He fully assented to the great truth that the ceremonies in religion, and even what they call the ordinances, are nothing compared with the living substance.

Grellet's account of this journey in his *Memoirs* follows Allen's closely, but it is more specifically religious. 'The Bishop speaks good French,' he writes 'and appears to be a man of religious liberality united with piety, which it is peculiarly pleasant to meet with in a person in such a station.' He goes beyond Allen's response to the dinner protocol: seated next to the Archbishop, he

took the opportunity to ask him respecting their having thus stood in silence before sitting down. He said that it is his regular practice in his family; he considers it much preferable to the formal habit of uttering set prayers, which often the heart does not feel; but that in silence there is an opportunity for the heart to feel after and receive a qualification for secret prayer to God.

He mentions several matters not regarded by Allen, writing, for example, that they were 'much pained, since coming to Finland, to find that so many women are in these prisons for the crime of infanticide. It appears to exist to a very deplorable extent.' After returning from the castle he 'felt so distressed . . . under a sense of the sufferings and misery which I had beheld, that I could not sleep.'

Another dinner was given by the Governor General, Count

Steinhielt, with whom, as with Julin, he was able to share his scientific interests:

> The Governor and I soon withdrew to his cabinet of minerals, which contains some of the rarest and most choice specimens of the country. Several were quite new to me, and he offered me some of his duplicates; Cornish specimens are rarities here, and I am to send him some, together with strontian, both carbonate and sulphate, &c., &c.

Allen departed for Helsinki on 2 November, after a disturbed night: 'There was a great dance at our inn this evening, though it was first-day. We have been much pained at several things in this house'(at the prison he had noted 'the increase of crime, in consequence of war and the use of strong liquor'). He took 'affectionate leave' of many new friends. Haartman 'said it was indeed hard, after having met with such friends, to part with them so soon'.

> After some delay about the horses, we set off between eight and nine, with our man Peter, who is coachman. We passed several poor hamlets, and have seen some wooden crosses, which we learn are to mark the distances. They now measure by Russian versts, and a verst is just about three-fourths of an English mile. The travelling in this country is, beyond all comparison, better than in Norway, and cheaper than in any part of the world we have yet visited. We are not obliged to send on a fore boot [a receptacle for stowing baggage], the horses being always ready.
>
> The accommodation at some of the stations was miserably poor, and though, in many parts, the roads were excellent, yet, in some places, they were sandy and heavy.

Settled in Helsinki, he 'waited by appointment on the State Counsellor d'Ehrenstrom'. This was Johan Albrecht Ehrenström, the chairman of the committee in charge of rebuilding the city after the great fire of 1808. 'He showed us the plans of improvement for the new buildings, &c, which, when finished, will make this a beautiful place.' In contrast to the old city plan with narrow and winding alleys, Ehrenström planned for Helsinki wide streets placed on a grid like cities of ancient Greece. 'This is a very interesting place,' writes Allen, 'and we seem to have arrived just in the right time.' Russia had relocated the capital from Turku to Helsinki in 1812, and building was now gathering pace. Just twelve years later Captain Frankland saw the results of Ehrenström's work:

Sept 23 – I arose early and sallied forth to look at the city. It indeed surpasses any expectation I had previously formed. It is the most beautiful and most interesting new city I ever beheld.

Allen's interests, though, were not architectural:

[Ehrenström] received us civilly, and seems to have a clear head and a right conception of things. He thinks the most effectual way of doing good is to interest the benevolent persons in a place, and form a committee for the care of the poor. This has been done here, and much has already been effected. We had a good deal of conversation with him, and were quite pleased in becoming acquainted with him. He says great improvements are going forward here, and the Emperor intends it for the seat of government in Finland. He is quite alive to the advantages of our system of education for the poor, and engages that a school-room shall be built; I left a manual with him. In the afternoon G. W. Sundman called upon us – he is an agreeable man, and one of the committee for the care of the poor.

This was Gustaf Wilhelm Sundman (1777–1835), a strong contributor to the development of Helsinki as a port. His house on the South Shore, designed by Engel, later became the most acclaimed restaurant in Finland.

Ehrenström accompanied them to inspect the 'poor-house and schools', and they then crossed to Suomenlinna, where

We met with a hearty reception from the Governor, Count Heydon, to whom the Governor General of Finland had given us a letter of introduction. We soon entered into agreeable conversation, and found him an excellent warmhearted man of very liberal sentiments. He quickly gave us to understand we might see all we wished, upon the condition of our dining with him, and we accordingly accepted his invitation. His sentiments on capital punishment and prison discipline are in perfect unison with our own, and he much regretted the present system. He sent his aid-de-camp, a very fine young man, to show us the prison, hospitals, &c. There is no sort of classification in the prison; in one room containing forty prisoners, there were nine boys committed for not having passports . . . Some of the men were heavily ironed. There are no women confined in the fortress. The hospital for the prisoners is in good order, and we were much pleased with the neatness which prevailed in the marine hospital, where there are two hundred and twenty-one patients; the linen is changed twice a week.

Our kind conductor, Dessen, took us to see the school, where ninety poor boys, taken from the whole province, are boarded, clothed, and educated. It was now two o'clock and we returned to Count Heydon's to dinner. He introduced us to his wife and family of fine children; their eldest daughter, Mary, reminded me of my own dear child; we had much conversation at dinner, and after retiring to take coffee, spent about an hour very agreeably and profitably, with these excellent persons; they are, both, earnest to see our school plans adopted, and the Count, who is a benevolent man, desired me to tell d'Ehrenstrom that, if a society were formed to promote this measure, and other objects connected with the welfare of the poor, he would become the first member of the committee. The Countess is anxious to have a school for girls; when we were coming away the Count accompanied us to the water side, where we found his own barge manned, with three pairs of oars, ready to take us back to Helsingfors. We parted under mutual feelings of affectionate regard, and afterwards went, by appointment, to spend some time with d'Ehrenstrom.

Despite the enlightened views of many he had met, Allen's last visit in Helsinki left him in a despondent mood:

We afterwards visited the schools and prison. In general, the education of the girls is much neglected. The prison was a trying and heart-sickening scene; most of the men were ironed, and one man had a great weight of iron upon his legs, an iron belt round his middle, and an iron collar round his neck, with a projecting piece eight or nine inches long, with chains beside. We could not help expressing to the gentlemen who accompanied us, our strong disapprobation of this barbarous mode of securing prisoners. The delay of justice is so great that, by Sundman's account, a prisoner sometimes is in prison two years, and often in irons, before his case is decided.

At Hamina '[we] delivered our letters of introduction from the Governor General, and, as usual, met with much kind attention.' They visited 'the prison, military school, and hospital', but, as in Helsinki, it was the prison which dismayed them: 'None of the persons here seem to have the least idea of a rational and Christian system of prison discipline, and [they] look upon the reformation of culprits as a thing next to impossible.' Apart from that, there was much which impressed them:

The military hospital is a large wooden building, and, like the rest of the houses, is roofed with wood. Every thing was in very clean nice order. The peasants, when ill, are admitted here as well as the soldiers.

We could not avoid dining with the Commandant, where we met a large company, many of whom were young officers. On Stephen [Grellet] remarking pleasantly to Colonel Taraschoff that we were men of peace, he, smiling, took off his sword, and put it in the corner of the room, and his example was followed by the officers round him. The freedom, openness, and hospitality we experienced, were very remarkable. In the evening we were visited at our inn by the Colonel, and several others who came to take leave. We have met with nothing but the greatest kindness and respect.

Continuing to the East, their experiences echo those of a dozen or so of the early travellers chronicled in *Not so Barren*:

About nine we arrived at the station Pytterlax, a filthy dirty house, but here we must breakfast. There was a cock crowing upon the table in the midst of the dirt: we, however, found another part of the premises rather more decent, and took our breakfast there, standing; we had brought our bread and tea with us.

In Vyborg, 'a strongly fortified town', they 'found pretty good accommodation at the inn, which is kept by an Italian, who speaks French well'. Here they did much as they had done in Turku and Helsinki, visiting the prison, the military school, and the *gymnasium* (high school) . 'We left several books and tracts, but regretted that our stock was nearly exhausted. I believe this visit will long be remembered by many here'.

In the city the weather had been 'very fine, but cold, the thermometer . . . equal to 14° of Fahrenheit.' As they left Finland winter was setting in. 'The snow is every where on the ground, and the roads are very rough. About two o'clock we arrived at the outposts of Petersburg'.

William Rae Wilson

Captain James Edward Alexander arrived in Turku in 1827, shortly after the fire which destroyed three-quarters of the city, including the university. '[A] most melancholy spectacle,' he wrote, 'Never did I see such desolation and ruin.' William Rae Wilson experienced some of the last days of Turku before the fire; his account was actually published shortly *after* the fire, and this gives his description a particular pathos. Of matching importance is the sparkling account he gives of every stage of the journey from St. Petersburg. No other British traveller from this era gives such an attractive picture of Finland.

Wilson was a modest lawyer who practiced as a solicitor in Glasgow until, inheriting a large fortune, he was able to 'gratify his taste for travel'. He was an intensely religious man, whose first recorded journey was *Travels in Egypt and the Holy Land*; this was followed by accounts of his travels in southern Europe, as far as Greece, and in northern Europe as far as Norway. His description of Finland is in the second volume of *Travels in Russia* (1828).

He was one of the many British travellers who had unforeseen difficulties in getting out of Russia, and he devoted half a chapter to chronicling them. The easy availability of horses was for him 'a proof we were approaching happy Finland'.'Happy Finland' becomes his theme, and the contrast with Russia is described animatedly wherever he looked:

> [we] found ourselves among a race of people altogether different from those we had hitherto met, in point of dress, appearance, physiognomy, and manners. Among these people, neither frowzy beards, slovenliness, nudity, nor grim visages, were to be seen; on the contrary, they appeared to be quite a superior race to the Russian peasantry. They are remarkably fair, their hair

almost resembling flax, cleanly in their habits, wear white clothes, and are marked by a striking simplicity of manners. We had soon an opportunity of observing them closely; for on changing horses we were surrounded by a number of both sexes, anxious to render us every possible assistance. The men were wrapped up in wide and thick long coats, as coarse, in fact, as a common blanket, with blue sashes round their waists, and had white pantaloons and boots. Farther on we met some hundreds of carts, drawn by diminutive animals, with a live cargo of Finns proceeding to the fair of Viborg, who showed the greatest politeness, taking off their hats, and making profound obeisance to us; marks of respect I do not recollect having observed at any time among the Russians.

West of Vyborg '[t]he views around were highly romantic', and life seemed to him little short of idyllic: 'Among all the peasantry here a great degree of comfort seemed to prevail; for we found no symptoms of misery or squalidity. All, in short, were well clothed, healthy, and apparently contented.' The closely-observed features he describes include a primitive snow plough, the detail of the fencing of the fields, the care taken of the potato crop, and the practice 'when horses are warm, for the drivers to take hold of them by the nostrils, and pinch and shake their heads violently'. In every village,' he notes, 'there is a large swing, with a seat large enough for two adults'.

In this part of the country, children, not more than four years of age, are actually dressed like old men, with high night-caps, coarse striped jackets, and enormous boots, so that they look like dwarfs.

Here we observed no females lolling, sauntering, and chattering about their doors in groups, as in Russia; but most of them were employed, many being occupied in knitting stockings, at the same time singing merrily, and enjoying the beauty of a brilliant sunny day.

Many of the travellers of this era regarded Finland only as an unavoidable distraction separating Russia from Sweden: a territory to be got over as quickly as possible. John Barrow, travelling in early September 1830, covered the whole 418 miles in four days, and mentions only that 'the face of the country' was 'of a pleasing character'. Wilson's account gives some idea of what he missed:

> From the fine state of the roads, – which are formed of gravel, and adorned on each side with beautiful trees, among which the willow and the verdant tapering fir were finely contrasted to the autumnal tint of the birch, – we might have imagined ourselves to be travelling along the avenue of some château.

Horses could be obtained with ease, but could be controlled only with difficulty:

> The Finns do not appear to have as yet acquired much skill in the art of breaking-in horses, for the animals are very restive, and almost as wild as if no attempt whatever had been made to tame them. Unless, therefore, they are kept tightly reined and harnessed, they are apt to turn out of the road and resist the efforts of the driver to urge them forwards; and it is a thousand to one but that the carriage is upset: indeed, it is necessary that a traveller should bring his own harness, as that in use here is very weak, and continually breaking. On this account we were often obliged to stop; and at one time the animals were so fierce and ungovernable, that they started out of the road, and ran among some large stones, while the wheels grazed against an enormous piece of granite, so that it was altogether a miracle that our vehicle was not dashed in pieces.

The women in Finland, were, by contrast, very biddable: they 'appear exceedingly good housewives of their time, for, like the Welsh, they employ themselves in knitting while walk-ing, although proceeding to ever so short a distance'. Wilson travelled with his wife, who is, presumably, included in the first-person plural of the narration, although she is never men-tioned. It would interest modern readers to learn what she thought of her husband's perspective:

> Health and robustness, rather than beauty, seem to be the characteristics of the females, except ruddy cheeks constitute any claim to the latter quality; neither do they appear greatly to study the art of setting off their persons to the best advantage, their principal attire being jack-ets and coloured petticoats. That they are not remarka-bly delicate in point of constitution, is evident from their not having recourse, even in such a climate, to shoes and stockings . . .

> After passing through several villages, we came first to Broby, beyond which the country is flat, but well cul-tivated; and afterwards to Pyttis [Pyttää], a considerable village, situate on a river of that name, which glides gen-tly past it. There is one church, with a prodigiously lofty roof, quite out of proportion to the body of the building, covered with small pieces of wood, one overlapping the other, in imitation of slate. In the church-yard the graves are covered with a roof resting on piles of wood at each corner, within two feet of the ground, and between it and the latter are railings, so that they have a considerable resemblance to hen-coops.

Hamina detained him only briefly, but he was quite taken by Lovisa:

> The roofs of the houses are covered with green turf; and it was a singular sight to see some of the natives reposing among the grass on them, basking in the sun, and with as much delight and satisfaction as if they had been in

an open field. The children are very beautiful, and have remarkably white hair; nor are the women less comely. Many of them were busily occupied with their needle and the distaff, within and without doors, and there was a peculiar modesty and calm demeanour about them, truly indicative of serenity and content. . .

Before the shops are lofty poles, twenty or thirty feet high, on which are suspended, by way of signs, figures of wood or tin, indicative of the trade carried on, or the articles sold; and when viewed from the end of a street, they present a very curious appearance.

A fine prospect is presented from the rocks hanging over the town, where the white chimneys, contrasted with the green "fields" on the summit of the houses, have a very pleasing effect.

The favourable impression continued on the way to Porvoo, especially at the inn where

we were received by a gigantic landlady, who was all bustle, like Mrs. Cheshire in the play; and seemed resolved that every thing should be shown off to the best advantage, for she ordered six large candles to be set upon the table. A bountiful supper of game was set out, with an enormous crystal bottle of spirits.

The following day brought a change of mood:

A miserable sight was presented of the remains of a person who had forfeited his life to the laws of his country . . . Three gallows, or rather strong posts, twenty feet in height, were erected a short distance from each other. That in the centre had the form of a wheel laid horizontally at top, with a ladder placed at the foot of it. The head of the criminal was first struck off, and fixed on the top of the wheel to the right, and the hand which directed the fatal blow on that to the left. In the centre was the body in its clothes, with the arms extended, and the legs hanging down. These dismal objects were fixed upon an elevation a short distance from the road, and the back was surrounded with dark wood, which threw a gloomy horror over the scene . . .

Helsingfors came into view at the extremity of a very extensive valley; and we afterwards travelled along the side of the water, where the prospect was prodigiously grand, both the islands and the opposite shores being covered with wood; and we were quite in raptures with the delightful scenery. The mile-stones hereabouts are pieces of granite, in the form of a pyramid, three feet in height, and two in breadth, set up on a pile of stones; and the letters on them are gilt . . .

From the number of new buildings in progress, quite on the Russian plan, (consisting of two or three stories, of stone, or of brick, coated with plaster, and roofs of sheet-iron, painted brown or green,) all traces of a Finnish town will soon disappear, and St. Petersburg will be represented here in miniature.

Wilson's taste was evidently for the small coastal towns; the only place that attracted and interested him here was 'the important fortress of Sveaborg [Suomenlinna], which was once the principal bulwark of Finland, will always render Helsingforth[sic] a place of note'.

Their request to visit the fortress was successful; they were escorted by 'Graf Erfelt, a young Swedish colonel in the Russian service, and aide-de-camp to the governor. This gentleman spoke English fluently'. At the harbour 'an elegant barge belonging to the governor, with a green awning, and rowed by twelve sailors dressed in white trowsers, striped jackets and caps, was in waiting'. He was given a prolonged tour, but decided not to make any notes: 'the attempt to do so might have excited suspicions, and have been attended with some unpleasant circumstances', so he was able to recall only rather general impressions: 'I can therefore only say, that both from its situation and natural strength, and the peculiar manner in which it has been fortified, this fortress appears to be altogether impregnable'. This diagnosis proved to be correct when it was put to the test in 1855, during the Crimean War.

This spot, which may be considered the key of Finland, as much as Malta is that of the Mediterranean, is situated on seven islands, composed entirely of rocks connected together by bridges of boats, and covered with houses, docks, barracks, hospitals, prisons, so that, in fact, it appears to be a cluster of small towns. The whole exhibits a most wonderful proof of the genius and activity which distinguished those who were employed in improving the advantages that nature had bestowed, by forming such tremendous bulwarks for the defence of the country.

The only disagreeable part of their tour – 'altogether disgusting' – was the prison. True Brits abroad, they could not resist giving unrequested opinions and advice: 'We took the liberty of remonstrating with the officers, and contrasted the filth and wretchedness here with that order, cleanliness, and classification which so much distinguish places of confinement in England.'

After viewing all the fortifications and the harbour, which is capable of containing upwards of 100 sail of the line, filled with astonishment at the incredible magnitude and extent of the works, where nature seems to have co-operated with the exertions of man, we returned to Helsingfors; and afterwards expressed, in a letter, our acknowledgements to the governor.

'On quitting Helsingfors,' Wilson writes, 'we . . . proceeded in the direction of Bomboli (probably Rembōle) where we arrived just at the time an assemblage of peasants had sat down to supper after the labours of the field.' Wilson presents it as a

SCENE AT AN INN:

Never was there such an exhibition! A more capital group could not possibly have been presented for the pencil of our Wilkie, or that of Cruikshanks. A long piece of burning lath stuck into the wall, served as a candle, and when it burned out was replaced by another. This glimmering light, with the crowded table, smoke from the hot victuals, and the competition of spoons in one dish, scrambling for the best supply of what it contained; the sparkling eyes seen through half darkness, the bushy locks hanging about the dishes, the yawning of the peasants from fatigue, the crowing of a cock perched over their heads, the snoring in chorus of an old couple lolling one in each corner of the fire-place, the hissing of a piece of meat in a frying-pan, superintended by an urchin, half roasted himself by the heat; with the bellowing of cattle out of doors, the rain rattling against the windows, and in addition, the screaming of a child in a cradle, and the growling of a mastiff under the table, who was affronted at not having come in for his portion of scraps, formed altogether such a combination of sounds and objects that it is extremely difficult to decide whether the preference should be given to the music, the scenery, or the characters.

The journey to Turku Wilson describes with extravagant enthusiasm. The recurring epithets are 'picturesque' (5 times), 'romantic', (6) and 'beautiful' (7).

On resuming our route, we travelled through many fine, well-cultivated valleys, with spring crops, remarkably green, and diversified with many murmuring streams. There were, also, several villages, and churches with extraordinarily high roofs, and mills for sawing wood into planks. The cedar, as well as the juniper tree, contributed to the embellishment of the landscape; nor were the inhabitants less cheerful than the country itself, for the countenance of every one we met beamed with satisfaction. At the post-house at Björsby '[t]he gratitude on the part of the landlady, on our paying the bill for lodging and breakfast, was such, that she actually laid hold of our arms and kissed them most cordially, a tolerable proof that travellers were rarities to her.

Travelling on towards Salo, Wilson bursts into a Wordsworthian hymn of praise for unspoiled nature, and scenery which included even wild roses. All was bright and beautiful:

The views in this part were delightfully romantic and varied, and the whole landscape one of the finest we had ever beheld. Dead must be the heart of that man who travels along insensible of the beauties of nature: every thing is expressive of gladness and joy; the perfume of flowers, the harmony of the feathered tribe, the gentle breeze, the flocks browzing, and winged insects sporting in the rays of a glorious sun; – moreover, the majestic woods, meandering streams, the silver waves of rivers, and verdure of the fields. Who can be indifferent, we ask, to her wonderful works? All that he sees around ought to prompt him, not only to admire the goodness of a bountiful Creator, who merely 'spoke, and it was done,' but reflect on the greatness of His wisdom.

We afterwards proceeded along the side of a rocky mountain covered with wood, to which succeeded well-cultivated valleys, extensive sheets of water, clusters of cottages, with meadows covered with flocks and shepherds, and numbers of windmills in full motion on a height. These mills are remarkably narrow, and resemble in shape a huge sentry-box. We next arrived at Sahlo [Salo], which is situated in an amphitheatre, surrounded by rocks in an undulating form; and proceeding along this extensive amphitheatre, which has a lake in front, we passed through a delightful woody country, until, after a drive along a most noble avenue, we reached Handala, which commands a most enchanting view of a fertile vale beneath, fringed with wood.

Wilson's account of Turku, as of Helsinki, is mainly of the principal buildings. The observatory, and the view from the hill he finds especially attractive:

On the highest rock, which bears some general similarity to the Calton-hill at Edinburgh, is a handsome observatory, with towers, and a statue on the summit. From this eminence a beautiful prospect is presented, not only of the town on each side of the banks of the river, and its serpentine stream, but of the country around, which is enlivened by the numerous windmills on the opposite heights; and, except it be at Lisle in Flanders, I have nowhere seen so many in one spot.

He describes the cathedral with some enthusiasm, with particular praise for the 'fine organ':

Little attention, at least externally, is perceptible in keeping it in proper repair, but the interior is remarkably neat, and a peculiar grandeur and solemnity reign throughout the whole. Its length is about 150 feet, breadth 80, it is upwards of 100 feet in height, and on each side supported by nine columns. There are two aisles, in which are recesses with windows, that appear to have been used as chapels during the period of Catholicism.

Under [the gallery] is a baptismal font, with an angel holding a shell: this figure is of wood, and has a massy canopy over it. The altar has a painting of the Last Supper, surmounted by one of the Crucifixion; and the pulpit, which is very handsome, is of black and white carved work, with the twelve apostles and Christ in the centre; its roof is also supported by two angels. Among the portraits of ecclesiastics are those of Luther and Melancthon.

In the castle, now a prison, '[w]e saw 100 criminals, 50 of whom were females. The males were most heavily loaded with irons round the neck, body, hands, and legs.' Nearby was a mineral spring 'which is annually resorted to by what may be considered a tolerable number of visitors, there being generally about 400 in the course of the season'. 'On the quay is a substantial inn, built by subscription, but on a scale too large and magnificent for such a town, and contains a ball-room, 143 feet long, by 60 broad, with a music-gallery, and seven lustres.' Many other such details make up his picture of the city.

Wilson was impressed most by the University. 'The building, which stands opposite to the Cathedral, was greatly improved by Gustavus Adolphus.'

There is a grand hall, 70 feet in length and 61 in breadth, which is used on extraordinary occasions, such as at the time of royal visits. At one end, in an alcove or semicircular recess, 15 feet in depth, is a bust of the emperor Alexander in bronze, on a high pedestal of polished granite, with an inscription in gold letters. There are four beautiful polished granite columns, 30 feet in height, on each side. On the walls are various emblematical devices in stucco; one of which represents Gustavus and his queen laying the foundation of this edifice; on which occasion the Duke of Gloucester was present. The music-gallery over the recess has a gilded railing.

There are 500 students in this seminary, to whom lectures are given gratis, government paying all expenses. Part of the revenue in support of the establishment is derived from land, the rest from a duty on exports from the town. Although there is a theatre, which rarely occurs in universities, all representations are prohibited during term; yet the Russian military are allowed to remain in the town, which never occurred when it belonged to Sweden. This has given great offence to the inhabitants, and most deservedly, since such amusements are calculated to divert the attention of the scholars from their studies. The botanical garden contains some thousands of exotics and indigenous plants. During the government of the Swedes, the School of Anatomy had the extraordinary privilege of demanding the dead bodies of those who held lands or pensions from the crown; but it is believed the Russians will take care that a law of this nature shall not extend to them. We were shown the Library, consisting of three handsome apartments; in the principal one of which is a marble bust, on a pedestal of granite, of M. Porthan, Professor of Eloquence, whose memory is here held in the highest veneration. This Library may be considered in its infancy, although it contains 40,000 volumes. A copy of each book published in Finland must be presented to it; but few are to be seen in this remote region. In glancing at the books, the most ancient of those pointed out to us were some writings of Hieronymus, in 1468; a Latin Bible of 1479; a collection of works on jurisprudence, by the celebrated Professor Chaubold of Leipsic. We were shown some English books; such as the "Archaeologia," by the Society of Antiquarians; Dugald Stewart's Elements of Philosophy; Black's Chemistry; Byron's Voyages, &c. Among the manuscripts is one of the History of Job, in thirty-five books, 1268.

Wilson was possibly the last visitor to see these books; a footnote to his own volume reads

Since the above was written a most terrible event has occurred at Abo. On the 4th of September, 1827, at nine o'clock in the evening, it was visited by a most awful conflagration, which, after raging twenty-four hours, ended with the almost total destruction of the town. The fire broke out in the premises of a tallow-chandler, who, to escape the penalty attached to carrying on such a business within the town, endeavoured to conceal the accident as long as possible; but the devouring element spread with such rapidity in three directions, that its ravages soon became universal. The cathedral, which had so long braved the hand of time, together with the archives of the consistory, and all the buildings of the university, were destroyed; and the scholar and the antiquarian will deeply lament the destruction of the library and cabinet of medals. The custom-house, court of justice, collection of instruments, town-hall, printing offices, and about 1000 houses, fell also a prey to the flames. Only thirty houses escaped, and 11,000 families were literally burned out and lost their all. To add to this overwhelming calamity, upwards of 100 human beings perished. Little did I imagine when I commenced the preceding account of Abo, that I should have to conclude with recording so dreadful a catastrophe. In addition to this, the religious world will regret to learn that all the Bibles and Testaments of the Bible Society, with the standing types for an octavo Bible in the Finnish language, and stereotype plates for a New Testament, fell a sacrifice to the flames; and the loss thus occasioned has amounted to upwards of 70,000 rubles. The Society of London have already generously made a grant of Swedish Testaments, and are making preparations to print an edition of the Finnish Testament for the general benefit of Finland. A second fire broke out in December, about three months after, which has reduced the remainder of this ill-fated town to ashes.

Wilson had found little to admire in Russia, and as he departs from mainland Finland, nearly a century before it declared its independence, he foresees its future with a certain amount of foreboding:

> During the whole of our journey, it was a subject of heartfelt regret to us that this fine country should have been added to the before enormous territory of Russia. Its invasion by the latter power was most unjustifiable, and the poor Finns were transferred to their new masters, without the least show of reason. Russia, in fact, seems to be grasping at the acquisition of fresh dominion far more ambitiously than prudently; for what is apparently gained in extent, with respect to physical force, is lost as to moral energy; and a power that could subjugate the globe, would have nearly as many rivals and enemies as it had dependant states. But let Russia never lose sight of one fact; that although it has obtained possession of Finland, never will she be able to acquire the affection of the natives, who are still, and ever will continue to be, attached to Sweden, which they regard with the feelings of one separated by force from a relation or friend. In seizing on this country, she stripped Sweden of a most invaluable possession; and, it is to be feared, that popular hatred will break out, sooner or later, like a volcano. It was easy to perceive that the Finns entertain a decided hatred against the Russians, and look on them as enemies; and although their language is cautious, yet their enmity and wrath are treasured up against the day when they may display them. In appearance in dress, in simplicity of manners, in their habits and dispositions, the natives are altogether opposite to the Russians. Much has been said of the ambition of Napoleon, whose object was universal empire; but the same charge may be alleged against Russia, since extension of territory seems to be her grand object.

Not so Barren or Uncultivated chronicles many accounts of the perilous crossings the Gulf of Bothnia, in all seasons of the year. It would be a couple more years before steamships finally replaced the sailing boat on this route; before that travellers were likely to experience the effects of prolonged calm or of violent storms. Wilson was unfortunate enough to encounter both. They secured a cabin on a boat 'literally crammed with passengers; among whom were some strolling players, stowed together like slaves for sale.' It was four days before they were able to sail down river, and then 'we were compelled to cast anchor in consequence of contrary winds, and forced to remain two days more.' When they finally got to sea

> a tremendous tempest set in, threatening our destruction . . . All the following day we were detained among clusters of islands, where, in many places, the passage was so extremely narrow, and the navigation so intricate and perilous from the numerous rocks, that it required a person, not only an expert pilot, but one who had a thorough knowledge of the place, to bring a vessel through of any burden.

Even after arriving in Stockholm they were not allowed ashore for another day, 'after a week's passage from Abo, which might have been accomplished by steam in twenty-four hours.'

*

The *Oxford Dictionary of National Biography* entry for Wilson concludes: 'Already criticized in his lifetime as trite and ill-written, his books were rapidly forgotten after his death.' It has been a privilege to rescue this one from oblivion.

Vyborg and the Saimaa Canal

In September 2019 I took a day trip from Helsinki to Vyborg, travelling by boat from Lappeenranta, by way of the Saimaa Canal. Talking with the manager of the excursion, I learned that she was a Karelian, her grandparents natives of Käkisalmi (Kexholm). She was understandably disappointed when I told her that few of the authors represented in my three books about the British in Finland had written about Vyborg. As Ernest Young had put it in 1912,

> Viborg is little visited by the tourist, but there is much probability that the man who 'does' Switzerland in ten days and Paris in two hours would find little to interest him. The majority of those who come to Viborg merely arrive *en route* for somewhere else.

I decided to look at the British travel accounts again, and found that in my reading I too had rather neglected Vyborg.

Until the mid-nineteenth century most of the British travellers to southern Finland were on their way to or from Russia, and Finland was rarely much more than a staging post. From about 1830 there was the option of travelling by sea, either from Lübeck to Cronstadt or from Stockholm by way of Turku, Helsinki, and Tallinn; Captain Alexander, a Scottish soldier and explorer, arrived in Finland in 1829 in 'the little smoke ship' from Tallinn to Helsinki. A later route was by train from Hamburg direct to St Petersburg, and before the end of the century there were regular sailings from England to Finland, now a destination in its own right. As tourism grew in popularity Vyborg became 'the most convenient starting-point for several of the show places of Finland,' as Young wrote, rather than merely the last stop before St. Petersburg. Several travellers I wrote about in earlier volumes had enthused about these places: Sortavala and Käkisalmi – now part of Russia

– Savonlinna, Imatra, and Punkaharju. For several of them Vyborg had been rather more than just a starting-point.

Sir Nathaniel William Wraxall, travelling in 1774, is an early instance of a traveller for whom the town was no more than a B&B stop. This is all that he has to say:

> The entrance into Wybourg, across the river, over two long wooden bridges, is striking; and I have seen no place since leaving Stockholm, where there seems so much the face of industry and commerce as here. It is a fortified city, and during the wars between Charles and Peter, when it belonged to the former of those princes, was reputed strong, the Russians having been more than once forced to raise the siege; but at present the fortifications appear to be very ruinous . . . I hope to reach St. Petersburgh to-morrow.

The last sentence says it all.

What particularly distinguished Vyborg from the other Finnish towns, something noted by many of these early travellers, was, as Edward Daniel Clarke put it, that it was 'still *Finland,* but it is *Russian Finland.'*

> The inhabitants of Wibourg are partly Russians and partly Finns. The former are generally distinguished by their beards: in their dress, they have the appearance of Jews, a long loose coat being tied round the waist with a sash. The Finland girls wear their hair drawn together, and fastened at the back of the head with a little circular roll, and a pin stuck through it.

John Thomas James characterised the population more precisely:

> The men seemed quite another race of beings; no longer the modest homely Fin, but persons of strong masculine habit, carrying a stubborn and listless mien, that,

combined with their majestic stature, seemed by no means devoid of dignity: while the coloured ornaments with which they were set off lent them an air of grotesque magnificence, not ill according with the showy buildings that surrounded us; every object, in short, which met our eyes, partook of the same character, and bore a hint of Asiatic origin.

Little had changed when Captain George Matthew Jones passed through in the late 1820s: 'we appeared,' he wrote, 'to have passed to a different race of people in every respect . . . with a population in a costume perfectly new to us'.

Arriving in this remote town, and knowing nothing of it but its name, some travellers experienced an enchantment perhaps lent by distance. James recorded:

On waking at an early hour after a sound sleep in my sledge, I gazed with wonder at the spectacle that presented itself in the streets of Wyborg: the glare of white houses, their green roofs and oriental cupolas, the noble mansions of the wealthy, and the religious fane, all so spacious and splendid in comparison of what we had lately been accustomed to see.

Some years later Thomas Denman Whatley, in the first edition of Murray's *Handbook for Travellers* (1839), also gave a rather striking and romantic picture of the city:

About seven o'clock we first came in sight of the distant towers of *Viborg* almost encircled by the sea, with a large harbour, in which we could distinguish the masts of numerous vessels; its churches and domes flashing in the morning sun and its long lines of batteries and bastions rising in massive strength from the water's edge. I have seldom seen any thing more striking than the first view of this frontier fortress – the country people in their gay Sunday dresses of red and yellow, thronging to the city, some on foot, others in various odd carriages, gave additional beauty and animation to the scene. It was full an hour from our first coming in sight of the city before we reached its gates.

At the end of the century Harry de Windt looked out from his hotel with disbelief:

Viborg is barely eighty miles from Petersburg, and yet I awaken to-day in another world in a cosy bedroom worthy of the Gordon Hotels. Its windows overlook a scene more suggestive of sunny Spain or Italy than the Frozen North. The picturesque town nestling against a background of pine forest, and blue waters of the harbour sparkling under a cloudless sky, the wooded islets with their pretty villas, the ruined castle of Viborg, with its crumbling thirteenth-century battlements, and last, but not least, the general air of life and animation are indeed pleasant to contemplate after the drab, dreary streets of the Russian capital.

He visited the castle, and walked back to the hotel 'through the public gardens, now crowded with fashionably dressed loungers, for Viborg, although it contains but some 20,000 inhabitants, is the Brighton of northern Russia.'

Captain Frankland summarised his impressions of 'a beautiful town, . . . regularly fortified. Green cupolas and roofs, facades of houses of yellow stucco, &c. are its characteristics. Good wide streets and spacious squares'. A recurrent epithet was 'handsome', sometimes just 'tolerably handsome'. Nearly all of the writers comment on the green roofs, while 'spacious streets and squares' are noted everywhere. There is just one recurrent disagreement; Clarke wrote that 'The edifices are all of brick, none of wood being allowed', but it seems that they *were* allowed, since according to Robert Pinkerton 'The houses are well constructed, exactly in the Swedish mode of building; being of wood, painted of a darkened colour'. De Windt agreed: 'many of its dwellings are built of wood, which, however, is generally stained a dark red colour'.

Every visitor noticed the churches, perhaps because Vyborg was probably the only Finnish town which offered much choice. 'There are four churches here,' wrote Rae Wilson, 'of the Russian, Catholic, Lutheran, and Finnish persuasions'. Pinkerton, who was an agent of the British and Foreign Bible Society, was perhaps showing his bias when he noted 'three Lutheran churches, one Russian church, [and]one Catholic church' but he left town immediately, having done no more than classify them. 'The churches,' wrote Jones, 'with cupolas painted green, were surmounted with a St. Andrew's cross and a crescent'. Back early in the century John Carr, outraged at being delayed by 'nine hours for a new post order, which must be signed by the governor or his deputy', pacified himself by attending divine service.

It was Sunday, and whilst this was negotiating, I visited the Greek church, which stands in a corner of the area where the parade is held, and is an elegant structure of wood, painted light yellow and white, with a roof and dome of copper, painted green. It had a very light and pleasing effect.

After reading the ritual in a low voice, during which his auditory crossed themselves, and one man, near me, in a long and apparently penitential gown of sackcloth, repeatedly touched the basement with his head: the congregation sung in recitative, and with their manly voices produced a fine effect. This will suffice for a description of the Greek church . . .

From this place we proceeded to a reformed catholic church, where the preacher was delivering, with apparently great pathos, a charity sermon, in German: every avenue was thronged almost to suffocation; whenever the orator had made a successful appeal, his hearers testified their approbation in savage acclamations, and the proper officers seized these impressive moments to collect from the congregation the fruits of their bountiful dispositions, received in a little silk bag, fastened to the end of a long stick, from which depended a small bell, shaken whenever charity dropped her mite.

Eventually the nine hours elapsed. Carr's journal for the day concluded, belated, with a prayer: 'Thank heaven! we are out of the town, although the road is very sandy and hilly'.

Travellers agree that Vyborg was, much more than Hamina, a military town. Clarke wrote that '[t]he town has a military appearance: drums are heard from morning to night: the troops are exercised every day, not excepting *Sundays*.' 'With the leave of the Commandant,' he continued, 'we walked round the ramparts, accompanied by the Major de Place.' Sir Robert Ker Porter in 1809 complained of 'the whole city being filled with Russian troops', and Jones wrote in 1822 that '[t]he town is regularly fortified, and has a strong garrison.' Whatley had 'seldom seen any thing more striking than the first view of this frontier fortress'. 'We saw the troops come out of the main church,' he continues: ' – I should think nearly two thousand; they had a beautiful brass band, and played some very pretty marches as the different regiments passed in review before the governor and his staff.'

The military appearance found little favour with the British ladies who were travelling in Finland around the turn of the century; they regarded it as a blight on the whole town. Rosalind Travers described how

At frequent intervals along my way I passed barracks – dreary, dirty structures of the meanest architecture. Soldiers pervaded the town singly or in companies, and did not add to its gaiety, being, for the most part, ill-nourished, ill-dressed, undersized men.

I find Viborg a depressing town. The streets are narrow and dirty, the houses indeterminate, the harbour shapeless; and the whole is ringed in with ugly, squat earthworks and fortifications.

Annie Margaret Clive-Bayley, a fervent supporter of Finland against Russian imperialism, had an additional reason for disliking the military:

... we heard the sound of drill, and also a long and echoing Russian hurrah, which certainly lacks English vitality and heartiness. It seemed rather as if uttered to order, for spontaneity is the last thing to be expected from a Russian soldier.

'I must own that Viborg gave me the impression of being the most dismal town that I had ever come across,' wrote Sylvia McDougall, while Mrs. Tweedie's assessment was close to dismissal: 'as a town Wiborg is nothing to boast of . . . On the high road to Russia, [it] ought to be handsome also and have good stone buildings, but it is not handsome, and has few good buildings.'

The only place which did not deepen Travers's depression was

a gay, crowded market-place, with a round tower in the middle, known as 'Fat Katerina'. The peasant-women are comelier than in Tavastian Finland or in Savolaks, and more pleasingly dressed; the hair is looser, the kerchief more becoming, and they wear a sort of Swiss bodice with touches of colour.

It was not only the ladies who relished the market, and described it with genuine feeling. Young's rather earnest book about Finland briefly becomes lyrical:

Viborg possesses a market that is not surpassed by that of Åbo. From early morn to noon it is a source of pure delight. The women at the stalls are so fat and cheery, the wild strawberries are so red and cheap, and the butter smells so sweetly that you want to purchase everything on the stalls and make the acquaintance of everyone you see. There are stalls, like other stalls, where meat and vegetables are sold, and where mistress and maid go picking and choosing and bargaining for the daily dinner; there are fish stalls and cheese wagons; ice-cream carts and tables where they sell sundry non-intoxicants of brilliant crimson and yellow hues; there are piles of round, flat, acid plasticiny [sic] loaves, and there are, in particular, rows upon rows of Kringlas cakes, the special delicacy of Viborg.

F. J. North, another generally restrained chronicler of his travels, describes how

Torkkelinkatu brings you to the Market Place, which, of course, must be visited in the morning, when it will be crowded with country folk who have come to sell to buy or to gossip . . . It has an air of intimacy that adds greatly to its attraction.

Travellers who trusted to Murray's *Handbook* would have found disappointingly little help with choosing their accommodation. It rather leaves it to them:

Viborg does not contain any regular Hotel; the post-house, kept by a German family, has very tolerable accommodations as far as we put them to the test; besides this there are numerous traiteurs and similar places of entertainment, but their exterior was by no means inviting.

Some visitors discovered that the interiors of these establishments were even less inviting. Ker Porter 'found the inns large and dirty', and his chosen hotel 'was rendered still more prolific in all manner of filthy abominations, by a party of soldiers quartered there'. The first 'Society House' (Seurahuone;

Societetshuset) had opened in Turku in 1812; by the end of the century they could be found in most of the main towns of Finland, and had won favour with British visitors. Sylvia McDougall must have been relieved to see that there was one in Vyborg. 'I hoped that at the hotel things would be different; the name Societetshuset sounded at least pleasant and familiar. But, alas! my hopes were not realized.'

> 'Can I have hot water and some coffee?' I said meekly. 'The chambermaid is on duty at eight o'clock, and the kitchens are open at 8.30,' he replied briefly. Then he strode silently out of the room, and closed the door.

Poor lady! Sir George Renwick suffered a similar disappointment, discovering that although the Helsinki train arrived at 5 a.m., the Societetshus did not open until 8.

'The hotel at which we put up,' wrote Rae Wilson, 'was kept by a native of Como in Italy, and is delightfully situate within view of a lake'. Another traveller, Francis Bayley, wrote in his journal on 10 October 1823 'dined at Wyborg – inn at an Italians, Molti. Very dear and tolerably good'. George Green recommended this as 'a tolerable inn kept by an Italian, and an ordinary [main meal], wine included, for one silver rouble and a half'. Charles Boileau Elliott wrote warmly that this 'excellent inn, the only good one I have seen since leaving Hamburg, is in the hands of a plausible Italian, who kept us in good humour while he filled our mouths and picked our pockets'. Carr was shocked at the assault on his own pocket by the landlord, 'a thorough-paced Italian' who

> had the impudence to charge us ten rubles and fifty copecs for a breakfast, a plain dinner, and a bottle of claret. 'Gentlemen,' said he, in reply to our remonstrance, (which by the bye was a successful one) 'why do you object to high charges? they are the inevitable consequences of approaching the capital.'

Captain Jones, by contrast, felt that he at least got something extra for his money: 'Our landlord, an Italian, had two accomplished daughters, who gave a concert on Sunday evening, which was attended by several officers of the garrison'. Only Captain Frankland seems to have had no problems with hotels: 'We drove to the post-house,' he wrote 'where we found excellent accommodation.'

Bernard Newman's *Baltic Roundabout* (1939) describes cycling from Copenhagen to Rostock. His longest stop on this journey was in Vyborg – he uses the Finnish name Viipuri –, where he had to apply for a visa for the Soviet Union. When the application was refused he had to resume his journey in Tallinn, but he made good use of his enforced stay while he waited. 'If you are wandering in Finland and want history, Viipuri is the place to come for it,' his account begins.

> I asked in vain to see the statue of Peter the Great which for a couple of centuries stood in the centre of Viipuri. It had, however, disappeared – they told me that in 1919 the burghers of Viipuri pulled down the statue and sent it by rail to Russia, carriage forward . . .

This was more or less the extent of his interest in history; he found the present more to his taste. His is the last British account of Vyborg for more than fifty years.

Newman did not hang about: he watched the '[local] paper put to bed, attended a concert by a local choral society, dined open-air in a very pleasant park, argued politics in the local press club, and fell into the sea . . .' The next day was given over to sightseeing. 'We passed by a squat bastion, gaunt and forbidding; it is almost the sole remnant of Viipuri's ancient walls. It is now ignominiously called 'Fat Catherine' – and is used as a restaurant.' He viewed the town from a church tower:

> We descended and wandered about the crooked streets of the old town. Most of the houses were built of stone,

which explained their survival and gave Viipuri an air of antiquity which is missing in Helsinki. The ancient cathedral was delightful, and I appreciated its sombre and restful interior after the glamour of Valamo.

'Fat Catherine' is still a restaurant, and is indeed the most impressive coffee-house I have ever visited.

In 1934 J. M. Richards, an eminent writer on architecture, and author of *Eight Hundred Years of Finnish Architecture* (1978), visited Alvar Aalto, who took him on a tour from Turku to Vyborg, viewing some of his buildings, including the Paimio sanatorium, on the way. He recorded the occasion:

> It was a cosmopolitan city with a long tradition as a cultural and educational centre, and the reason that we had come so far was to look at the library that Aalto had been building there after winning another competition. The competition had been in 1927 but the building was still not quite complete. The reason for the delay was the local council's mistrust of his first design because of its foreign appearance.

I have not located any British account of the library from before 1940; after the war Vyborg, along with most of Karelia, became part of the Soviet Union. As David Langdon has written,

> When its neighbours – including the cathedral itself – were reduced to rubble under Soviet artillery, the library was abandoned and allowed to fall into disrepair. Hidden behind the increasingly impenetrable Iron Curtain, knowledge of the building was lost to the western world, and it was presumed destroyed.

Fiona MacCarthy recorded dining with Aalto at the Savoy in Helsinki in the 1960s:

Aalto talked with some emotion about Viipuri Library,

one of his seminal early buildings which had disappeared with the Russian occupation and was believed to have been destroyed. Its rediscovery in the late 1980s, neglected but not irrevocably damaged, was for Aalto admirers a little miracle . . . It is sad to think that Aalto, who died in 1976, will never know it exists once more. Restoration of the library was first mooted in 2003, and was finally finished in 2013, having cost nearly 9 million euros. Since then it has been on every tourist's visiting list.

For many travellers, such as myself, an added attraction of travelling to Vyborg is the Saimaa Canal. The first one, the 'Canal of Emperors', with 28 locks, opened in 1856, and was enlarged in the 1920s to accommodate larger vessels. It enabled ships from Saimaa, Finland's largest lake, to access the rest of the world; there were customs houses as far north as Kuopio.

Sylvia McDougall's description of ascending the canal, the most detailed, and indeed one of the best parts of her book, is given in *No Particular Hurry*; here is another part of her description, shorn of its more effusively romantic embellishments. She likened the journey to ascending 'a ladder of water', with the locks punctuating the glories of the adjacent countryside:

It sends a thrill through the most phlegmatic pulses as the steamer glides into a kind of cavern, and the massive, ironbound gates through which one enters are slowly closed. The water is black in the shadows of the high walls on either side. All the light and the sunshine seem to have been left behind. Facing us similar gates stand threateningly in our way.

Suddenly an unseen hand pulls away a shutter in the mighty barrier, and through the opening a tongue of water almost like a flame leaps forth. One by one a dozen shutters open and the water dashes forth from each, in a cascade of foam, surging down upon us.

Our steamer rocks to and fro, and beads of perspiration gather on the brows of the sturdy sailors as they hold on for grim death to the ropes that bind the steamer to the sides of the lock, to steady the vessel in her ascent. The waters sobbed and hissed. At last the tension is lessened, the battle is over, and the water, trembling and moaning, endeavours to calm itself. The sailors relax their hold and throw the ropes up on the banks. Slowly the great doors open and we enter another cavern, if possible deeper and more dismal than the first. It is like going back into prison, and one thought that beyond those doors liberty and sunshine were waiting.

'The wooden landing-bridge of Rattijärvi,' she wrote, 'was all aglow with the rays of the setting sun. From the surrounding forest there came the soft tinkle of cow-bells, and a herd of little Finnish cows, heavy with milk, came into view.' With this pastoral adieu she disembarked to start the next stage of her tour, to Imatra.

At about the same time Sir George Renwick, a British shipowner and M. P., who had a 'lifelong interest' in Finland, travelled down the canal (later, more adventurously, he went down the Olunjoki in a tar-boat).

At Juustila the voyager must change from the steamer which had brought him from Viborg and continue the journey on the canal steamer.

The Saimaa Canal is thirty-seven miles long, and is the gateway from the sea to the great Finnish lake system on which one can go almost across the whole country. It took eleven years to construct, about half of it having to be cut through hard Finnish granite. There are twenty-eight locks, and the entire rise is about 300 feet. Before Rattijärvi is reached there are eight locks to be passed, but there is not a great deal of canal, cuttings connecting several lakes. The rate of travel on the canal is very slow, for passing a lock is a long and somewhat tiresome business. During the summer months, too, enormous barges, laden with timber, pass down the canal.

The canal is a silvern staircase through the lovely lands of Karelia, a dainty waterway stealing, a sunlit sheen of mother-o'-pearl, through forests of charming green, where the air is laden with the delicate odour of flowers; now across far-rolling green lands it goes, then through Nature's great ramparts of granite. It is when looking at these sombre cliffs that it is realised what a task it was to drive this road of water to its distant goal. Children play by the canal side; cattle graze there; many a little wooden hut is seen; the song of the bargeman is often heard, and all round everything is at its fairest.

Vyborg and the canal were lost to Russia in the Moscow Peace Treaty of 1940. War damage had made it inoperable, and political as well as financial considerations made its restoration unlikely. In 1963 Finland obtained a fifty year lease on the Soviet section, and constructed a deeper 42.9 kilometre canal, which opened in 1968. This is known as the 'Third Building', and follows only part of the original route; it has just eight locks. Summer cruises, such as the one I took from Lappeenranta, are now an important addition to the commercial traffic, but I have come across no account of travelling the new canal which seems worthy of resurrection.

Crossing the Russian Border

Long before the imposition of the Iron Curtain, which divided
Europe from 1945 until the end of the Cold War in 1992, travel
into – and often out of – Russia could be both a difficult and
a daunting experience. The westernmost branch of the river
Kymi, one of the largest rivers in southern Finland, served as
the border between Sweden and Russia until 1809, when Finland was ceded to Russia. The parts of Finland east of the river
were later known as Old Finland, and were incorporated into
the Grand Duchy of Finland in 1812. Most of the early British
travellers in Finland were on their way to or from Russia and
were therefore, until 1809, crossing from Sweden. For them
the border was marked by the bridge on the River Kymi.

William Coxe crossed the bridge while returning from St
Petersburg in 1779:

> Being admitted through a wooden barrier, guarded by a
> Russian soldier, we crossed a bridge to a small island,
> passed another bridge over a branch of the Kymen, and
> went through a second barrier, at which stood a Swedish
> centinel. On quitting the Russian dominions, our bag-
> gage was slightly searched, and entering Swedish Finland,
> the same ceremony was performed by the custom house
> officers of that district.

Leaving Russia was at that time a good deal simpler that
entering the country, as travellers began to discover. Sir Nathaniel William Wraxall had passed through Finland five years
earlier than Coxe, and crossed the border with no unexpected
problems:

> It was nearly midnight, when I arrived on the bank of
> the river Kymen, which here divides the empire of Russia
> from the dominions of Sweden. The stream is above two

hundred feet broad, and across it is a wooden bridge, one half of which is constantly repaired by the one, and the other half by the other nation. I was stopped by the guards on either side, and underwent a very minute search before I was permitted to proceed.

Twenty years later a 'very minute search' no longer sufficed: corruption had arrived. Edward Daniel Clarke, arguably the most notable of all British travellers in Finland, was on his way to Russia, (and finally Constantinople) in 1800, after a prolonged visit to the University in Turku. He was 'stopped by a Custom-house officer; who intended, as we supposed, that we should unpack all our baggage: but he at last observed, that if we would give him something, be would suffer us to pass.'

Having crossed the *Russian* bridge, we were ordered to halt, by one of the sentinels, a dwarfish meagre figure with a sallow complexion and a long cloak, who, with scarcely strength enough to shoulder a musket, stood shivering before a large fire. A little above was the wretched hovel which serves as a guard-house. Notice being given of our arrival, we were ordered to approach; and after a few necessary ceremonies, we passed to the Custom-house, a little higher up on the left hand. Here we were ushered into a tolerably neat little room, where sate an officer with a lame foot on a couch. He could neither talk *French* nor *English,* and very little *Swedish;* so that we had no means of communication, until at length he surprised us by asking if we spoke *Latin.* Our passports were then examined, and returned. We had reason to fear that our servants would be detained; for although they had been included in the passports of the *Danish* and *Swedish* Sovereigns, and expressly mentioned in that of our own Government, they had not been included in the *Russian.* Our passports were, however, signed and delivered to us, with an assurance that we were at liberty to proceed.

They may have been at liberty, but they still could not proceed. 'It was necessary also,' Clarke continues 'to have our *Swedish* paper changed for *Russian* money, that we might be able to pay for our horses on the other side of the frontier.' An 'Inspector of the Customs' attempted to swindle them with dud banknotes, which they refused to accept – 'the imposition was too glaring to pass'. '[H]is honour had been wounded by the detection of his villainy; and therefore, making a virtue of revenge, he would for once fulfil his duty to his Sovereign, by exactions of the most vexatious and frivolous kind.' He reacted by refusing to allow Clarke's servants entry into Russia.

> He had also, without doubt, a hope that our servants would be left in his hands; by which means a new demand might be made upon us, subject to the most flagrant imposition. The *Swedish* officer, with the politeness and hospitality of his nation, and justly indignant at what he had witnessed, conducted them back to *Louisa* [Lovisa], assuring us that they should be taken care of, until we were able to send for them from *Petersburg*.

John Carr, in 1804, was permitted to proceed, but, like Clarke, only after a great deal of ludicrous and exasperating protocol. At the guardhouse

> we were ushered into a small shabby room; in the windows were some flower pots, and upon an old table the poems of Ossian in French, open, and by their side a vast snuffbox and most filthy handkerchief; presently a little old Russian major entered, in a white linen dressing-gown, and in French demanded our passports, with which he was satisfied, and immediately made out our order for post-horses, without which no one can travel in Russia, called a *fiodoragiria;* upon presenting the paper to us, he demanded six rubles and forty copecs.

Because they had no Russian currency they were threatened,

as Clarke had been, with the confiscation of their Swedish money. Feeling 'like two ill-starred mice, who unexpectedly find themselves within the basilisk beam of a cat's eye', they were finally permitted to proceed, only to find that

> we were most vexatiously detained on the opposite side of the way by the custom-house officers, who, under a broiling sun, ransacked every article of our luggage; even the private recesses of the writing-desk were not sacred.

Carr became intrigued by the saga of 'the Swedish and the Russian bridge'

> which crosses a branch of the river Kymen, and divides Sweden from Russia. The *exclusive right* of *painting* this little bridge had very nearly inflamed these rival nations to the renewal of all those horrors which have so long and so prodigally wasted the blood and treasure of both countries . . . This marvellous dispute, after a stormy discussion, with the sword half-drawn, was settled in the following manner, viz. Sweden was to use what sized brush and what colours she preferred, upon one half of the bridge, and on the other Russia the like materials in the way that best suited her fancy. But it is useless to talk about a few piles and planks; they were the ostensible, but the *real* cause of the difference was, and ever will be, the *vicinity* of the countries, for, unhappily! nations are more disposed to mutual attachment, if they cannot see each other.

The jealous partitioning of this wooden bridge was a recurrent subject of interest for travellers who crossed it, even after it had ceased to be the border. In 1813 John Thomas James, together with two fellow Oxford academics, travelling through Finland on their way to Russia 'to make scientific and industrial observations'

passed the bridge that once marked the point of separa-
tion between Swedish and Russian Finland. It claims a
sort of historical notoriety from the mad caprice of the
late Gustavus Adolphus, who, outstripping the limits
of his jurisdiction, ordered the half of the bridge on the
Russian side, as well as that on his own, to be painted
with the Swedish colours: this pitiful act of aggression
afterwards formed one of the pretexts of a war that led
his country to the very brink of destruction, and, by its
consequences, deprived the ancient blood of Vasa of their
inheritance.

This story was variously retold by later travellers. In 1827,
long after the border and its bridge had been consigned to history, Captain George Matthew Jones described passing 'the
boundary between the old and the new Finland':

> It is said, that the ex-king of Sweden, having caused the
> arms of that country to be painted on the Russian end
> of the bridge, it formed one of the pretexts for the war,
> which ultimately cost him the whole of the duchy.

Several years later Captain James Edward Alexander wrote
of 'the celebrated bridge which formerly marked the boundary between Russia and Swedish Finland, but which the
dethroned Gustavus had caused to be painted entirely with the
Swedish colours; and this aggression, with others, led to the
war which lost him Swedish Finland.' The story of the bridge
became a traveller's tale, but one which soon faded: Murray's
Handbook (1839) simply records that a 'long wooden bridge
traverses the river, over which we whirled like lightning, and
were in a moment at the door of a post-house.'

The river and the bridge made the geographical border clear
– indeed, visible – but British travellers discovered how a very
different country lay the other side of the border. Coxe had
had depicted the change fairly gently:

The peasants of Finland differ widely from the Russians in their look and dress: they had for the most part fair complexions, and many of them red hair: they shave their beards, wear their hair parted at the top, and hanging to a considerable length over their shoulders. We could not avoid remarking, that they were in general more civilized than the Russians; and that even in the smallest villages we were able to procure much better accommodations, than we usually met with in the largest towns which we had hitherto visited in this empire.

Clarke, travelling east, was very much more judgemental, writing with palpable disgust of now travelling 'through a country more inhospitable than the deserts of *Tahtary*':

> When the mind has been accustomed to repose implicitly on the fidelity and virtues of those around us, it is difficult to submit it all at once to a system of suspicion and caution. The confidence which had originated in the long-experienced honesty, goodness, and placid benignity of the inhabitants of *Sweden* [which, of course, included Finland] did not entirely forsake us, as it ought to have done, on entering *Russia*. A few miles, nay, even a few yards, conduct you from a land of hospitality and virtue, to a den of thieves. We suffered for this want of caution, in the loss of the first moveables on which the *Russians* could lay their hands. We had, indeed, been forewarned of their pilfering disposition, but did not imagine that we should so soon experience the truth of the information which we had received respecting this part of the *Russian* character.

For Rae Wilson*, travelling west in the 1820s, problems began long before he got to the actual frontier: he was delayed for weeks in St. Petersburg by 'many irksome and tedious formalities [which] were to be submitted to before we were at liberty to quit it'. His catalogue of formalities occupies nearly two pages:

> Having at length obtained the passport that had cost us so much trouble, and hired a Swedish servant, we took our final leave of St. Petersburg; and such was our irritation at the moment, from the provoking detention we had experienced, that so far from feeling any regret at leaving this splendid city, we exulted as much as if we had been prisoners escaping from captivity.

He does not describe the actual border; crossing into Finland, though, was a transformation. West of St. Petersburg posting arrangements began to improve: 'now the animals were furnished on merely being called for, – a proof we were approaching happy Finland' where

> [we]found ourselves among a race of people altogether different from those we had hitherto met, in point of dress, appearance, physiognomy, and manners. Among these people, neither frowzy beards, slovenliness, nudity, nor grim visages, were to be seen; on the contrary, they appeared to be quite a superior race to the Russian peasantry.

For the rest of the century there is no significant printed account of crossing the border. There were more convenient ways of reaching St. Petersburg – by steamer from Stockholm or Lübeck, or by rail via Germany and Poland; those who travelled to Finland went principally with the purpose of seeing Finland. Only after 1914 did the picture change. Charles Fillingham Coxwell's *Through Russia in War-Time* (1917) gives a graphic account of the problems of exiting Russia, echoing those described by Rae Wilson some ninety years earlier, but now exacerbated by the war. He 'had failed to understand that Tornea, a town on the dividing line between Finland and Sweden, is not the only frontier', and had innocently assumed that since Finland was part of Russia entry would be trouble-free. He was astonished to find that at customs 'all papers, postcards, letters, diaries, negatives, prints, and two faithful cameras were segregated on a counter, and declared forfeit'. He 'pleaded, as a mother might for her young', and after an unfriendly interrogation was required to 'return to Petrograd and observe several formalities'. His account of the customs officials, and of the bureaucrats in Petrograd (renamed in 1914) is both comic and ominous: it took him three days, with three different authorities, to collect all the permits and waivers required to travel on into Finland. Finally a messenger brought him 'a large packet carrying the seal of a great and formidable department of State. Each of Mr. Inspector's three requirements had now been faithfully carried out, so in buoyant spirits I soon quitted the capital.'

To his dismay he found subsequently that it was as difficult to leave Finland as it had been to get out of Russia. The 'liberal attention from the Custom House officials' which he received in Tornio replicated his earlier experience.

The examination was thorough, and lasted perhaps an hour. Once more it became necessary to battle for precious negatives, films, and rolls. Not quite liking to see unopened and unexposed material thrown away, I announced in Russian that such and such film packs were 'novy,' or 'new.' Whereupon an unsympathetic gendarme solemnly asked, 'What is "new"?' a Socratic form of investigation with which I could not cope. But, with sardonic humour, he added he supposed 'new' was not 'old', a speculation so much to his taste that he uttered it at least as often as I asserted that anything was new. After a while a superior appeared, who, with ability to speak French, displayed a reassuring and not ungenial disposition. When all spoils from my belongings had been set aside with view to a later investigation, I was searched in a considerate manner, and requested to attend at eleven on the following morning.

At the appointed hour he presented himself at the Customs House:

> I answered questions and tried to shepherd my property. While any undeveloped film was forthwith confiscate, every negative underwent careful scrutiny . . . Meantime, at the officer's request, a linguistic genius who stood near satisfied himself that my correspondence and notebooks were innocuous. At last even the picture postcards were done with; whereupon, having lost little, I collected my scattered goods with a gendarme's help, and felt that I had been treated fairly and justly. At a barrier on a pier, passports were expeditiously restored to their owners, who could then embark in a small steamer for Haparanda, where, at the Stadt's Hotel, all very gladly partook of a meal.

Until 1917 the problems involved in crossing the border were considerable, but never life-threatening. After the Bolshevik Revolution crossing could become literally a matter of life and death. One of the first to cross at this time did get through lightly: Arthur Ransome, a Bolshevik supporter, was expelled from Sweden in January 1919, crossed to Finland, and duly arrived at the new Russian border at Beloostrov (Valkeasaari):

> . . . we walked down to the little wooden bridge over the narrow frozen stream that separates Finland from Russia. The bridge, not twenty yards across, has a toll bar at each end, two sentry boxes and two sentries. On the Russian side the bar was the familiar black and white of the old Russian Empire, with sentry box to match. The Finns seemingly had not had time to paint their bar and box.
> The Finns lifted the toll bar and the Finnish officers leading our escort walked solemnly to the centre of the

bridge. Then the luggage was dumped there, while we stood watching the trembling of the rickety little bridge under the weight of our belongings, for we were taking with us as much food as we decently could. We were none of us allowed on the bridge until an officer and a few men had come down to meet us on the Russian side . . .

The contrast was noticeable at once. On the Finnish side of the frontier we had seen the grandiose new frontier station, much larger than could possibly be needed, but quite a good expression of the new Finland. On the Russian side we came to the same grey old wooden station known to all passengers to and from Russia for polyglot infamy and passport difficulties.

Ransome had been close to Lenin and Trotsky in Stockholm, and so was spared any scrutiny or luggage search at the bridge. In contrast, Paul Henry Dukes, newly appointed to the Secret Intelligence Service, needed to avoid bridges at all costs:

At last the train stopped at Rajajoki, the last station on the Finnish side of the frontier. It was a pitch-dark night with no moon. Half-a-mile remained to the frontier, and I made my way along the rails in the direction of Russia and down to the wooden bridge over the little frontier river Sestra . . . The Finnish sentry stood at his post at the bar of the frontier bridge, and twenty paces away, on the other side, was the Red sentry. I left the bridge on my right and turned to look for the house of the Finnish patrols to whom I had been directed.

Dukes was a fluent Russian speaker, but he had to be given a Russian identity; he was duly issued with papers identifying him as Joseph Hitch Afirenko. At 3 a.m. he was accompanied to the crossing point:

We walked stealthily along the road the Finn had pointed out to me on paper overnight, bending low where no trees sheltered us from the Russian bank. A few yards below on the right I heard the murmur of the river stream. We soon arrived at a ramshackle villa standing on the river surrounded by trees and thickets. Here we stood stock-still for a moment to listen for any unexpected sounds. The silence was absolute. But for the noise of the water there was not a sound.

We descended to the water under cover of the tumble-down villa and the bushes. The stream was about twenty paces wide at this point. Along both banks there was an edging of ice. I looked across at the opposite side. It was open meadow, but the trees loomed darkly a hundred paces away on either hand in the background. On the left I could just see the cottage of the Red patrol against which the Finns had warned me.

The cadaverous man took up his station at a slight break in the thickets. A moment later he returned and announced that all was well. 'Remember,' he enjoined me once more in an undertone, 'run slightly to the left, but – keep an eye on that cottage.' He made a sign to the other two and from the bushes they dragged out a boat. Working noiselessly they attached a long rope to the stern and laid a pole in it. Then they slid it down the bank into the water.

'Get into the boat,' whispered the leader, 'and push yourself across with the pole. And good luck!'

I shook hands with my companions, pulled at my little bottle of whisky, and got into the boat. I started pushing, but with the rope trailing behind it was no easy task to punt the little bark straight across the running stream. I was sure I should be heard, and had amidstream the sort of feeling I should imagine a man has as he walks his last walk to the gallows. At length I was at the farther side, but it was impossible to hold the boat steady while I landed. In jumping ashore I crashed through the thin layer of ice. I scrambled out and up the bank. And the boat was hastily pulled back to Finland behind me.

This is only the first of several perilous crossings, in both directions, which Dukes made every time he needed to report back to Helsinki or Stockholm. They are described in thrilling detail in his *Red Dusk and the Morrow* (1922).

Getting *out* of Russia continued to be a daunting experience. Richenda C. Scott describes the experience of Theodore Rigg, a Quaker who had been working with famine relief in Russia with his companion (and later wife) Esther White. They had reached the border at Byelo-Ostro from Moscow in a train which had been arranged for a group of French residents of Moscow after the Bolshevik Revolution:

> There followed a time of suspense and anxiety for the whole party as luggage and papers were searched and scrutinised by the Soviet guards and officials. At last all was ready for the transference of the group to Finnish territory. A bridge spanned the small river which here marked the boundary; at the Russian end stood a Soviet Commissar with his guards, at the other a Finnish commandant with a detachment of soldiers. A list of the names of those composing the party had been prepared in alphabetical order. The names were called out one by one; as his name was called each person stepped forward and was handed his passport, then alone he walked over the bridge to Finland. It was fortunate that the names Rigg and White came relatively near together, but Theodore Rigg experienced some bad moments, when time stood still in his dread [sic], as he walked over the bridge into safety and had to wait at the far end till Esther White's name was called and she could join him.

During the inter-war years, individual travelling to and within the Soviet Union was more or less impossible. Bernard

Newman's *Baltic Roundabout* failed to live up to its title
because he was unable to obtain a visa for the Russian section.
Even the carefully-managed groups which were permitted did
not always escape scrutiny or intimidation. A particularly
colourful account from 1939 is given by Noel Coward; his
description of crossing the border is a modern-dress version of
what the travellers had been noting since the eighteenth century – even the bridge saga is revived in updated form: 'In
1939 the railway bridge crossing the river that separates Russia from Finland was painted half red and half white. I presume that now [1954] it is entirely red.'

When his train pulled out of the Finland Station in Leningrad Coward had felt, much as Rae Wilson had a century
before, 'exactly as though I had been let out of prison after
serving a long term'. Like Coxwell before him, though, he
found that he was not yet out. At the border station

> My luggage was again examined, but less meticulously
> than before; I was again questioned and cross-questioned,
> and made to wait interminably while a yellowish gentle-
> man with a cropped head and a spectacular wart on his
> chin thumbed through my passport and handed it in turn
> to several of his colleagues. Finally I was permitted get
> back on to the train . . . I really had the sensation that I
> was escaping by the skin of my teeth, and might at any
> moment be hauled out of the train and sent back to Len-
> ingrad for further interrogation.

By contrast

> The Finnish frontier station was most beautiful in my
> eyes; most beautiful and gay and clean. The officials were
> smiling and courteous, and one of them even seemed to
> like my passport photograph. The Customs men, god-like
> creatures with blond hair and gleaming teeth, marked my
> baggage without even looking at it.

Some years later, in 1962, Diana Webster, taking an officially organised visit in the opposite direction, described what seems have been a well-established procedure:

At the frontier the blue and white posts gave away to red and green. The Soviet guards, one in a fetching outfit of dark lime shirt and dark blue trousers, were very careful and thorough, studying our passports, looking under the seats, and even opening up each wheel casing on the train and looking into it. They seemed mostly interested in what books and papers we were carrying. I declared some manuscripts I was working on for the BBC, and Mike [Webster] declared *The Tar Trade*, a vast thesis by a Finnish professor whose English he had been asked to correct. These were both taken away but were later returned to us without comment . . . [I]t seemed to me that we were an unlikely group to be carrying capitalist propaganda.

A formal border zone had been established after 1917. On the Finnish side entry was allowed only with a permit, but residents could continue living in the area. Jim Ingram, a young British adventurer to Finland in 1931, stayed in such an area. He obtained a pass in Vyborg, and duly presented himself at the border zone: 'A wooden gate like those used at level crossings barred the road, with a military post on one side and a sentry post on the other'. He was arrested, briefly, because of suspicions about his red shirt. During the Cold War Finland's long border with Russia became part of the perimeter of the Iron Curtain, and crossing it became next to impossible; all border zones were off limits – no more 'level crossing gates'. For reasons which are self-evident, Finland did not worry over-much about its citizens defecting to the East, but on the Soviet side the preventative measures were extreme. Patrols were supplemented with extensive electronic systems, and there were successive deterrents: raked sand strips, alarmed trip wires, and a ten foot high barbed wire fence.

A remarkable border crossing from the Cold War era came to light with the publication in 2018 of *The Spy and the Traitor*, by Ben Macintyre. In 1985 Colonel Oleg Gordievsky, chief of the KGB's London operation, who had for three years been responsible for gathering intelligence and for espionage in the UK, was summoned back to Moscow. He feared, rightly, that he had been detected as a double agent. After interrogation and the administration of 'truth drugs', he was released. He may not have cracked, but he knew that his career was finished, and that exposure was inevitable. He had been told that he 'was suspected of espionage for a foreign power', and would not be permitted to work abroad again. He remained under close KGB surveillance, but somehow was able to make contact with MI6. An elaborate pre-arranged escape plan was put into action: he evaded surveillance to take a train to Vyborg where he was met by British Embassy cars, driven by two Embassy staff, Gee and Ascot, with wives, children, including a baby, and all of the equipment for a pretended picnic. They managed to shake off their 'tails' briefly, turning into a forest track where Gordievsky was quickly bundled into the boot of one of the cars and covered with an aluminium sheet. They drove on.

Ten miles west of Vyborg 'they reached the perimeter of the militarized border area, a wall of mesh fencing, topped with barbed wire. The border zone was roughly twenty kilometres in width. Between there and Finland were five separate barriers, three Soviet and two Finnish.' Helped by their diplomatic number plates, they were waved through the first, and then the second border check, but delayed at the third, where they discovered what travellers had been recording for nearly two centuries – that 'filling out paperwork for leaving [Russia] could be a time-consuming business'. When a sniffer dog started showing interest in the car which contained Gordievsky, Mrs Ascot first distracted him with a couple of cheese and onion potato crisps, then, 'as the dog circled the boot', she reached for a weapon that had never been deployed before in the Cold War, or any other. She placed [baby] Florence on the car boot directly over the hidden spy, and began changing her nappy – which the baby, with immaculate timing, had just filled. She then dropped the soiled and smelly diaper next to the inquisitive Alsatian. The dog slunk off, offended.

Even after they passed the last barrier, passport control, they did not feel it was safe to tell their passenger that he was free, but they put in a tape which played 'the haunting opening chords' of Sibelius's *Finlandia*.

III

POST-WAR VISITORS

John Grundy and the British Council

'The rise of English to its present status is striking,' wrote Professor Bill Mead in 1948. Although English teaching had made some headway in Swedish-language schools, it had had to compete with German; it was not until 1924 that a Finnish-language secondary school first appointed a full-time teacher of English. Just two years after this the first Finnish-British Society was founded in Helsinki, declaring that Finland should 'learn from English people and have the opportunity of making its national aspirations known, and the foundations and character of its international life understood by them.' These aspirations could scarcely be met without a knowledge of the English language. By 1948 the membership numbered 1400, and a varied cultural programme operated throughout the year; there were 'eight anglophil societies in the capital [and] nearly forty provincial organisations'. *Helsinki Times* reported recently (2020) that only around 'ten per cent of Finns do not speak any English'. After the war the British Council became the focus of British cultural liaison with Finland, making contact with numerous learned and professional societies. In 1948 its library in Helsinki held 4,000 books, and significant gramophone and film collections.

The British Council, established in 1934, had been granted a royal charter in 1940 for advancing 'a wider knowledge of [the United Kingdom] and the English language abroad and developing closer cultural relations between [the UK] and other countries.' As Marek Fields wrote, it had the general task of 'promoting abroad a wider appreciation of British culture and civilisation, by encouraging the study of the English language and the British contribution to the fine arts, literature and music.' 'The Council,' concluded Mead, 'meets a very real need in an East European country such as Finland which adheres to a Western European way of life.' Largely inactive during the war, it swung into action in 1945. Britain had resumed diplomatic relations with Finland after the Moscow Armistice in September 1944, and later that year Sir Francis Shepherd arrived in Helsinki to serve as British Political Representative.

As I began looking closely at English translations of the *Kalevala* I had noted that my copy of Kirby's Everyman edition, reprinted in 1956, had a short 'Introduction by J. B. C. Grundy, M.A., PH.D'. It did not take long to find out about him, and to hunt down his autobiography, *Life's Five Windows*, published in 1968. Grundy studied French and German at Cambridge, and between the wars taught modern languages and published several textbooks. Two years spent at Göttingen University enabled him to complete his doctoral thesis (on 'art and literature in Germany during the Romantic period'); at the *viva voce* examination one of his examiners was a Finn, Tancred Borenius*, Professor of the History of Art at University College London. It would be more than twenty years before Grundy came into contact with Finland again.

This was shortly after VE-Day, May 1945, when, not yet demobilised and still in uniform, he found himself in 'a crowded small room in Hanover Street', the headquarters of the British Council. 'The Foreign Office had told the Council to open up along the Iron Curtain as fast as possible and they wanted someone in Finland at once.' Grundy was willing, and was given his brief:

I was to set up an office and a library in Helsinki, arrange exhibitions and summer schools and language courses, give suitable Finns bursaries to take them to the universities or industries in the United Kingdom, and establish anglophil societies wherever it could be done. As food was very scarce there I was to enjoy the use of the diplomatic bag. The salary was £900, [and] living expenses would be paid for.

This was not quite as tall an order as it seemed, as Grundy found on a reconnaissance trip: Denis Frean, who had gone to Finland during the Winter War as a volunteer fireman (along with, among others, James Byrom), and was now lecturer in English at Helsinki University, had much of the necessary work in hand, and had already managed to establish an office, make academic contacts, and generally provide a firm base for Grundy to work from.

The Council advanced the position of English teaching in Finland partly by supporting and encouraging the anglophil societies which were being set up in towns and at factories all over the country. Many of these Finnbrit Societies (as they are now known) still exist: the Federation of Finnish British Societies currently lists eleven branches, but in Grundy's time they were not yet an organisation. The British Council oversaw the recruiting of teachers: these were recent British graduates, hired for nine months by local Finnish British Societies. Described as 'teacher- secretaries', they set off into often distant parts of Finland. In the early years they had little or no preparation for what lay ahead, but practical details and sensible advice soon became part of their London orientation. The Council sent out 'Particulars of Post' to candidates; the 1976 version listed the 'personal qualities particular looked for', which included

a cheerful and well-balanced temperament, initiative, resourcefulness, adaptability – and an ability to appreciate a society whose attitudes and way of life differ in many respects from those which prevail in Britain.

There must have been several hundred of these teachers over

the years; it is a great pity that, with these personal qualities, hardly any of them recorded their experiences, at least in print. The few accounts of Finland which we do have, based on their experiences and observations during nine or more months, often show an educated understanding of the country which no visitor, tourist or journalist could easily match.

One early recruit to Finland as a Finn-Brit teacher-secretary was Katharine Whitehorn (famous later as a columnist and author), who recorded that when she arrived in Mikkeli in 1950 'there was no-one to meet me; I didn't speak any Finnish, and the station people didn't speak any English. Nobody, it seemed, was expecting me.' She was, she wrote, 'the first teacher-secretary they'd had; no-one knew what should be done any more than I did'. Diana Ashcroft*, a few years earlier, was welcomed by Finnish-British Society members at the station when she arrived in Kaajani, but faced a very steep learning curve as both teacher and as secretary. When Diana Webster arrived two years after this, as one of about twenty teacher-secretaries, they had already had an introductory course about Finland from the British Council in London and had been given a booklet *A Record of Living Conditions in Finland*, full of pieces of good advice. Webster gives a selection of these in *Finland Forever* (2013); for example, a caveat – 'the climate has on some persons (more on women than men) a depressing and devitalising effect and allowance should be made for this fact.' Julia Hammett, in 1976, was asked at her interview in London whether 'she was the sort of person to put her head in an oven'.

Webster's group was met at the harbour by the British Council Representative, and enjoyed several days of what would now be called orientation, before setting off to all corners of Finland, Webster herself to Turku.

Today the idea of teaching English as a Foreign Language without any training, preparation, or qualifications is unthinkable, but it was some years before the Council introduced some species of crash course for teacher-secretaries in London before they left. Sandra Haill, enrolled by the Berlitz School (the British Council did not have a monopoly) to teach in Turku in 1963 was given 'two whole days of instruction in the "method"'as well as a handbook'. For decades now EFL has been a big business, especially for publishers; yet in 1947 it was thought, as Ashcroft describes, that simply being a native speaker was sufficient. Haill found that some of her pupils 'just wanted a native English speaker with whom to chat'. Even in the late 1960s, when it was part of my British Council sponsorship to give talks (six a year) to Finnish-British Societies throughout the country, it was often clear to me that a main attraction was neither me, nor my chosen topic, but simply the opportunity of hearing an English voice.

*

The Grundy family arrived by boat soon after Christmas, to 'a land of ruin and hunger', as he put it. Frean had, amazingly, found them a four-bedroom flat. At this time the housing crisis, caused by war damage and the evacuated Karelian refugees, was very acute. (Even the Rector of the University was obliged to house a student, in his study.) As well as access to the diplomatic bag for food and drink, the Grundys also had space to 'do some entertaining'. They quickly noted a Finnish habit which persists to this day, and has discomposed many British residents in Finland, who are used to the '7.30 for 8.00' formula.

> The Finns . . . arrived for dinner on the dot – and there-fore all together. Looking from the window we would sometimes see expected guests stamping in the snow in their curly Finnish boots until the precise moment.

During Grundy's first winter he and Frean, neither of them experienced drivers, took the Council's, 'narrow 14-h.p. Humber' and 'made the round of a dozen of the remoter anglophil societies clamouring for attention'. For a century or more British accounts of travelling in Finland had described increasingly comfortable journeys. Grundy's accounts read like throwbacks to the eighteenth century:

> As there were no radiator muff and no heater we replaced them by cardboard, an extra set of underwear and football stockings. We had pushed so much cotton wool into the chinks that the car had about it the hint of a Christmas bazaar. There were chains for the rear wheels, a stout steel cable, two pairs of folding Finnish skis and their sticks, a compass and much hard food . . .
>
> We would arrive in the afternoon at one of the two towns destined to hear a lecture on the Outer Hebrides or National Pensions later in the day, stagger up the icy steps with apparatus and luggage and separate for the evening. Despite the acute shortage of food and drink, dinner was ample and fiery, and it was sometimes hard to call to mind the after-dinner topic, let alone arrange the slides in order. Later came supper, often indistinguishable from what we had enjoyed a couple of hours before: it was all that the black market had. Finally to a comfortable bed with paper sheets in the factory guest house or the local hotel, where there was heating but no hot water. By now the temperature might be down to -50 °C.
>
> Finnish roads were at this time waterbound and steeply cambered. A plough would clear them once or twice a week, but its passage left an even glossier surface between ever closer walls of snow. We skidded into the latter once or twice a day, usually when I was driving, but it was no great problem. After perhaps an hour, during which ice formed inside the car as well, some other vehicle would turn up. Four or five stocky Finns would alight and, in a trice, lift us and the car back upon the highway. It was a rule of the road, just as it was understood that any stranded motorist might 'borrow' fuel or food. Some-

times the winter route would dip down to cut across the frozen surface of a lake and for a moment one had a view of tiny cyclists, horsemen, sledges – occasionally drawn by an elk – and lorries on the vast sheet below. It was as if all the toys in the nursery had been set out on the billiard table.

The Grundys, quite undismayed by the Finnish winter, were positively stunned by the summer:

Our first Finnish summer took us completely by surprise, though we found out later how it came about. One day at the end of April you notice that the bushes have ceased to be mere blocks of white, the trees are asserting their personality, jaded tips of grass have reappeared above the greyish snow. A day or two later the branches have come surreptitious into bud, there are green shoots in the sheltered corners. By the end of the week there is no further doubt. What takes a month or more in England has happened here in a few days. In June Finland is transformed. Women put away the sober clothing of the winter, the inner windows are removed, men discard hats and collars and ties, flowers and fruit and fresh salmon appear like magic on the stalls of the market by the water, open-air restaurants spring from the ground, skiffs and launches ply busily upon the inlets and lakes, school children wheel upon their bicycles like swallows. It is summer.

The whole Grundy family took a summer trip which they 'all found exciting' on a wood-fired steamer from Savonlinna to Kuopio, which transported them 'by lake and canal into the heart of the country':

Once or twice the sturdy little black and white boat had to negotiate rapids. At one village, of perhaps a hundred houses, there was time to explore, and we noted that the wooden church had seats for two thousand. We were told that it was full on Sundays. At another place there was a stop of four hours to allow passengers to have their weekly sauna.

Apart from Mrs Tweedie, who devotes a chapter to '"Kokko" Fires', which she witnessed near the Saimaa Canal, British travellers rarely mention the Midsummer Eve celebrations, which are such a distinctive feature of Finland in summer. For Grundy they were a memorable experience.

The Midsummer Eve festivities began at about 7 p.m. Most of the women and some of the men were in local costume, dyed with local herbs. There was song and frolicking and country dances, accompanied by *kantele* and *joujikko*. Then came refreshments in some farmhouse, able to cater for sixty or seventy guests only because each had brought his contribution. And, at precisely midnight, the vast bonfire. With a crackle and a roar flames leaped into the air. The songs and dances began all over again. Presently one would walk to some high high ground and look out over the lake. Its shores were outlined by pinpoints and whorls of red. Boats with lanterns moved across its surface like glow-worms. All Finland rejoiced that summer had come back. It would be there for three splendid months.

'The climax to our first year in Finland,' Grundy continues 'was a summer school.' He does not give the location, which was simply 'a ramshackle place for a hundred teachers of English.' The only luxury was real coffee, courtesy of the diplomatic bag; 'the Finns were overjoyed to taste it once more' – there had been no coffee available at all in Finland during the latter part of the war. Grundy catches movingly the spirit of these teachers, just emerged from the nightmare of war, as they attended lectures, swam, sculled, enjoyed tea parties, singing around an evening bonfire, and even a cricket match with improvised, hand-carved bats and stumps. As the teachers departed Grundy reflected on what the occasion revealed and meant:

> Some of these people had spent a year's savings on our course, many had left families which could ill do without them. How gay and sturdy and full of pluck they were! Round the bend by the sauna rumbles the lorry [to the station], full of waving hands and brave smiles.

Back in Helsinki 'it was autumn and berry time'. After raspberries and wild strawberries it was now time for 'cranberries and cloudberries and bilberries and *lingon*.'

Grundy barely touches on Finland's precarious political situation, and the unease caused in Helsinki by the Soviet-dominated Allied Control Commission, which did not leave until late in 1947. His attempts to go beyond his semi-official Russian contacts even with the 'pleasant cultural attaché, Blivatny' came to nothing. He sketches in some events of the 1948 Communist *Putsch* and its failure. 'It was,' he writes, 'one of diplomacy's most brilliant miniatures'. He gives much more space to his visits to Sibelius, who 'admired our [British] music and did much to help it on its way in Finland, writing a holograph message of goodwill for our first concert in Helsinki, which was reproduced on the programme.' 'When I came to leave Finland,' Grundy concludes, 'he sent me a letter of two pages in his own hand'.

Diana Ashcroft

One of the first teacher-secretaries recruited by the British Council [*see above: John Grundy*] was Diana Ashcroft, whose *Journey to Finland* describes her year in Kajaani during the immediate post-war period, 1947–1948. The British tourists who had published their sometimes alluring accounts of Finland only ten years before would hardly have recognised the country she describes; for her the real state of Finland was all around, inescapable:

> At that time life was far from easy for the Finnish people. The energy which should have gone to post-war reconstruction was being expended on reparations for the Soviet Union, and the crying needs of countless refugees [from Karelia, Hanko and Porkkala] were taxing the nation's already meagre resources to the utmost. Shortages of all kinds were acute and casual intercourse with the outside world virtually at a standstill. Fear of Communism was widespread and a deep sense of isolation prevailed.

The advice she had obtained from the Political Representative of Finland in London was not encouraging: 'Conditions were hard, shortages numerous, and, if I went, I would do well to take all that I should need for a year with me; sheets, blankets, soap, tooth-paste – everything.' In Stockholm the staff at the British Council office 'were gloomy beyond belief. They obviously thought us crazy to be going to Finland where, they assured us repeatedly, living conditions were very bad indeed. Did we realise how much of their valuable time was spent in sending food parcels to their staff in Helsinki and Turku?'

On board a badly overcrowded SS *Bore*, in the wake of an ice-breaker, Ashcroft's Finnish adventure began:

> There was something very strange and exciting about the

way in which we steamed slowly and deliberately down this narrow channel with the recently shattered ice boulders clanking against the ship's side and the distance shrouded in mist. There was about it an overwhelming sense of adventure; a sense of moving, slowly and deliberately, into the unknown.

They docked in Turku at 7 p.m., twelve hours late. Bank, money exchange, and customs took up the next morning, before they took the train to Helsinki, which 'was scheduled to take six hours . . . because of the enforced detour round the Russian base in Porkkala.' British Council staff met the train and took them to their hotel. The following day, Good Friday, included lunch with the Representative, John Grundy*, and a brief introduction to the capital. The weather was 'bleak and cold'; everything was closed, 'shop windows were almost empty, and everything looked inexpressively sad.' In the evening she boarded the night train to Kajaani.

On Kajaani station the following morning members of the Finnish-British Society 'stood stiffly in a row' on the platform to greet her. She was driven to the large paper mill on the edge of the town. As the principal local employer, the mill had a 'Club', where business visitors could stay, and the firm's personnel could have their meals. Here she was to lodge, and here she taught many of of her students. It was not until her return from the summer holiday that she moved permanently to live with a family in town. Kalle Frey was a doctor who 'worked from home'; Ashcroft's small room doubled as the patients' waiting room.

'Living at the fringes of the medical world in Finland,' she wrote, 'was very interesting.' There were so few doctors that home visits were a rarity, and in any case there was only one car between six doctors, and there was no ambulance. 'As for the Finnish hospital buildings,' she wrote, 'they vary from the primitive and inadequate to the super-modern and magnificently equipped.' Kajaani belonged to the former category. Dr. Halliday Sutherland, in Helsinki ten years earlier, had admired 'the four most modern hospitals in Europe', but that was there and then; Ashcroft was in distant Kajaani in 1947.

Arriving at the Easter holiday weekend gave her the opportunity to meet members of the Society and their families, as it was not until Wednesday that students were enrolled. Then it was that the reality of her position suddenly became apparent to her: she was surrounded by people paying their own money 'for the benefit of learning English from me twice a week for the next ten weeks, and I had never given a lesson in my life.' The role of teacher-secretary, she now realised, was much more teacher than secretary: lunchtimes she taught at the factory, afternoons in pupils' own homes, and evenings at the Lyceum (secondary school).

Luckily for Ashcroft many of her students had copies of a book unknown to her, *Brush up your English*, by Marie D. Hottinger '– a godsend; there was no end to the number of topics it suggested for conversation':

> What the hero and heroine, Charles and Mary Smith did not do was not worth doing, and what they did we did with them. They went sight-seeing and shopping, that was child's play; they went to the bank and they played bridge . . .

(Twenty years later, the Smiths' successor was alive and well in Finland. This was 'my boyfriend Cyril', who had the leading role in *Living English Structure: a Practice Book for Foreign Students* by Allen and Stannard.) In time other materials, especially books, arrived in Kaajani from the British Council, so play-reading could be added to the attractions. Very occasionally a visiting English speaker would include Kajaani in a lecture tour.

The Society met on alternate Wednesday evenings. Establishing anything, let alone a programme, was an accomplishment as far beyond Ashcroft's experience as language teaching; her first attempt offered party games, and herself reading English poetry, beginning with 'The Pied Piper of Hamelin', and concluding with Belloc's *Cautionary Tales*.

Although she was living at the Club, Ashcroft was closely involved with the domestic life of many of her students. The men, mainly factory employees, were usually taught at the Club, but the women were taught at their own homes. Because of the shortage of coffee, which had been not been available at all during the latter part of the war, she did not suffer from the poisoning which affected some teachers in the 1960s, as a result of drinking coffee with every home student. What she saw and recorded was genuine Finnish households: she admired the ingenuity employed in housing families in a very few rooms, and the ways in which they managed despite severe rationing and shortages of almost everything.

Sylvia MacDougall, staying in Kajaani early in the century, recorded that the town 'was enjoying the height of her season, and hotels were full up'. She described the shops in the main street, where 'anything from home-made hjortron jam to a ready-made pair of trousers could be bought'. Forty years later Ashcroft 'strolled along looking at the shop windows. There did not seem to be anything to buy that was not made either of paper or wood'. Only ten years earlier, in his introduction to *Finland on Ten Pounds,* Sydney A. Clark had written 'In no other country covered by the £10 Series will £10 stretch quite so far.' Those days had disappeared with the war: Ashcroft's book is a chronicle of austerity. '[T]he cost of living was appalling. Meat was the equivalent of 12s. and upwards a pound, and eggs anything anything from 1s to 1s.8p. each. Most people reckoned on spending three-quarters of their income on food.'

On her travels around Finland Ashcroft often took her own food with her, an expedient which had been a frequent and necessary resort of travellers in the eighteenth century. For her trip to Lapland she was strongly advised to 'take all the food we should need, because no-one in Lapland was, at that time, in a position to cater for visitors.' Even the food that was available was restricted by rationing; at the Club her diet was mainly 'raw salt fish, potatoes and porridge . . . It was a lucky thing for me that I liked potatoes and porridge,' she wrote, 'because I do not take at all kindly to raw salt fish.'

One mark of the famine conditions during the later years of the war had been a return to peasant economy. Ashcroft sees several indications that even in this time of extreme austerity 'things were beginning to look up': the Freys had 'eaten the last pig', one which had presumably lived in town with them, and a neighbour who had accommodated chickens in her attic reclaimed the room for the family.

Many features and occasions which had in the past been noted intermittently by travellers and tourists as they passed through Finland were for Ashcroft part of living in the community. On the first of May, Vappu, she was invited to 'a large dance at the club', and escorted by Yrjö, one of her students:

Together we joined the party in the big room, which had been elaborately decorated for the occasion. Paper screens adorned with a series of pictures hid the windows and bookshelves. The caption beneath each mural was the same: *Jo rittää* which means 'that's enough'. Every picture was a variation of this theme: champagne being poured into a glass; a couple kissing in the moonlight. The artist had worked hard and had, so it seemed to me, exhausted all possibly variants . . .

As the meal progressed it was punctuated by singing, which seemed to begin quite arbitrarily whenever anyone felt like tuning up. All the songs were Finnish except *My bonnie lies over the ocean*, which all assembled sang with great gusto. All over Finland this tune is very popular and may be heard sung, with equal frequency, both in English and in Finnish.

After dinner they let fly streamers in all directions, drink was plentiful, and everyone was very merry and in the mood to appreciate fully a cabaret put on by the younger members of the staff.

When this was over the room was cleared for dancing, which went on until midnight. Then on the stroke of twelve all those who had ever graduated from school to the University – whether or not they had actually been there – put on their caps and, irrespective of age or sex, continued wearing them throughout May Day . . .

Dancing went on until around three in the morning; then everyone went home. It was a good party, merry but sober, and did not at all bear out the contention which I heard almost daily that Finns drink too much.

I do not know if anything special happened next morning, because I slept late, and only staggered up in time for the eleven o'clock meal. After that I walked into the town to see if there was anything doing, but all I saw was a brass band that had finished for the day and was being driven home in a lorry.

Another occasion was the school-leaving ceremony for the graduating students:

Practically all Kajaani was there, wedged between the schoolchildren who were congregated at the back and the graduating students who occupied the front two rows of chairs. In pre-war days the graduating girls would have been dressed completely in white; now they had been reduced to white blouses. The boys all wore their Sunday best . . .

Shortly afterwards the party broke up, and the graduating class went first to be photographed and then, in a body, to put their flowers on the graves of the war dead.

Then at the homes of the new 'graduates' it was open house, for friends and relatives to call and congratulate them. Ashcroft was disappointed with the seriousness of the whole occasion:

After eight years' grind I would have expected far more gaiety, and I felt sorry for the students. But I need not have done so; that night they had a party all of their own at the club, a rip-roaring affair if the noise they made was any criterion. I know all about that, for I had very little sleep that night.

As far as I can recall – and I have read well over a hundred British descriptions of Finland – Ashcroft is alone in describing a Finnish Christmas; she spent it with the Frey family. First Santa Claus (*Joulupukki*) came with presents for the children, and after they had settled playing with their new toys, the family party of ten sat down to dinner.

We ate by candlelight. On the sideboard beneath the portraits of Kalle's great-grandparents, four candles burned in silver candlesticks. Normally these pictures lacked vitality but now in the soft light they lived as never before. The table, too, was lit by candles whose mellow radiance dimmed all contours and threw new features into relief . . .

There was no holly and no mistletoe; instead there were evergreens, paper hangings, and, as at Easter, the inevitable straw decorations. There were straw angels, straw animals and the peculiar pendant straw boxes known as *himmeli*. But of all the Finnish decorations it is the candles that strike the dominant note. They are everywhere, indoors and out, for on Christmas night they burn outside in the churchyard and the cemeteries. As soon as it is dark, the people come and light them on their family graves and soon the whole churchyard is alive with twinkling points of flame.

'In 1947,' Ashcroft wrote 'the country as a whole was in no position to cope with tourists. There was little food and less accommodation. Conditions that were bad in the south were even worse in the north.' By the 1930s most large towns had boasted a Seurahuone, hotels which were highly regarded by tourists, and recommended by travel guides. Now even these were bare and utilitarian, and Ashcroft did not care for them. The Maakunta in Kajaani, where she stayed periodically when her other accommodation was otherwise required,

> was like a hundred and one other such places, as throughout Finland there is a great sameness in hotel accommodation. With a few exceptions, hotels are places where travellers may pass a night or two, but they are not designed to live in. Bedrooms, restaurant and *sauna* are provided, but nowhere to sit or lounge.

At the Seurahuone in Savonlinna, for example, 'the dining-room in which we ate was singularly charmless and the whole building merited the adjective 'commercial.' The Hotel Finlandia at Punkaharju gets some grudging approval, but the 'sitting-room felt unlived in, and the dining-room had [an] impersonal atmosphere.' At Koli she describes a brave attempt to capture the pre-war mood: 'The waitresses were all dressed in their national costumes: long-sleeved blouses, tightly-fitting bodices, aprons and full, striped skirts . . . though exasperatingly slow at their job, they were a cheerful lot, and I think the probability is that they were all amateurs.' One thing which austerity could not spoil was the view:

> Beneath us lay the lake; its surface calm and unruffled and its shores fringed by an infinity of small bays and inlets, while alongside the low ridge of tree-clad hills reached out into the distance. There were splashes of clear leaf green in the forest; there were stretches of golden sand at the water's edge; there were bare rocky headlands and smooth rounded islands. The lake threw back a thousand mirror-clear reflections and, once again, there was a

sense of immeasurable distance. It was a scene of supreme loveliness.

By the 1930s the Finnish Tourist Association was taking care of every imaginable requirement. As well as offices in major towns, the Association provided guides 'found in most of the nodal places of tourist traffic', as F. J. North put it. '[Y]ou will very likely find', he continued, 'that he is a University student chosen for the job during the tourist season because he can speak four or five languages in addition to his own,' and is able to 'discuss matters intelligently with you.' Ashcroft's experiences show how things had changed: the office in Helsinki, which she trusted to have booked her two weeks in the lake district, had done nothing, the young manager 'blandly remarking that it was far too late to do anything about it, as all the hotels and boats would be full.' For most of her travels she had to depend on her wits, and on her confidence that all would turn out well.

By arriving in April Ashcroft had the whole summer holiday for exploring Finland. In later years the teachers arrived in late August, so were able to return to Britain the following May, and usually did so; this greatly limited their whole experience of Finland. The description of her journey, with a girl friend, through Eastern Finland reads like a black-and-white version of many pre-war technicolour accounts. She concedes that they 'caught the steamers at a bad time': they were no longer 'the height of comfort . . . the much-vaunted spotless linen had perforce given way to paper sheets.' Food was, as everywhere, 'expensive and difficult to obtain', but 'that the dining saloon should be unbearably hot, the seats on deck inadequate and the view restricted from almost everywhere but the bridge cannot be blamed on the war.'

In Helsinki Michael, a friend from England, joined her, and they set off for Lapland with 'three small suitcases a large rucksack and a haversack.' Some of these items were left at different places to be picked up later, since they would be hiking and hill-climbing; they never lost any of them. Their resilience was astonishing, as they reached their destinations with a mixture of hiking and use of the very sporadic bus service. Even when they found their bus, the apparent eccentricities of the driver could confuse them, and on at least one occasion had them believe that they had been abandoned during a 'pit stop'.

Lapland had been visited in the eighteenth century by Englishmen who were more explorers than travellers. It did not become a resort for tourists until the railway reached Rovaniemi in 1909; the completion of the Arctic Highway in 1931, and the arrival of the motor coach, put it firmly on the tourist map. The comforts and pleasures of Lapland, recorded by several visitors in the 1930s, had entirely vanished by the time of Ashcroft's trip. A prerequisite of the peace negotiations with The Soviet Union in 1944 had been that the German troops in Finland should be expelled. The final part of the war, driving them out of Lapland into Norway, produced what D. G. Kirby calls 'some of the bitterest fighting of the war.' Their scorched earth policy left a trail of destruction through the whole of Lapland. Ashcroft and her friend found sparse accommodation and no certainty of any food . There appeared to be no telephone, bus services were skeletal, and as for tourist offices – forget them.

Although Ashcroft and her partner had a hiking holiday in mind, they often found themselves walking even longer distances than they had planned Their first destination was Pallastunturi, travelling for the final stage in a lorry full of students who were joining a camp there. A very modest hotel was being erected in place of the grand edifice which had, very evidently, been dynamited by the retreating Germans. This was their base for a few days hiking. In Lapland she saw the results of the war in stark reality; unlike in the bombed towns elsewhere in Finland, reconstruction here was only just beginning. In Kajaani the aftermath of the wars was ingrained (rationing, reparations, the war-wounded); in Lapland it was grimly visible, for instance from the bus which took them to Muonio:

> Scenically, the early part of the drive was not particularly interesting, but from the human angle the whole journey was a shining example of indomitable spirit. The people of Lapland had all returned to their ruined homes and, in the straggling little villages that we passed, almost without exception, every house was brand new. From Aavasaksa to Kilpisjärvi there was nothing to choose between these villages, about whose houses there was a terrible sameness. Every one had been erected at high speed and every one was bright yellow, rectangular and devoid of all decoration. And, as if this in itself was not depressing enough, each one of these little houses overlooked a square of blackened earth in the midst of which stood a charred brick stove and, rising to the height of two stories, a gaunt chimney stack. Impervious to fire, these mute relics were all that the flames could not burn. No effort had been made to demolish them, nor yet to turn the blackened squares of earth. While there more important things to be done, these stark relics must stand and the ground remain in mourning; in the meantime the stoves served very well for boiling the cauldron full of laundry.

Finally they arrived at the frontier station. Ashcroft does not describe the three days spent in Norway, only that she took a train from Narvik to Stockholm. '[R]eturning to Finland,' she wrote 'felt almost like going home'. She was unimpressed by Turku, even by Bryggman's cemetery chapel, but enchanted with her stay with friends of friends at Kiikala, near Salo. She spent a few days in Helsinki, consuming 'vast quantities of crayfish' and stocking up on books for the coming term.

Living in town now, and in a family house, Ashcroft became more closely involved with some of the wider issues that were concerning people: the stigma of the war responsibility trials, the role of the communists in the government, and the elections. The Civil Service Strike in November 'paralysed the country, and cut it off from the outside world completely.... In Kajaani, as elsewhere, the inhabitants were marooned.' The 'Communist Prime Minister... put out a false report that the strikers in the capital had gone back to work and that all those in the provinces who did not promptly follow suit would lose their jobs.' Ashcroft, like so many British observers of Finland, had remarked on the 'habitual Finnish phlegm', but on this occasion she saw Finns falter.

She returned from an Easter skiing trip in Lapland to find

the town bubbling over with rumours. It was now a fortnight since the delegation [summoned by Stalin to discuss a 'friendship and mutual assistance pact', as had just been concluded with Roumania and Hungary] had left for Moscow, and still there was no news and, as a result, my last days in Kajaani were coloured by the undercurrent of anxiety that flowed through the minds of all. There were startling stories in circulation about Russian territorial demands; this or that port was to be relinquished, Lapland was in danger of total annexation now that the railway line from Kemijärvi to the Russian border had been completed, and there was a real fear that the young men might be conscripted into the Soviet Army. In all, it was a crop of rumours of unparalleled fertility and a wave of people anxious to leave the country were caught and held on the Swedish frontier.

The realities of Finland's position, even in peace, was felt in every household. Russia loomed like a frightening shadow over everyone's life. 'The day before I left Kajaani, Yrjö's brother came out of prison, where he had been sent in 1947 for what is generally referred to as 'The Concealment of Arms Affair'. 1450 men were charged with holding concealed weapons, and 'so many were sentenced to varying terms of imprisonment that I got quite used to hearing people refer casually to the time when their husbands, fathers, sons, brothers, uncles, and cousins had been in prison.' The Freys may have been eating their last pig, with Finnish life beginning to resume, but the country which Ashcroft was about to leave was very far from carefree.

The next day nearly thirty people were at the station to say goodbye, many bringing flowers. She was, she wrote, 'feeling overwrought and struggling painfully to say the unsayable.' As the train drew out 'someone burst into "Auld Lang Syne" and everyone else joined in.'

Walter Bacon

'We went to Lapland in 1955 and did not leave it till the end of 1958.' The opening sentence of Walter Bacon's *Highway to the Wilderness* (1961) introduces a Lapland very unlike that described by Diana Ashcroft*. She saw everywhere grim reminders of the scorched earth policy of the German army on their retreat in 1944, and describes the new little houses, 'like identical boxes', which 'overlooked a square of blackened earth in the midst of which stood a charred brick stove and, rising to the height of two stories, a gaunt chimney stack.' Bacon's time in Lapland began only eight years later, but he makes just one passing reference to 'blackened chimney bricks, of the sort I had seen that first day in Ivalo', although the town had been severely damaged.

Bacon, a lecturer in electronic engineering in southern England, had been feeling dissatisfied with the pattern which his whole way of life was imposing on him: in electronics 'I was, I realised, a heretic and deviationist' he wrote. He became attracted to the attitudes of the Society of Friends, and at a seminar organised by them in Holland in 1953 he met Arja Aromaa, a Finnish dentist; they married the following year. When she became pregnant she returned to her family in Helsinki for the birth, and Bacon followed a few months later. One day there she said 'How about going to live in Ivalo? Inari commune are advertising for a school dentist . . . You could teach English.' The discussion was fairly brief:

'You couldn't possibly manage it with a young child.'

This was an unwise thing to say; to suggest to a Finn that some task is beyond him or her usually makes the hearer even more determined to do it.

'Of course I could,' Arja replied, a trifle angrily. 'Most Finnish women do.'

So Bacon returned to England, gave three months' notice to the college, and settled the practicalities. Early December found him at Rovaniemi airport, waiting for the bus which was to take him to Ivalo, 180 miles to the north. His introduction to Lapland was an eight hour journey where, for part of the time, it was standing room only.

'We could go for year,' Arja had said, 'and then come back, but we should have seen what Lapland really was like all the year round.' Most British accounts of Lapland before this time are inescapably limited and partial, often restricted to comments on the mosquitoes in summer, and on the cold, the dark, and perhaps the reindeer in winter. An outstanding feature of Bacon's book is his description of the changing seasons:

Then the snow came. I stood at the window and watched it falling steadily and rhythmically down, flake after flake dropping on the dead landscape, transforming it into its winter form. The world of the sun had gone, but a new world was being born. It exercised an almost hypnotic effect, this steadily, inexorably falling snow; and through it one could hear the soft melancholy clanging of the bell as a horse went past dragging a sledge.

His accounts of the winter months take the dark for granted. He and Arja often walked at night:

On many nights above our heads there would be great swirls of creamy colour, the aurora, transforming itself from long searchlight beams into single and double arcs right across the centre of the sky, fading into patches and cones until – after minutes or hours – it finally disappeared.

The manifestations of the aurora were varied; but the moon changed its whole character in a single night. It pulled itself up slowly over the northern sky, a huge orange balloon with scarcely enough lift to be airborne.

Five hours later it was high overhead and directly above us – or even south – a pure, silvery sphere, the passionless priestess of the skies from whom no corner of the sharp clear landscape could be hidden. Light came from the sky and the snowy earth, from every leaf on every tree. Nothing, it seemed, could remain in darkness. Such a night of truth might follow the day of Judgement. As morning came one looked out again; the priestess had vanished; instead a big bloated old night rake was staggering home towards the north pole.

Eventually '[t]he white turned to brown'. Then 'the brown was washed away by the flood of green which came pouring over the landscape. Nature's scene-shifters work fast in Lapland.' Soon came 'the second spring':

> The ice on the Ivalo river had broken up and was floating down to lose itself in Inari Lake. I ran outside: the inert white plain between us and the school had disappeared, and instead a sapphire torrent was rushing past, carrying with it a multitude of strangely-shaped white pyramids. The river had come out of hibernation.

In England the changes of the seasons are not especially distinct: 'Nature's scene shifters' are leisured, even lethargic. While a Finnish wardrobe typically contains four coats, one for each season, in England a winter coat and a mackintosh for summer usually suffice. Spring typically has several false starts before it finally arrives, and by then summer is at hand. There is no mistaking spring in Lapland.

> Spring came; not rose-in-hand, but accompanied by something better than roses – indeed, the source of all springs and all roses – the sun. The sun leapt up into the sky with no false diffidence or modesty, but with gay exuberance as though it were coming back to its rightful kingdom. Each day the dark hours shrank perceptibly until one morning

Arja said: 'We're passing them now.' By 'them' she meant the rest of the world south of the Arctic Circle, the people who had seen light throughout the winter, whilst we had lain in great darkness.

The greater part of Bacon's discovery of Lapland took place, not surprisingly, in summer.

Life quickened towards its summer pace – but not without hesitation. Many people suffered from 'spring tiredness" – a well-known Lapland phenomenon – a lack of energy when the springs came after an exhausting winter. It was only a pause; in summer energy seemed boundless and – to many – sleep hardly necessary.

Bacon glosses over one hallmark of summer in Lapland: only half a page is given to the 'hellish summer for mosquitoes', and the need to wear thick clothing in June and July, whatever the temperature. 'In autumn', though,

there is a sudden and unbelievably brilliant flash of colour – the swan-song of the departing summer. The sharply falling temperatures combined with the very dry atmosphere gives the dying leaves a vividness of colour all the more remarkable because it is so short lived. This is the time of *ruska*, at the beginning of September, when the birches stand like tongues of yellow flame and the ground is a voluptuous mosaic of red ripening berries, dark oval green leaves with the brown mushrooms pushing through, and underneath the light green reindeer moss. The atmosphere is clear and clean and there is still light well into the evening. The magnificent sunsets paint the sky as alluringly as the earth, but with a different technique; the interweaving of a myriad separate strands is replaced by great masses of glowing colour flung on with careless genius.

A little later in life Bacon published a novel, set in Finland, but if he wrote poetry it was never published. This seems to me a pity; his writing about nature and the weather reflects British poets such as Thomson, Shelley, and Hardy.

All this could not really be described as merely the background of Bacon's life in Lapland: it was a felt part of his whole experience. At a hostel, during their excursion to the Arctic Ocean, one of the guests – 'neither Finnish nor British' – remarked to him

'Some people come here for fishing. I can appreciate that. But some of them don't fish'. He waved his hand to the panorama of mountain and river and forest. 'They just seem to like to be here'. He shook his head sadly. 'I can't understand it.'

Bacon does not attempt to explain things to him, because '[f]or the true Lapland lover, the emphasis is frequently on being – in Lapland – rather than doing.' Nonetheless Bacon did 'do' quite a lot. The foreground presents another calender: the realities of family life with a small child, Arja's formidable work load, and their journeyings beyond Ivalo.

*

In a chapter titled 'Dentist and Doctor in Lapland' Bacon describes the problems which they confronted in such a sparsely populated commune – the biggest in Finland – served by one doctor and one dentist. 'From morning to late in the evening,' he writes 'the whirring of the drill was rising and falling in the surgery'. He took over the developing of the X-rays, which had to be done in the bathroom. There was only one doctor 'for the commune of Inari and also for the still more northerly one of Utsjoki'. The commune doctor and dentist were required 'to examine each school child once a year.' It was out of the question for all the children from twelve different schools to travel to Inari, so the doctor and dentist had to travel to each school, with portable equipment.

Bacon sometimes accompanied Arja, helping with the preliminary examinations by filling out the card which recorded the state of each child's teeth, as she called them out.

On Arja's first visit to Menesjärvi Bacon followed 'a day or two later in one of the Ivalo taxis':

> The taxi turned left just before reaching the centre of Inari village, along a stony, winding narrow road that led towards the forest. It ran between the hills, curving away from the river which flows into the Inari Lake . . . We went on like this for between one and two hours, then the road suddenly dwindled to a footpath and we decided that we had come too far. We turned round, went back, and found a track going off to the left; half a mile along this we came to a steep hill, with a lake at its foot and a little to the right a school building.

They made the second visit to this school in late winter, when the snow was getting soft. 'The road was closed and there were only two possible ways of getting there – by plane, landing on skis; or by reindeer. We planned to go by the first and return by the second.' The first went well, despite leaving late afternoon when the snow had hardened a little, but the second, a few days later, presented problems. The 'post reindeer' were slow, and as with horses in traditional posthouses, there could be a long wait between changes. They learned that 'a neighbour on the other side [of the lake] had some faster reindeer', so they skied over to ask him, but the message they got was that 'the snow was almost too soft for reindeer travel and why didn't we go by plane?' So that is what they did.

Among Bacon's accomplishments was learning to ski. No-one who has first put on skis as an adult in Finland ever forgets the humiliation of trying to extricate himself from an undignified position in a snowdrift as four-year-olds ski past him with expressions of infuriating unconcern. One night Arja and a friend 'lashed skis on my feet and gave me a gentle push'.

Up until that moment there had been foolish pictures in my mind; dreams that skiing would be the art which I never tried yet for which I had an undoubted natural talent, that I should glide along masterfully whilst the bystanders called out: 'Surely you must have done this before!'

It wasn't at all like that. I travelled along, very slowly, for about half a yard; then the ground dipped downwards abruptly, my velocity increased uncontrollably, and I sat down. That, for many many times, was the pattern of my efforts.

DETERMINATION – CONSTERNATION – FRUS-TRATION

His training took place on a nearby hillock:

I stood at the top, pushed off, and went down to the bottom, hoping to remain upright, and trying at least to land on a different part of the body each time. It was sometimes a relief when darkness made it possible to retire inside without dishonour.

After regular Sunday trips by bus to Kaunispää, 'the real Mecca of the ski-ers', he was competent enough to go with Arja for a week of fell skiing, taking day trips and returning to Ylämaja to eat and sleep.

During the years in Lapland the baby, little Lillian, was growing up, but she has only a small role in her father's narrative. Despite her parents' reservations, she went with them to the sauna, and accepted it 'quite naturally'; Bacon speculated that a small child 'could find in the warmth of the *sauna* a pleasant reminder of its unborn life.' At the other end of the temperature scale, Bacon had been very agitated when Lillian, aged three months, was put outside in her pram. Arja responded

'Well, why not?'

'Because there's fifteen degrees of frost. Twenty-seven if

you work in Farhenheit. She'll freeze to death. She's only a tiny baby.'

'She won't freeze to death at all. She's been going out ever since we came.'

We never learn what provision the parents made for Lillian during their skiing excursions, their visits to distant schools, or during their longest expedition, described in a chapter entitled 'To the Arctic Ocean'. They left Ivalo with nothing more than backpacks, and took the bus north beyond Utsjoki, finally to 'Tenokoti, a guest house by the [river] Teno itself and on the very edge of Finland.' Leaving the next morning they took the post boat at midday , 'when it started on its day-long journey up the river.' With them were the postman and the postboy; every few miles 'the boat slowed down, the post-boy rose grasping a a bundle of papers, and as we drew level with the yellow box he hurled the bundle towards the bank where it landed on the ground and set pebbles rolling into the river'. It was so cold on the river that they needed to empty their knapsacks to put on all their clothes. Seven miles short of their destination, they reached a rocky section where the passengers had to get out out. Another boat took them across the river, and they got a lift to Nuorgam, 'a tiny village as far as it is possible to get from Helsinki whilst still remaining in Finland'. The next morning the bus took them to Kirkenes, and from there a small steamer set off for Hammerfest, a day and a night away, calling at several 'attractive little ports' on the way. Finally at Hammerfest 'the clouds had disappeared; from our room in the Grand Hotel we looked out over the blue water, with the sun streaming down so brilliantly that the scene looked Mediterranean.' From there the journey home was straightforward; two days of buses 'delivered us to Karis-joki, not far from the border of Finland and Norway. The circle was almost completed.'

Bacon does not bring Ivalo alive in the way that Ashcroft

animates Kajaani: there is little about the geography, or about society, school, or church. It was only the shops which give any sense of place:

> There were few things they did not sell. From a button to a bicycle, from a kilo of butter to a motorized saw – these shops had them, and what they did not have in stock they would order. Of course, the ordering took time; it might be weeks before a major article arrived; but it invariably came, and in the waiting period one had to console oneself with the saying: No hurry in Lapland. But what a wonderful saying it was! All my life there had been hurry.... All this time I had thought this hurry a virtue; and now, suddenly, I realized that it might not be. There could be a different way of living: No hurry in Lapland.
>
> In a small community a shop becomes something of a social centre. At first their interiors were a pattern of dark and light, the heavy browns and blacks in which the customers were dressed contrasting with the white uniforms behind the counter. Then, as we got to know more and more people, the sombre colours receded and in their place the shop was filled with familiar faces.

After three years, on a December afternoon, the Bacon family, now with two children, set off on their return to England. To the end 'it seemed impossible to leave Ivalo.'

> But, finally, we went. We drove a couple of miles out of Ivalo, to the rubbish dump and tipped out all the old jars and bottles; then we went round to our friends distributing the plants which had graced our house, and about one o'clock in the afternoon we were ready to go.

Bacon's thoughts make a fitting adieu. He had experienced at last the pattern of life which he had, years before, been vaguely seeking:

I should not again see Lapland with quite the same eyes, puzzled and seeking, sometimes hopelessly lost, dimly conscious that somewhere here might be a signpost to what I was looking for. We could not again live those difficult, sweet years, the first years of Lillian's life. No moment in the future would be quite like the one in which I had stared down for the first time at that small golden-haired figure. I should not again cycle back through a summer evening with the sun still impossibly high in the sky and a little girl on the front of the bicycle, calling out "Home! *Kotiin!*" in her two fragmentary languages.

John Sykes

'An Encounter during the Winter War' is the title of the opening chapter of John Sykes's memoir *Direction North: A View of Finland*, published in 1967. Sykes was a Quaker, a conscientious objector who had volunteered as an ambulance driver in 1939; his account of the encounter on the Karelian front during the Winter War has its place in *A Life of Extremes* (pp. 201-05). At the field hospital he had got to know Lars, a Swedish-speaking doctor, and kept in touch with him over years, years during which he himself had become the writer of a cosmopolitan range of books.

One of the wounded soldiers Sykes had transported through the barrages from the front to the field hospital for some reason caught his attention. From the doctor he had learned that he was a mechanic, a radical socialist from Tampere. His name was Pekka Suusanen. Lars adamantly regarded him as a hero. '"A war hero?"'asked Sykes. "Oh more than that," was the reply "In ten, twenty years from now he is the sort who must speak for Finland."' It was some twenty-five years later that Sykes, returning to England from Leningrad, decided to spend some time in Finland. Lars's cousins still worked as directors in the factory complex that accommodated 'the rebel Sussanen', so Lars had been able to follow his career from a distance; he knew that the socialist rebel was now an assistant works manager, and was able to put Sykes in touch with him. The reply to the letter he sent to Suusanen came as a phone call from his daughter. A complex arrangement led to the daughter using Sykes's flat in London and him lodging with the Suusanen family in Tampere. It was there that he began writing *Direction North*.

It is very evidently the work of an experienced writer – Sykes had published several travel books and seven novels. *Direction North* showcases his abilities in both of these genres. Finland is seen principally through the members of the Suusanen family, most of all through his relationship with Pekka, whose history and character emerge as the narrative progresses. This is Sykes's first impression:

He was excessively cautious, it seemed, these days lest he comprise his essential self, put a stout working man's foot wrong, in a world that was changing just a shade too rapidly. He was ponderously suspicious of innovation.

Suusanen's radicalism dated from his eighth birthday, when his father was executed by the White Guards; the Civil War is hardly mentioned in the book, but it is a permanent background. Pekka himself, 'a brooding figure', dominates Sykes. Although he spent time away from Tampere, 'making other friends and ceaselessly discussing Finland with them', 'the rest fades beside the looming figure of Pekka':

Pekka seized by his personal conundrum. Pekka brooding, evening after evening, as though a false move between himself and the Company, and then again (just trust it to have come up) between himself and his errant sister, would call his entire life into question. Had he perhaps always seen himself askew: through an image imposed by the previous generation? Or was he just ageing, weakening? Who was he? Above all he must act by principle . . . but which one?

Sykes confesses to something like an obsession: Pekka haunts him, here, there, and everywhere.

He roars from the shadows, he throws his shape across my thoughts, each time there is a light tinkle of drinks . . . He stands behind our chairs at at dinner worrying why we eat so slowly, why we talk and spin it out.

Pekka fears that he has betrayed himself, that the fearless Hame socialist has been tamed. But his grouse is not economic; he now accepts free-enterprise society, stringently checked and taxed by the State; materially speaking, he is as bourgeois as any of them, and this is indeed part of his travail. Affluence has become his right, yet has he been tricked in the process of attaining it?

The central matter in the brooding mind of Pekka, and indeed of his family, Sykes learns, is that the company has offered him a plot of land by the lake at Pyhäjärvi, where he can build his own house. He is agonising about this: is it a sell-out to the White bosses of the Company? He is a socialist, but after losing several jobs because of his activities, he has learned to channel rather than to douse his enthusiasms. At work he was still a fighter: 'within his orbit he was commander, all his energies given to the task, the exacting daily production schedule. This was now his fighting outlet, whatever the past issues had been. He was not a man to cease from struggle.'

Pekka's story, writes Sykes, 'reflect[s] his times and country'. It certainly does that, but *Direction North* is also a family chronicle, and in this respect is comparable with many classic novels: Angus Wilson's *No Laughing Matter* and Jonathan Franzen's *The Corrections* are examples which come to mind, novels in which the family members broadly present a section of society reflecting the state of the nation. Mrs Suusanen – we never learn her first name – is almost a stock figure, self-effacing, hard-working, a trainer of seamstresses in a local factory, returning from work only to prepare supper, and rising early to pack sandwiches for the menfolk before they leave for work in the morning. She is a church-goer, to Pekka's intense disapproval. He has actually disowned 'his errant sister', who is not only a Revivalist but has married a White farmer. One daughter, Marjatta, in Sykes's flat in London, is largely out of the frame, but is a reminder that Finland is now part of a larger world. The other children are all part of the story. Living at home are Aarne the youngest, a mechanic, and into jazz and motor cycles. Another son, Toivo, lives nearby as does a daughter, Helmi, who is distinctively of her time in her Merimekko dress. Finally there is the eldest son, Olavi, who teaches in a college in Helsinki and is married to Anna, a Karelian whose family came from Vyborg; this significantly broadens the picture of post-war Finland. He has lectured in America, and she has published poetry; Sykes forms an impression that Olavi is seen as having '"climbed" on to some higher platform, and that this was resented'. There is also Pekka's Uncle Matti, an aged unrepentant communist. These characters present some of the different faces of Finland in the 1960s, but there is no sense that they have been in any way contrived to give a representative picture. After all, they are not fictional.

Sykes's view of Finland is very much his own view, based on describing and interpreting what he sees and experiences and thinks worth recounting. There is no attempt to be historically complete, or to present any of the touristic attractions of Finland – he brushes aside a suggestion that he might 'see much of Finland, on the old steam boats, by our lake system'. His description of a Sunday morning in Tampere – people jogging, going to church, beating carpets, washing and polishing cars – is surely authentic, but, like many of his descriptions, does nothing to make Finland appear worth a visit. The family Sunday lunch is described just as it was:

> there was pea soup first; and we rounded off the meal with ice cream; and then of course there was coffee and pulla, the home-made sweetened bread. But nobody talked. We ate in silence.

The Finland seen of this book has almost nothing in common with any of the numerous pre-war British accounts. There is no mention of the idyllic countryside, or of the amazing modern buildings; the only Helsinki building described is Marjatta's little flat:

low chaste lighting and chaste birch chairs, leather-backed on a vinyl flooring, and all this so swept and polished one could not believe that anyone used it, and lithographs, with a leaning to the abstract, and neatly tucked away, tape-recorder, and television, and radiogram.

The PRO who gives Sykes a guided tour of Pekka's factory strikes a particularly modern note. It seems to belong so closely to Huxley's *Brave New World* that is hard to believe that Sykes is not spoofing:

He was indicating that we should climb some stairs. He was already at the top. He was in good trim. 'I will show you first the recreation rooms – these are the ones for office employees. You see – piano . . . discussion room . . . and here is the hair shop . . . and here changing rooms . . .

For recreation, a variety of courses . . . in home cooking, baby care, orchestration, chess, civics; and an equal variety of sports arrangements. 'You see we work for a happy people – in the broadest sense, for a happy Finnish people. The Company is firstly patriotic. Humanity requires more than bread.'

Sykes's evident disdain for this is part of a wider distaste for Tampere:

I was obsessed and depressed by surly faces, by rancid faces, by unsteady faces on the verge of breakdown into melancholia or some shocking violence. The quality of life-annihilating drunkenness met daily in the street unhinged one; in restaurants there would always be somebody gone that much further than his fellows, but reflecting, as his façade collapsed, their unhappiness taken to its destructive conclusion. They were an unhappy people, they made one sad – and this despite their their tremendous valour, and uprightness, and social achievements that, as I say, spoke from every side. I had always thought

Yorkshire on a wet Sunday the ultimate in public gloom, but it was Mediterranean beside a walk through Tampere.

Tampere was Sykes's urban nadir, but his disappointment was widespread, and especially depressing in Savo and Karelia, which he had hoped would offer a more cheerful prospect. 'Kuopio,' he found 'was too busy becoming a city to bother much about June having struck', so

> I imagined that it would be interesting to return to Joensuu where we had worked with war evacuees. Not at all. It was a draughty market town, with commercials crowding the hotel bars, and the streets flitting with ghostly teenagers.... They bothered me, these phantom creatures, the girls especially thin and waiflike ...

Neither Savonlinna nor Lappeenranta seemed any better.

Sykes was not a tourist. He did not want to be a sightseer, but to experience something more profound, perhaps something closer to what he had sensed back in 1940. His response to walking in the forests, for example, shows his more refined apprehension that somewhere there lies 'the heart of Finland', something distant from Tampere drunkards and the accumulated views favoured by the Kodak generations:

> You do not talk much in this immensity of forest. You inhale it, imbibe its drifting moods, its minute variations; and then by the lakes you keep on halting, standing, and listening, knowing this to be the very heart of Finland. Whichever spot it is, ... in front of you [is] the sky, already changing a fraction since you looked, interchanging with the light on the water, which is a soft-toned light, which could link eternity and all the worlds that have ever been to this particular lakeside moment ... You don't have to travel about, in order as it were, to accumulate views, so as to understand the country: it is all there by the nearest lake. That lakeside is essentially Finland.

Many published, as well as anecdotal accounts of Finland – and there is no shortage of them – comment on the preference of many Finns for silence, and make jokes about it. Sykes actually became something of a connoisseur. 'You have to get used to silence in Finland. It is a major part of social communion,' he wrote. He identifies different orders of silence, experienced on different occasions. In a public sauna, for example. This

> was not the mean, barbed silence, nor the anxious, over-whelmed-by-life silence, nor any of the other impenetrable silences drifting among Finns like a fog, but an inclusive, a friendly, a reverend silence gathering us properly into the occasion.

Pekka's habitual brooding is, of course, is a very individual species of silence, of which Sykes is constantly aware.

Swedish Finns have a chapter to themselves. Pekka hated all the associations of Swedish to the extent that he could not bear to hear Swedish spoken, though Sykes needed it to make up for his lack of Finnish. He takes good care to conceal from the Suusonens his friendship and connection with Lars and his Swedish-speaking family. His visit to them at their manor house near Lohja gives a view of a Finland far distant from Tampere's factory economy. Sykes describes it without comment, distancing himself from the scene only by a careful choice of vocabulary. Sylvia MacDougall could comfortably have included this visit in her tour of Swedish-speaking country mansions, described some sixty years earlier in *A Summer Tour in Finland*.

> 'A peasant girl' as Mrs Eksberg called her – that is, a country Finnish Finn, with face and hair like Sophia Loren's – saw to the drinks and a tray of canapés, then clocked out on the stroke of six, to be collected by a local sawmill engineer, to be driven down to Hanko for the evening. Sometimes he took her as far as Helsinki. That made her

in Mrs Eksberg's view (who naturally referred to the capital as Helsingfors) into a motorised peasant.

Sykes gives what he calls 'a very Chekovian picture' of a way of life with tasteful surroundings, elegant interiors, and leisurely meals. As they took lunch on the terrace, with a few guests of Mrs Eksberg's persuasion, and 'a chill dry hock', there was 'still a "peasant" to wait upon us, an old dame who had always been with the family'.

This chapter follows one describing the family's visit to Uncle Matti; the juxtaposition of this octogenarian communist and the privileged Swedish speakers is striking. Both are hospitable, both have a regular routine, both display old-world courtesy, and both care deeply for tradition.

Sykes's *View of Finland* has a number of set-pieces. The Lohja villa is one; another is driving. Several British travellers in the nineteenth century recorded being driven in springless carts on dangerous roads, at high speed, by very small boys (obviously the ancestors of the modern race of Finnish rally drivers). Toivo, 'an accomplished driver, and one who looked about for challenge', drives some of the family on their visit to Uncle Matti. 'About half an hour out of Tampere we were challenged by a Buick that was just shaking loose from a Mini, like a pekinese snapping at its heels'. This was a prelude:

We had caught the Buick up but could not overtake it. Toivo promptly crossed the line and had two wheels abreast of the other, when, round a bend, a bus appeared, itself well into the middle. For a fleeting second it looked as though Toivo would head for the opposite verge so that we and the Buick would pass the bus, if at all, one on either side of it; but just in time he drew back, to our chagrin allowing the Mini to catch up. He was drained of colour. '*Hitto! Hitto!*' Then, a gear lower, he was charging again.

Again we had to brake, and this time the Mini tried

to pass us on the near side. Toivo quickly had him in the ditch; so that we could see him abruptly coming to a standstill, then continuing but effectively out of the race. We concentrated now now entirely on the Buick. As it chose to slow behind a lorry, then swerve out too late to take the lead again at speed, we passed it on a gradual curve, inching it nearer and nearer to the side, so that the other driver suddenly lost his nerve, a fact communicated to each of us, so that we equally entered into Toivo's skill in taking control of the other car, so that it was slowed, slowed, and dismissed behind us. Whining through the gears we sped ahead.

That was nothing. Now we had to hold the lead against a slightly faster car . . .

Toivo wins this third round as well. Sykes reflects that for a Finn this 'was a way of checking up on one's nerve. Something they all believed in doing'. For the first time in the book 'Pekka was elated'.

The sober, sombre mood of what Sykes at one point calls the 'Lutheran underworld' he experienced in Tampere evaporates sensationally on the last of May, graduation day, when students get their caps. Even Pekka 'smiles at their happiness'. It is an occasion when 'a great deal of money has been spent on new dresses and shoes and coats' and even more 'spent on their day and evening wardrobes for the elaborate academic celebrations'.

They bloomed with all this fantastic expenditure. Finns who usually have to keep an eye on the cost-of-living index go wild in decking out their children for this climax of the educational year. Roses abound. No girl feels fêted unless the diploma or title she is receiving is crowned by immense bunches of roses. No one stints. The papers are full of it, and television: it's a national bean-feast. and as another twelve thousand or so white caps appear (and stare for weeks from photographers' windows) every reasonable Finn gives a cheer for this best proof of national progress.

The contrast between this and Diana Ashcroft's* description of the same occasion in austerity Kajaani in 1948 could hardly be greater. There the girls' attire 'had been reduced to white blouses', and there is no mention of even a single rose. Yet less than twenty years separate the two occasions.

In 'The White Nights of June', the final chapter, Sykes writes that 'the stage was set', as the Suusonen family starts assembling at Olavi's lakeside summer house. Another strand is added to the presentation of Finland as a few of them visit the elderly farmer ('first the old windmill, then the threshing shed') who had sold the plot of land to Olavi for his house. In retrospect, he realised that he had sold it 'for nothing'. He was still sore at having lost land for the resettlement of Karelian refugees. He

> tended to reiterate grudges and to pour scorn on city thinking. All but one of his children had deserted him, complaining of the farm's servitude: only to become serfs in factories, clocked in to a fixed daily pattern. The independent Finnish yeoman had at last become the property of masters. It was the farmers who in the Winter War had saved Finland's freedom! Factory serfs did not know about fighting.

Back at the villa

> Pekka was animated, his whole appearance bigger and fleshier, for all that he was wearing a thick check shirt instead of his usual bulky jacket; his eyes were clear and edging to jokes; his mouth had lost its contracted line and was wide, ready to talk to people. His handgrip was of steady iron. He was standing more or less on one spot, as he always did, as though the weight of his life did not allow of too much movement, but he was disporting this

weight with a new-found confidence. Some major mile-
stone had been passed . . . He was off the treadmill of
sustained anxiety.

Anyone who knows Finland will recognise this change of
mood – almost a change of personality – when town is left
behind, and the lakeside cottage beckons. After sauna, a lot
of drink, and dinner ('We started off with poached salmon,
with plenty of summer dill'), Pekka, 'flushed, redder than a
salmon', made a speech, with pauses for Anna to translate. For
a man who so hated his wife's church attendance, his tone is
strangely biblical:

> I ask God to look down on our gathering, for it pleases
> Him that we are a family and here. I speak for this family
> in asking His blessing. I give thanks for this meal, and
> for this summer evening. It is right to be in harmony with
> Nature. Summer is short in our country, like our lives. We
> say Amen to His goodness to us . . .
> 'So that ends God,' she interposed; translating, 'I speak
> first of my wife, for she has been by my side, a good
> mother to you, and to Anna and to Toivo . . . Your mother
> has worked long for us all, and now she claims rest. I shall
> continue working.
> . . . We have an English friend sitting with us, whom
> I met long ago, I think it was twenty-five years ago. In
> the middle of a war which . . . in modesty we claim . . .
> preserved the freedom we enjoy at this minute. Where
> is Anna's Viipuri now? Would not this lake also have
> become Russian?
> I invite you next year, and you, our English friend . . .
> to a dinner like this to be held, God willing, at the house I
> shall build ... as I say God willing, on Pyhäjärvi.

Pyhäjärvi! Pekka has at last resolved his dilemma, and accepted
the company's offer. The scene, and the book, end with Sykes

and Pekka together on the beach as dusk finally descends. 'He stood happily facing the water, modest, decorous, his fires unflagging. I could feel his friendship unreserved towards me, but, true northerner, he made no show of it.' 'I am glad that I have come here' he tells Pekka in broken Finnish.

He replied as warmly. We shook hands. Then swiftly retreating as though nothing had been demonstrated, we continued silently to view the lake. An uninflected silence, tranquil, serious, into which seeped a little Finnish melancholy, and an awareness of other worlds beyond us which touched us only to point the more surely to the duties and challenges of this one.

'The coffee is ready!'

We returned to the terrace, to the area of family life.

Kate Clanchy

Kate Clanchy's publisher outlines her literary career:

Kate Clanchy is a writer, teacher and journalist. Her poetry collection *Slattern* won a Forward Prize. Her short story 'The Not-Dead and the Saved' won both the 2009 BBC National Short Story Award and the VS Pritchett Memorial Prize. Her novel *Meeting the English* was shortlisted for the Costa Prize. Her BBC 3 radio programme about her work with students was shortlisted for the Ted Hughes prize. In 2018 she was awarded an MBE for services to literature, and an anthology of her students' work, *England: Poems from a School*, was published to great acclaim. In 2019 she published *Some Kids I Taught and What They Taught Me*, a book about her experience of teaching in state schools for several decades.

She spent part of 1999 at the University of Helsinki as British Council writer-in-residence.

What are you doing here? is the question most frequently asked of a writer-in-residence. In Britain, the questioner is usually aggressive: he means what are you doing breathing the local oxygen, and how do you expect to pay for it by writing something as silly as poetry. In Finland, though, the question seems to mean something very different: why, my Helsinki students wanted to know, would I want to come to the edge of Europe, especially in March when the weather was neither hot nor glitteringly cold, what material and ideas could I gather here – what, in short, could Finland offer me? But Finland has everything to offer a writer. All writers want to be heard, and the Finns – once you've got used to the askance looks and shut faces which in fact indicate absolute involvement –

are wonderful listeners. My Helsinki students handed in not just academic essays but whole diaries of passionate involvement with poems in response to some of the lectures I gave on contemporary British poetry. Finns think a great many things they do not always presume to say: a surprising range of people will launch into conversation on the meaning of life, poetry, modernism, and Finland over coffee and cake. The Finns are also wonderful readers. Finland has the most literate population in the world, and to judge from the statistics (Finland also has the most statistics in the world, I think) and the scrum in the Academic Bookshop, the most interested in world literature. Finland is still border country, still defining itself between East and West, telling itself its history, working out its relationships to Finnish and Swedish, still building its literature and its national aesthetic. The arts, therefore, are still serious here, still serious about building a monument, or a town like Aalto's Jyväskylä, rather than novelty, money or catching a headline. It is stimulating simply to be surrounded by such an atmosphere. A Finnish paradox: the family is nationally cherished, public services are wonderfully organised and cohesive, but people also expect to live alone if they haven't got a family, and to be left alone, even within the family, for generous stretches of time. No one will take your time unless they ask, probably anxiously, first. This makes for ideal conditions for a writer. I have rarely covered so much ground and paper – in six weeks. As for the weather, and the season, I have enjoyed both. When I came here the sea outside my window was frozen, Helsinki was sunk in feet of snow and small boys were sledding, with un-Lutheran glee, down the cathedral steps. During my six-week residency, the snow has melted, I have experienced the excitement of an Easter which really is the end of privation and a frozen Lent, seen the sea melt and spilt and finally reflect a blue sky. Students are sitting on the cathedral steps and, outside my flat, the brown battered earth has appeared. I am packing a bagful of printed sheets to take back to green, crowded, muddled England. I feel that Finland has given me a great deal, and only hope – perhaps the national modesty is catching – that I have given enough back.

IV

BRITISH EXPERIENCES AND RESPONSES

The Kalevala in English

The Kalevala, first published in 1835, was revised and greatly
enlarged in the 1849 edition, which contains 22,795 lines. It
is a Primary or Folk Epic, like *Beowulf* and *The Iliad*, written down at some point by a scribe from oral transmissions.
In Finland the identity of the scribe was actually known: it
was Elias Lönnrot (1802–84), a doctor and folklorist, who
arranged the numerous pieces he had collected in eastern Finland and Karelia over a long period to form the work as it is
now known: *Kalevala the Land of the Heroes*. The poetry was
usually sung or chanted, sometimes assisted by a kantele. It
was, in modern terms, performance poetry, performed often
by a duo singing or intoning alternate lines.

Folk song collecting had become popular in many parts of
Europe in the early nineteenth century. Thomas Percy's *Reli-
ques of Ancient English Poetry* (1765) heralded a widespread
enthusiasm in western Europe for ballads and other antiquarian material, and influenced the direction of literature during
the Romantic period. Against this background it is not surprising that word got round, and that from the middle of the century scholars and translators were seeking out the *Kalevala*.

The first British record of its existence is in the unpublished
journal of Sir Henry Austin Layard, who visited Finland in
1838. He records that 'Dr Loendrott, a physician, collected the
ancient sagas of Finland, termed Kalevaleh.'

'Finnish folk poetry was first written down in the 1670s,'
wrote Keith Bosley. 'Of the material collected, about a million and a quarter lines were eventually published in *Suomen
Kansan Vanhat Runot*' in the twentieth century. Lönnrot was

far from being a lone pioneer collector in the field, nor were all the collectors Finns. George Borrow, for example, an agent of the Bible Society, spent two years in Russia (1833–35) charged with supervising a translation of the Bible into Manchu. His precocious abilities as a linguist led to the publication of *TARGUM. Or Metrical Translations From Thirty Languages And Dialects* in St. Petersburg in June 1835. The book contains translations from about twenty languages, two of them from Finnish. One of these, 'Woinomoinen', echoes Runo XLI of the Kalevala.

WOINOMOINEN.
From the Finnish.

Woinomoinen was, according to the Mythology of the ancient Finns, the second Godhead, being only inferior to Jumala. He was master of the musical art, and when he played upon his instrument produced much the same effect as the Grecian Orpheus, enticing fishes from the stream and the wild animals from the forest. The lines here translated are a fragment of a poem which describes a musical contest between Woinomoinen and the Giant Joukkawainen, in which the latter was signally defeated.

> Then the ancient Woinomoinen,
> On the bench himself he seated,
> Took the harp betwixt his fingers,
> On his knee about he turn'd it,
> In his hand he fitly plac'd it.
> Play'd the ancient Woinomoinen,
> Universal joy awaking;
> Like a concert was his playing;
> There was nothing in the forest
> On four nimble feet that runneth,
> On four lengthy legs that stalketh,
> But repair'd to hear the music.

The same passage, in a different translation, appears in John Bowring's* article in the *Westminster Review* in 1827 (see below).

The first translation of the Kalevala, published in 1841, was into Swedish, by Matthias Alexander Castrén, professor in Finnish and Norse languages at the University of Helsinki, and a close associate of of Lönnrot. French came next, with a prose translation in 1845 by M Leouzin Le Duc, followed by Franz Anton Schiefner's German translation – of the 'second edition' – in 1852. Thomas Milner, in *The Baltic, its Gates, Shores, and Cities* (1854) describes how

> Finnish poetry embraces a number of popular songs, mythological compositions, and proverbs, orally handed down from the times of Paganism. A collection published by a native, Dr. Lænnroth [sic], has been translated into French by M. Leouzon le Duc. From this translation, some extracts were given in English by the author of 'Eastern Europe' in 1846. One poem, The Kalevala, of a mytho-logical cast, celebrates the adventures of Wainamoinen, a female [sic] divinity, and extends to not less than thir-ty-two books or runes. All Finnish poetry, ancient and modern, is in alliterative verse, the harmony depending upon a number of words in the same line beginning with the same letter. This kind of versification is improvised by the peasantry with great facility.

The author he mentions was Charles Frederick Henningsen, whose *Eastern Europe and the Emperor Nicholas* (1846) devotes some forty pages to the Kalevala, more than half of them retelling parts of a work which, he writes, 'though sin-gularly disjointed, obscure, and confused may be termed an epic.'

> It is compared to the Odyssey by some of the learned Finns, who in their patriotic enthusiasm even give it precedence.

Though it is difficult for any one but a Finn to acquiesce in this judgement, the Kalevala must be admitted as an interesting monument, of a distant age and of a numerous people, which probably overspread a large portion of Europe long before it was occupied by its present races, and of which the only notable remnant is now to be found in Finland . . .

That the reader may be enabled to judge of the nature of Finnish national literature, a brief analysis with extracts from the Kalevala and Kanteletar [a companion work to the Kalevala, published by Lönnrot in 1840] is herewith given, – the one an ancient epic in two-and-thirty books, the other a collection of the lyrics of the people.

It is evident that Milner either had not read these forty pages, or else had read them very superficially. Even so, there is no reason why he should not have enjoyed Henningsen's pleasant lilting prose summary:

The beauteous virgins of the air, the sun dazzling in splendour, and the soft-rayed moon, have alike paused to listen at the further end of a long light cloud, in the luminous vault of heaven. There they were weaving the wonderful texture of the skies, with a golden shuttle and a silver comb, when astonished by the strange voice and the melodious accents of the hero's song.

The comb of silver fell from their hands, the golden shuttle breaking the threads of the woof, escaped from their fingers. All the living things of the waters, all the fishes waving at once their myriad fins, swam up to hear the voice of Wainamoinen, to listen to the harmony of his song

The salmon and the trout, the pike and the seal, the large fishes and the small, drew as near as was possible to the voice of the charmer.

A much fuller English version appeared in 1861, when John Oxenford, a noted linguist and popular dramatist, published an account of the Kalevala in *Temple Bar,* a leading literary magazine. 'To a certain class of modern philologists,' he writes 'no poem in the world is more familiar than the Kalewala' but 'that class is scarcely a drop in that ocean of humanity, the British public. Hence, humbly relying on the assistance of the great Finnish scholars Castrén and Schiefner, I venture to narrate a curious cycle of legends that will be perfectly new to thousands.' His narration runs to an astonishing 10,000 words, written in lively, at times jaunty style, as befits a dramatist. The opening gives a fair indication of what its appeal would have been to a public much larger than 'the modern philologists':

An allegorical female, called the Daughter of the Air, finds herself in a fair way to become a mother, through the influence of the wind while she is disporting on the surface of the water; but her expectations are so far from speedily fulfilled, that she floats about for 700 years before she increases, or rather commences, the population. In this condition, she offers a prayer to the supreme deity Ukko; and a duck at last appears, and builds upon her knee, which it takes for a mountain, a nest, in which it lays six golden eggs and a seventh of iron. When the eggs have been sat upon for some time, the Water-Mother (as the maiden is now called) feels a painful sensation of burning, and shakes them off, so that they fall into the water. The shells form the upper and lower vaults of the universe, the yolk becomes the sun, the white is coagulated into the moon, some particles are converted into stars and clouds.

The Kalevala is mentioned also in a few non-academic magazine articles on 'Poetry in Finland'. One, in *Household Words* (edited by Dickens) in 1854 is is typical:

Amid [Finland's] woods and moorlands wanders invisibly but yet felt, the good old Wäinämöinen the god of song, with his lyre framed from the wood of the sighing birches, strung with six golden hairs of an enamoured maiden, and with its golden screws dropped from the tongue of the melodious cuckoo.

It was at about this time that a more academic interest began. Max Müller, Professor of Modern European Languages at Oxford University from 1850, claimed an interest in Finnish literature dating back to the 1840s. 'In one of my earliest courses of lectures,' he wrote in 1888 'delivered at Oxford, I gave a full account of the now famous Finnish poem, the Kalevala'. Müller wrote to Gladstone, then Prime Minister (20 December, 1884), 'It is a pity that the Kalewala has not been translated into English; some portions of it are quite worth it.'

In 1884 Andrew Lang, an Oxford folklorist and anthropologist, published *Custom and Myth*, which contained a chapter 'Kalevala, or; The Finnish National Epic'. These are his opening words:

> It is difficult to account for the fact that the scientific curiosity which is just now so busy in examining all the monuments of the primitive condition of our race, should, in England at least, have almost totally neglected to popularise the 'Kalevala,' or national poem of the Finns. Besides its fresh and simple beauty of style, [it is] a storehouse of every kind of primitive folklore.

The neglect of the Kalevala in England should not have surprised him, since it would be another five years before an English translation appeared; one must assume that Lang read the work in Schiefner's German version. The few quotations among his plot-summaries are in prose, yet when he writes that '[f]urther proof of ancient origin is to be found in what is the great literary beauty of the poem – its pure spontaneity and simplicity' he implies at least some acquaintance with the original.

In *Custom and Myth*, according to William Donaldson, '[t]he focus upon "Aryan" civilization was far too narrow, since comparative anthropology showed the same practices, customs, and beliefs occurring in widely scattered societies.' 'Among the Finns,' Lang writes 'we find no trace of an aristocracy; there is scarcely a mention of kings, or priests; the heroes of the poem are really popular heroes, fishers, smiths, husbandmen, "medicine-men", or wizards; exaggerated shadows of the people, pursuing on a heroic scale, not war, but the common daily business of primitive and peaceful men.'

All this was fresh meat for anthropologists: an epic of popular society, no less. Lang gives a plot summary with short quotations, in prose: '[T]he value of the "Kalevala" is partly this,' he continues, 'that it combines the continuity and unison of the epic with the simplicity and popularity of the ballad, and so forms a kind of link in the history of the development of poetry.' He then explains 'the literary history of the Finnish national poem' before giving 'an abstract of its contents.'

In 1888 William Forsell Kirby, a entomologist at the Natural History Museum, and an amateur folklorist, issued a proposal for a translation of the Kalevala. For a year this became the subject of antagonistic discussion in the pages of two fashionable London journals, *The Athenaeum* and the *Pall Mall Gazette*. Some of the writers loosely classed by Oxenford as 'philologists' took issue with this proposal to provide a 'popular edition', which was to be translated from the German of Schiefner, but, as Kirby explained in the *Pall Mall Gazette*, he would 'collate with all the other versions' and consult 'the Finnish text in any case of real difficulty.' Dr. G. A. Schrumpf rubbished this idea, writing that Kirby 'proposes to give us a Kalevala at third hand' and exclaiming 'Why, he has not even informed us "plainly" whether he knows Finnish or not!' Edmund Gosse and Lang shared his concern that a popular version would cut the ground from under any future provision of a scholarly translation, which was their ideal. They conveyed, too, a sense that Kirby was an unscholarly upstart who needed to be stopped in his tracks. When Kirby refused to be persuaded, Schrumpf showed his true colours; it was, he wrote 'impossible to make him sacrifice a little self-satisfaction in the interests of science.'

An irony underlies this semi-scholarly dispute: as the philologists were busy squabbling in London John Martin Crawford, an American physician and scholar, was completing his translation of the Kalevala from the German of Schiefner, and this was published in America and England in the following year. Müller's contributions to the Kalevala debate in 1888 had been exclusively on the topic of whether it could be usefully compared with 'the Homeric poem'. He actually knew of Crawford's work – his help is acknowledged in the preface – but he seems not to have mentioned it to the others. Crawford's preface is dated October 1887. England had been slow off the mark in terms of translation: in fact the first English versions, of selected passages only, were by North Americans. John Addison Porter, Professor of Organic Chemistry at Yale College, produced *Selections from the Kalevala. Translated from a German Version.* The Publisher's Notice explains that the translation was done 'to while away the hours of the long illness which terminated his valuable life.' He had died in 1866, but his work was not published until 1873. After a very long introduction and analysis, the selection, in verse, occupies about ninety pages. On 17 March 1869 Edward Taylor Fletcher, born in Canterbury, and later Surveyor General of Quebec, read from his own translation before the Literary and Historical Society of Quebec. James Gifford has explained that

Fletcher's translation was published a year too late in 1869 to be the first English translation, but John Addison Porter's 1868 partial translation derives from Franz

Anton Schiefner's German translation, which it uses as a bridge. Fletcher's is the first to translate the work into English from the original Finnish, and it includes a significant introduction discussing the poetic structure of the poem, its unique meter, and the linguistic traits of Finnish.

Crawford's translation was published in 1889. In the same year he was appointed as consul-general of the United States to Russia, presumably in St Petersburg, and while no more is heard of him, *The Kalevala: the Epic Poem of Finland* alerted British readers to the poem's existence; several of the British accounts of Finland during the next two decades quote from it. Their books, especially Mrs. Tweedie's popular *Through Finland in Carts* (1897), made the Kalevala better known; British writers about Finland sometimes seem to be showing off their acquaintance with the poem, possibly wishing to give their writing more authority. For several of them, male as well as female, this was linked with their interest in status of women: Tweedie wrote 'men and women are practically equals, and on that basis society is formed. Sex equality has always been a characteristic of the race, as we find from the ancient Kalevala poem.'

Extracts from Crawford's translation appeared in 1892 'Selected by Lady Paget (Cambridge)', 'Printed for private circulation only.' (see p.13.) In the Preface she claims that her book 'will show the high tone of moral and religious feeling existing in a race among whom such sentiments are not usually supposed to have flourished.' She prefaces each extract with her own comments, such as '. . . the curious and unsatisfactory custom of washing clothes by beating them on a rock or stone is alluded to' and 'These few lines give us the various names by which the bear was known among the Finns.'

A book published in the following year, in which 'Mr. T. M. Crawford's metrical translation of the Kalevala has been quite closely followed' would have had much wider circulation. This was *Finnish Legends for English Children*, by R. Eivind, part of a popular series, *The Childrens' Library*:

> The following stories cover almost all of the songs of the Kalevala, the epic of the Finnish people. They will lead the English child into a new region in the fairy world, yet one where he will recognise many an old friend in a new form. The very fact that they *do* open up a new portion of the world of the marvellous will, it is hoped, render them all the more acceptable, and perhaps, when the child who reads them grows up to manhood, will inspire an actual interest in the race that has composed them.
>
> And this race and their land will repay study, for nowhere will one find a more beautiful land than Finland, nor a braver, truer, and more liberty-loving people than the Finns, although, alas, their love for liberty may soon be reduced to an apparently hopeless longing for a lost ideal. For the iron hand of Russian despotism has already begun to close on Finland with its relentless grasp, and, in spite of former oaths and promises from the Russian Tsars, the future of Finland looks blacker and blacker as time goes on.

I can find no details, not even the sex, of the author. The name suggests a Norwegian connection. 1892 had seen the première of Sibelius's *Kullervo*, which marked a new era of Finnish patriotism. Eivind's book was an early prelude to the support in Britain for Finland's opposition to Russification; it was Nicholas II's February Manifesto of 1899 which fully alerted liberal opinion in Britain – indeed in Europe – to Finland's plight.

We left William Forsell Kirby back in 1888, unconvinced by the philologists, and possibly unaware that Crawford was about to forestall him. Kirby spent the following years (he had his day job) mastering Finnish – but not before having learnt Estonian. It was not until 1907 that his translation of the Kalevala from the Finnish finally appeared in two volumes; it was reprinted in 1914 and 1923, and reissued in 1985 with a Preface by Michael Branch. The publisher identified the book as 'Romance', but Kirby's two-page introduction opens 'No national *epic* lies so firmly in the heart of its people'[my italics]. He explains that the Kalevala 'is very unlike any poem familiar to general readers, but it contains much that is extremely curious and interesting; and many beautiful passages and episodes which are by no means inferior to those we find in ballad literature of better-known countries than Finland.' By this date Finland was becoming well-known in England, but Kirby nonetheless feels the need to assure readers that Finns 'are a pious, industrious, and law-abiding people, the upper class being highly educated.' He adds, modestly, that 'perhaps the best translations' are by Schiefner and Collan. His own translation, in an accessible format in Everyman's Library, now became the one which British writers on Finland read, and from which they quoted.

Kirby's translation was very timely, coming at the opening of the second period of Russian oppression, under Stolypin in 1907. During the nineteenth century, as Keith Bosley has written, the folk songs which reflected national identity found particular favour 'among nations with little by way of recorded history or literature, small nations that for centuries had been mostly unlettered peasants under masters speaking another language.' As Finnish nationalism crystallized into opposition to Russification, the Kalevala had become a powerful symbol of Finnish identity. Professor Mead suggested an interpretation in which the battle between good and evil presented in the Kalevala was an allegory for the need for an independent Finland. In Britain liberal concerns about Finland were reignited, and led four years later to the foundation of the Anglo-Finnish Society. The music of Sibelius was now being performed in England, becoming part (a small part, admittedly) of the pro-Finland movement in Britain. Today the Kalevala stories are widely – perhaps best – known through Sibelius's music, especially the *Lemminkäinen Suite of 1895.*

One of the early readers of Kirby's translation, in 1911, was a Birmingham schoolboy, John Ronald Reuel Tolkien. His fascination with the work continued after he went up to Oxford the following year. There he wrote a prose version of 'The Story of Kullervo', not published until 2010, edited by Verlyn Flieger; it was, she wrote, 'a general precursor to his entire fictional canon'. (It is worth noting that Kullervo was singled out by Kirby in his Introduction: 'His history is a terrible tragedy, which has been compared to that of Oedipus.') In a talk which he gave to an undergraduate society, Tolkien exclaimed that 'you discover the Kalevala . . . and at once you are in a new world; and can revel in an amazing new excitement. You feel like Columbus on a new Continent.' He assures his audience that it is only in print that the 'sing-song character' of the metre is boring: 'they are in essence sing-songs chanted to the harp as the singers swayed backward and forward in time.'

Tolkien is lyrical about the scenery of Finland; 'short of going there,' he writes 'I imagine one could scarcely get a better picture of the land than the Kalevala gives'.

> One sees the lakes and reed-fenced flats with slow rivers: the perpetual fishing: the pile-built houses and then in winter the land covered with sleighs and men faring over quick and firm alike on snow-shoes.

He is amusingly aware that the rough and tumble of the world of the poem might not attract all of his audience, 'people of irreproachable education and faultless urbanity' – this, after all, was Oxford. '[T]he heroes of the Kalevala do behave with a singular lack of dignity and even decency, and with a readiness for tears and and dirty dealing', but that, he explains, 'is part of their special attraction'. These were among the significant features of the poem which Lang, too, had singled out.

'The language of these poems,' Tolkien continues 'makes a

strong bid for the place of most difficult in Europe'. He had borrowed from the college library *A Finnish Grammar* by C. N. E. Eliot, hoping, without success, to be able to read the Kalevala in its original language. 'I never learned Finnish well enough,' he wrote long after to W. H. Auden, 'to do more than plod through a bit of the original, like a schoolboy with Ovid.' Finnish nonetheless made a strong impression on him; he later wrote 'It was like discovering a complete wine-cellar filled with bottles of an amazing wine of a kind and flavour never tasted before. It quite intoxicated me.' When his Moderations (the first university exam) 'should have been occupying all my forces I once made a wild assault on the stronghold of the original language and was repulsed . . . at first with heavy losses'. The effort failed, but was not wasted: the grammar of *Quenya*, one of the fictional languages he devised for use by the Elves, was influenced by Finnish. 'The ingredients in Quenya are various,' he wrote 'but worked out into a self-consistent character not precisely like any language that I know. Finnish, which I came across when I had first begun to construct a 'mythology' was a dominant influence.' The Kalevala gave 'a mythology for Finland', and Flieger suggests that it 'might have made as deep an impression on Tolkien as the songs themselves, and have played a major part in his his expressed desire to create his so-called mythology for England'. 'With *The Lord of the Rings*,' wrote John Garth 'he wanted to give England its own Kalevala'.

Both the story and the language of the Kalevala played a significant part in all his writing. The 'tragic hero' archetype was used for the character of Turin Turambar in *The Children of Hurin*: he, like Kullervo, inadvertently marries his own sister, and commits suicide. Numerous commentators on Tolkien have identified a whole raft of borrowings and influences from the Kalevala. It has been suggested for example, that the Sampo influenced the One Ring which drives the plot of *The Lord of the Rings*, and that the character of Gandalf was inspired by Väinämöinen, as well as by the Norse god Odin, and so forth. The Kalevala, especially the tale of Kullervo, was a major influence on *The Silmarillion*.

Influences apart, the sheer exuberance of Tolkien's final response to the Kalevala has not been matched by any other British writer:

> All the world to reel about in, the Great Bear to play with and Orion and the Seven Stars all dangling magically in the branches of a silver birch enchanted by Väinämöinen; the splendid sorcerous scandalous villains of old to tell of when you have bathed in the 'Sauna' after binding the kine at close of day into pastures of little Suomi in the Marshes.

In a wartime letter to his son Christopher he wrote 'I wish I could have visited the Land of Ten Thousand Lakes before this war. Finnish nearly ruined my Hon. Mods., and was the original germ of the Silmarillion.'

Kirby's translation replaced Crawford's, which was not reissued in England until 2017, and in 1977 Ursula Synge used it as her source for an abridged version in prose. 1963 Francis Peabody Magoun, a Harvard Professor of English, had already published a prose translation, having learned Finnish in order to further his researches in oral-formulaic poetry, but this was not published in England. In 1989, two translations marked the 150th anniversary of Lönnrot's original publication. A blind, septuagenarian, Finnish-born American, Eino Hjalmar Friberg, worked from a Braille copy of the Kalevala, and Keith Bosley, who had been preparing the way for more than twenty years with translated extracts in a variety of publications, published his translation with the support of the Finnish Literature Society. 'It was felt in Finland that a more contemporary English translation was needed,' he wrote 'I was also dissatisfied with the previous attempts on the field, so I decided to take the task on.' 'The only way I could devise of reflecting the vitality of Kalevala metre was to invent my own . . . based on syllables rather than feet.' Bosley's transla-

tion 1989 has now more or less superseded all other versions.
In 2013 he completed a reading of his version, lasting more
than thirteen hours, and available on twelve cds. His version
may here be compared with Kirby's, which follows.

At that old Väinämöinen
began to play prettily
the sounding thing of pike-bones
the kantele of fish-bones;
his fingers rose nimbly, his
   thumb lifted lightly;
   now joy waxed joyful
delight echoed like delight
music sounded like music
song had the effect of song;
   the pike's tooth tinkled
   the fish-tail poured forth
   the stallion's hairs called
the hairs of the steed rang out.

*

Then the aged Väinämöinen,
Quick commenced his skilful playing
On the instrument of pikebone,
On the kantele of fishbone,
And he raised his fingers nimbly,
And his thumb he lifted lightly.

Now came pleasure after pleasure,
As the sweet notes followed others,
As he sat and played the music,
As he sang his songs melodious,
As he played upon the pike-teeth,
And he lifted up the fish-tail,
And the horsehair sounded sweetly,
And the horsehair sounded clearly.

John Bowring and Early Finnish Poetry

John Bowring, who passed through Finland on his way back from a commercial trip to Russia early in 1820, makes only a brief appearance in *Not so Barren or Uncultivated*. In Turku he met 'the leading men, notably Archbishop Tengström and John Julin'; he would keep in touch with both of them, as well as with Franz Mikael Franzén. 'I found among the Finns,' he wrote 'a civilisation far superior to what I had anticipated'. His account of the dangerous journey through the ice to Sweden in an open boat is one of several such accounts from this period. He later recalled some dramatic details:'I was once frozen in for some hours in the Gulf of Bothnia, crossing from Abo to Upsala, the cold being so intense that we used a hatchet to cut our bread, while the brandy was frozen. I lay down under some furs, expecting to die, but at length the ice around us broke, and we were enabled to make a perilous way between the ice-islands that were floating about.'

Back in England Bowring wrote to Tengström, thanking him for his hospitality, and sending brochures of the recently founded Peace Society, which he hoped might be translated and distributed in Finland.

Bowring was a man of many parts, and many languages. A ubiquitous figure in the literary and political scene of early nineteenth-century England, he was a close friend of Jeremy Bentham, and became editor of the *Westminster Review*. Known, in Thomas Hood's words, as a 'man of many tongues', he claimed once to know two hundred languages, and to speak one hundred of them! This passion for languages, combined with his radical political views, led him to compile a series of translations from the folk poetry of a number of European nations. Folk songs, as Keith Bosley has written, 'because they reflected national identity', found particular favour at this time 'among nations with little by way of recorded history or literature, small nations that for centuries had been mostly unlettered peasants under masters speaking another language.' In *Minor Morals for Young People* Bowring wrote 'The poetry of the people is one of the most delightful resources and comforts of nations that have been subjected by strangers. In it they often give expression to thoughts, which would otherwise find no vent.'

A year after his visit to Russia Bowring published the first of two parts of *Specimens of the Russian Poets*, which went into a second edition. These launched him on a period of verse translations which was to last a decade. The Russian volume was followed by translations from the 'popular poetry' of Holland, Spain, Poland, Serbia, Bohemia, Hungary, and Friesland. It is now clearly established that Bowring made use of existing translations, usually into German, to aid his own 'translations'. In 1830 was advertised 'Songs of Scandinavia, in 2 Vols., containing a selection of the most interesting of the Historical and Romantic Ballads of North Western Europe'. There was an extended correspondence between him and the co-author George Borrow, but the book was never published.

In Turku, he wrote, he had discovered that the Finns, like the Poles, had 'an earnest longing for the return of their independence, but that they were fully convinced that it was hopeless to dream of such a felicity.' He saw Finland as 'among the oppressed nationalities', like other Russian dependencies, so it was an obvious candidate for one of his volumes; he set about it as soon as he returned to England. He must have been back by early spring 1820, because in *The Monthly Repository* for April, above the initials J.B. is printed 'A Finnish Runo. Verbally Translated, and the original measure preserved'. To the poem (nineteen lines in each language) is added a footnote: 'Runo is the Finnish name for a song; the singer or poet is called Runolainen.' A much longer note on runes and on Finnish mythology follows: '[M]any of the Finnish Runes, consisting of several hundred stanzas, have been orally conveyed down to our times, from a period of very remote antiquity, in a state of perfectness, of which it would be difficult to furnish any other example'. The poems are 'wholly founded on the mythology of distant centuries'. Bowring can only have got this information from Schröters *Finnische Runen* (1819), which he would probably have brought back with him from Finland or Sweden. All this shows that he was already doing some homework in preparation for a collection of Finnish popular poetry, something which would occupy him intermittently during the 1820s. It was advertised in *The New Monthly Magazine* for November 1827:

> The publication of the Runes of Finland is delayed for addition to them of sundry Laplandish and Esthonian Compositions, which Mr. B. has collected, and which will enable him to give a more comprehensive view of the state of Letters among the three principal branches of the Fennic state.

Even this added attraction did not arouse enough interest in the work; no Finnish anthology appeared, and, like the *Songs of Scandinavia,* the scheme faded away.

There are only a couple of surviving letters from Bowring to Finland from the early 1820s, to Tengström and to John Julin, but in June 1822 he wrote to Friedrich von Adelung in St. Petersburg 'Je vous prépare d'excellens matérieux pour la littérature finnoise.' Adelung was planning to compile dictionaries and grammars for all the languages spoken in Russia, many of which had no established written tradition.

One of the many articles which Bowring contributed to *The Westminster Review* was 'Runes of Finland' (April, 1827), ostensibly a review of Renvall's *Suomalinen Sana-Kirja*, and Schröter's *Finnische Runen*. He later claimed this as the first presentation of Finnish poetry and folklore in England. Yrjö Hirn (professor of Aesthetics at Helsinki University) wrote in 1939 that readers of this article should not expect 'the results of independent and thorough research', and pointed out that the English translations are taken without acknowledgement from Schröter's German version. The research may not have been independent, but it was new to English readers. Bowring's important achievement in this long article was to give the first detailed account in English of Finnish poetry. It is a passionate plea for looking beyond established, published literature.

It has been no part of our project to make English poetry, by decorating or mis-translating the Runes of Finland. We wish to give a correct, and, at the same time, a distinct, idea of the popular literature of that country. With it the literature, as well as the language, of Lapland is closely associated, and we should deem the adventurer most deserving the favourable regards of the public, who should lead the way into that remote and almost unknown region. While so much of life is wasted, so many energies idly engaged, in 'beating and beating again the beaten track of literature,' we can assure the intelligent inquirer, that there are many unvisited gardens, whose first-fruits and earliest flowers he may, if he pleases, cull. We are sure an honourable, and, we believe, an enduring, reputation might be created by directing the inquisitive attention into the untrodden paths of study. Even in Europe there are languages, and, connected with those languages, literary treasures, a thorough acquaintance with which would richly reward the labour of acquiring them. The time is past, we hope, in which learned ignorance can pour out its vials of scorn and contempt upon every thing which did not flow forth from the Alpheus or the Tiber.

One sample of the translation Bowring provides must suffice here:

KANTELEEN SYNTY.
Birth of *the Harp.*

He, the aged Wainamoinen,
Up the rock his boat has lifted;
On its height the harp created.
Whence the concave harp created?
From the body of the birch-tree.
And the harp's keys, whence created?
From the oak-tree's equal branches.
And the harp's strings, whence created?
From the tail of mighty stallion,
From the stallion's tail of Lempo.
He, the aged Wainamoinen,
Call'd on youths and call'd on maidens,
That their fingers might awake it ;
Rapture answer'd not to rapture,
Song was not by song repeated.
Then he call'd on men unmarried,
Then he call'd on married heroes;
Rapture answer'd not to rapture,
Song was not by song repeated.

The harp, as invented by Wäinmäinen (Kantelet), is still
the national instrument, and is used, even in our day, to
accompany the singing of the ancient Runes, not indeed
without some improvement since the old god tore the
hairs from the tail of the wild stallion for its strings.

Bowring writes about Finland with the assurance of a man
who has actually been there:

The university of Åbo is the principal source of the cul-
tivation of Finland. Many of the professors have distinguished themselves in the annals of philosophy, and have
added important contributions to science and literature.
The chemical works of Gadolin, the Swedish poetry of

Franzen, the philological writings of Ehrstrom and Otte-lin, are known far beyond the Finnish borders. Trans-lations of the Bible, of the laws of Sweden, and many religious publications, circulate pretty extensively.

Of the living poets of Finland, the most industrious and the most popular is Jacob Juden, of Tavastehus, now an inhabitant of Viborg. He has published a variety of critical remarks on Finnish literature . . . and, by his own contributions to almost every class of poetry, has placed himself at the head of the modern literati of Finland.

Bowring sent copies of the article to John Julin, asking that they be delivered 'as addressed' in 'the hope that I shall obtain from those who are thoroughly instructed in the matter such hints & such help as may enable me to bring out a proper volume after a proper time.' A half-dozen additional copies he asked Julin to forward to anyone who might be willing to assist him 'in making a more complete portraiture of the Finn-ish Poetry than can be found.'

However willing they might have been, events intervened. Just two months after this letter was sent most of the uni-versity, including the library, was destroyed in the fire which burnt down three-quarters of the whole city of Turku. The news of the fire duly reached Britain, and more than £800 was raised for relief. The news spurred Bowring into action, and he wrote a two-page address, *Conflagration of Åbo*, widely distributed – 'at least 10,000 copies' he at one point claimed – and had it inserted in *The Foreign and Quarterly Review.*

In a country like Finland, so little visited, so far removed from the attention and sympathy of the civilised world, the destruction of the only large public library is a calam-ity, the greatness and extent of which can hardly be esti-mated here.

'I have been addressed by some valuable Finnish friends on

the subject,' he continues, to ascertain if 'literary and scientific individuals' might donate some of their works 'to assist in the reformation of their library.' Bowring took the lead in obtaining such books and organising their dispatch to Finland. The progress of this can be followed in a series of letters to John Julin, seven of which are preserved in the Fiskars archive. Bowring kept him in the picture of his activities, which included using his trading connections to establish collecting-places for books in Paris, Brussels and Strasburg.

Bowring was disappointed by the poor response to his appeal, which he attributed partly to a 'feeling that English books are of little value in Finland.' During 1829 the University Library (now in Helsinki, of course) received 287 books; there were copies of the *Westminster Review* to date, twenty-nine works donated by Jeremy Bentham, and other valuable accessions, but also a good deal of dross which today would scarcely have found shelf space in a charity bookshop. The recipients too were disappointed: Professor Pipping admitted in the Senate that it was Bowring's intentions rather than his achievement which merited recognition. Bowring had dropped several heavy hints that he would welcome some formal distinction from the University, but, for several complex political reasons, all he received was an address of gratitude written in florid Latin. Bowring's last archive letter, dated 5 May 1830, continues his search for material for his projected book of Finnish popular poetry, but his interest in Finland was now fading.

Born into a Unitarian family and educated in a Unitarian school, Bowring had at one stage wished to become a minister, and has indeed been described as 'the most prominent Unitarian layman of his time.' The contacts he maintained in Finland and Sweden were partly religious. He published popular books of hymns, one of which, *Matins and Vespers,* he discovered, was kept by Bishop Franzén in the pulpit of his church in Sweden. His religious and Finnish interests came together in

1830 in a contribution to *The Winter's Wreath*, an anthology of wholesome pieces in prose and verse. In one of these, titled 'Respice Finem', he passes off an overdone travellers's tale as his own experience; his actual journey would have been the fairly well-trodden route from St. Petersburg to Turku.

I have travelled through those sublime forest-solitudes, which, stretching landwards to an untrodden distance, terminate on the western side of that great bay, at whose highest point, like the topmost star upon the brow of Urania is the town of Torneå . . . The snow and rime falling thick among the fir-tree branches, soon suspend festoons, which, hardened by frost, form, ere long, huge fetters which bind the woods together. The wind awakes – the trees are torn asunder; tremendous crashes are heard on every side – the very echoes seem busy in adding to the din of the disorder. Pursued by the drifted snow – pelted by hail and icicles, and overwhelmed by the frozen masses which are shaken by the tempest from above – his eyes kept forcibly open by a plate of ice, formed from the moisture of the cornea – his garments hardened by the sleet, his hair stiffened – his breath congealed as soon as it is exhaled: the thought that naturally presents itself to the the traveller: what a bliss that I am not called to dwell in these desolate regions!

He describes the scenes more vividly than many writers who had actually experienced them, but what immediately follows is purely fanciful:

I have seen happiness there, and have head the joyous song and the cheerful story. In many a wooden hut, almost buried under the snow, rocked by the winds, surrounded by the wild beasts – solitary, shrouded – there are warm affections – aye, and gentle love, and sober wisdom, and poetry, and patriotism, and felicity – where they 'look to the end.'

Passing one of these 'rude habitations of the Finlanders', Bowring claims to have overheard the 'monotonous tones' of someone reciting lines from 'that famous old Rune "On the Birth of Fire"'. On entering the hut he 'found a cheerful old man chanting to his children and grandchildren the marvellous story recorded in the composition.' Entertained, warmed, and comforted, he was fed from one of the 'ring-shaped loaves' taken from its pole in the ceiling, and 'a large mug of beer', he sits back to ask the inevitable question: 'can you tell me the ingredients out of which you produce so much content, so much felicity?' The equally inevitable answer is a proverb: 'Don't waste your tears'. By looking to the end the old man has come through many hardships – military, familiar, and worst of all the fire of Turku which ended his university education. The effects of this old man 'throwing sunshine over all events, however gloomy' transform Bowring's life, and he hums a cheerful tune as he seats himself on his sledge and pulls the 'rough bear skin' around himself. I can only wonder if there could have been any reader who believed this story.

A mercifully short variant is found in 'Songs of the People' in a chapter of *Minor Morals for Young People*:

> There is poetry and beautiful poetry everywhere. I remember once, when in the woods of Finland, I heard a song, many centuries old, which described what song could do . . . The song I heard from the Finlanders reminded me of the classical fable; for it told of the powers of the harp whose strings were made of the tail of the wild horse, and its body from the oldest oak tree of the woods. And it is said, that when played on by a mighty hand, the birds gathered round the musician; the beasts crouched before him; the fishes looked out of the ocean, and all the auditory wept.

This seems to have been his last word on Finland, and that is perhaps just as well. He was elected to Parliament in the following year, 1835, and lived another forty years, with an active career as a politician, economist, and diplomat. In 1849 he was appointed British consul at Canton (Guangzhou), and superintendent of trade in China. In 1854 he became Governor of Hong Kong, where he was responsible for the hostilities that led to the Arrow War (1856–60).

[This chapter is based on my long article 'John Bowring and Finland' in *Neuphilologische Mitteilungen* 3 LXXV (1974). The whole of Bowring's *Westminster Review* article is available on line: http://www.doria.fi/bitstream/handle/10024/149248/bowring_on_the_runes.pdf;jsessionid=4094AFB9173073C64494545CB1EC2E2B?sequence=1).]

British Sauna Experiences

'The sauna cannot be recommended to a people so incurably shy
of their birthday clothes as the British.'
Harry Bell, *Land of Lakes* (1950)

'The *sauna*, or stream bath, is a national institution of Finland.
I had now been in the country for nearly a week, and hadn't had
one. My host stared with astonishment when I told him, evidently
considering the feat impossible.'
Bernard Newman, *Baltic Roundabout* (1939)

Although the Finnish word *sauna* did not appear in print in
England until the 1880s, British travellers had been describing
the phenomenon for well over a century. The Finnish bath was
first observed from a safe distance, then explored more closely,
and finally, after about a century, actually experienced.

Until the mid-nineteenth century travellers used the terms
'Russian bath' or 'Russian vapour bath'. The Swedish term
'bastu' was also used, with a variety of spellings. John Carr
describes with horror several sauna scenes: 'we beheld men
and women indiscriminately mingled together, in a state similar to that which preceded the slightest notion of breeches and
waistcoats . . .' His sauna viewing, described in terms which
verge on the sarcastic, was of the briefest:

> The vapour-room was capacious, women and men were
> piled one above another amphitheatrically: the vapour
> which filled the room, and gave it the atmosphere of a
> digester, was produced from water being thrown upon
> a great number of heated stones, some of them red hot.
> In this place, they exchange the little *tender and deli-
> cate offices* of flogging, soaping, and rubbing each other
> down.... These scenes, such is the effect of habit, are sel-
> dom productive of libertinism, even amongst the natives;

to every foreigner they cannot fail to be offensive and repulsive.

The British were were historically late in experiencing a sauna themselves; there is a description by Giuseppe Acerbi, an Italian gentleman whose host in Kemi 'wished to instruct me in all the Finlandish customs'. His *Travels through Sweden, Finland, and Lapland, to the North Cape, in the years 1798 and 1799* was published in London in 1802, and was reviewed at length in the first number of *The Edinburgh Review*: '[t]he plates, which accompany Mr Acerbi's travels, are in general good [but] the Finlandish bath has nothing to recommend it, but the naked accuracy of the re-presentation.' As if to prove their point, the editors reproduce this plate.

Edward Daniel Clarke, later to become Professor of Mineralogy at Cambridge, in Finland at the same time as Acerbi, gave a measured and objective account of the sauna:

There is not a village, nor indeed a dwelling, without a steam-bath; in which the inhabitants of both sexes assemble together, in a state of perfect nudity, for the purpose of bathing, at least once in every week; and oftener, if any illness occur among them. These steam-baths are all alike: they consist of a small hut, containing a furnace for heating stones red hot, upon which boiling water is thrown; and a kind of shelf, with a ladder conducting to it, upon which the bathers extend themselves, in a degree of temperature such as the natives of southern countries could not endure for an instant: here they have their bodies rubbed with birch boughs dipped in hot water; an office which is always performed by the females of each family, and generally by the younger females. It is to these baths, and to the natural cleanliness and temperate habits of the people, that the uninterrupted health they enjoy may be ascribed.

Few of the the early travellers were as non-judgemental as this, and got no further than peeping through the open door of a sauna. The Rev. Robert Bateman Paul, writing in 1836, does not conceal either his ignorance or his contempt for the 'Baths of the Peasants': 'The mode of bathing adopted by the peasants in the country is simple enough: the peasant creeps into the oven, from which he has just extracted his bread, or his mess of buck wheat, and having baked himself to his heart's content creeps out again'. The only benefit he concedes is that rheumatism 'is almost unknown among them.' Other writers assumed the 'swarthy' complexion of Finlanders was the result of such baking.

Sir Arthur de Capell Brooke, travelling in the 1820s through Muonioniska, was actually tempted to bathe, but his courage failed at the doorstep:

> There being a bastuen, or vapour bath, my travelling companions, with the exception of Frue Klerck, took advantage of its refreshing powers after their journey, and were bathed by the young women of the house. This curious operation is invariably performed by females, and those the youngest of the family. One of the bathers, on the present occasion, was a good-looking girl about seventeen. If I had not been so greatly occupied as I was, I should have been tempted, perhaps, to have tried the effect of the bath; and to have undergone the rubbing process, which is the most important feature of it, performed by so pretty a hand. The truth is, besides being busy, I did not quite like the idea of having this ceremony performed in the presence of so large a party, and which would seem to require no small degree of privacy. I therefore determined to pay a visit to the bastuen on some future occasion; and while the others were steaming, I proceeded to look at the church, at the distance of about half a mile.

The attractions of a naked nubile teenage girl were clearly not lost on him, but whatever it was that he envisaged would have required privacy – he was, after all, a baronet and a Fellow of the Royal Society – and remained unfulfilled. Perhaps he confessed his temptations at the church. A century later Cutliffe Hyne, in the wilds of Finnish Lapland, describes the sauna quite straightforwardly; he was a fully hardened explorer, and it would have required much more than the sight of a few naked bodies to discompose him.

Several travellers were able to regard the sauna more objectively, not so much as a symptom of barbarity, beneath contempt for a visitor from the civilised world, as actually a mark of higher civilisation; de Brooke's 'future occasion' arrived fairly soon, in Jahois, south of Muonio. Again he declined to bathe, but instead of visiting a church he ruminated

the whole of the family had just come out of the bastuen, or vapour bath; and the men had entered where we were sitting, for the double purpose of drying themselves by its heat, as is usual with them, and having a peep at their new visitors. A stranger from far more civilized parts of the world than Finland is greatly surprised at finding the intercourse between the sexes so unconstrained, and yet so innocent. In his own country, extreme as the stress which is laid upon female propriety of conduct, and rigidly as the rules of decorum are enforced between the sexes, he is sensible, that licentiousness prevails to an extent, unheard of in these parts of the North, where the inhabitants are comparatively in the state of nature, and where the freedom between the sexes is infinitely greater, without transgressing the proper bounds.

He here anticipates the way in which some later British travellers came to view the sauna. E. S. P. Haynes, in an essay published in 1936, put a classical shine on his own experiences of taking a sauna, calling it a 'curious instance of the progressive spirit':

A genial and buxom young woman who talked no language but Finnish saw me through this ceremony and subsequently washed me in stark nudity without the least embarrassment. The situation was perhaps easier because as I cannot talk a word of Finnish all communication was by gesture and dumb crambo. It almost recalled the atmosphere of Nausicca and her friends in the Odyssey, and there is no doubt that what is called progress is no more than a return to pre-Christian civilisation.

As William Sansom put it some thirty years later, 'This unassuming attitude towards nudity comes from a liberal rather than a libertine temperament.'

It was not until 1875 that we find a detailed *British* account of actually taking a sauna. Edward Rae, whose *Land of the North Wind* is one of the most entertaining of all British accounts of travelling in Finland:

> I was directed to leave everything at the door of the hut, and in a few minutes the bathing attendant, a decent hard-featured woman, came in without the slightest embarrassment or false delicacy, and bathed me much as if I had been in a Turkish bath. By-and-by she told me to mount by a wooden ladder to a small raised platform, when she threw a pailful of cold water upon the heated stones, and the hot steam came round me in clouds. I was directed to switch my limbs and shoulders with a bunch of birch-twigs, until the gentle perspiration came upon my forehead and face. Then I sat with my feet in a bucket of delicious cool water, while the bathing-mistress poured soft water over my head and shoulders: then I was soaped and drenched again until I felt as clean as an ivory statue. Then came the drying, and the delightful gradual cooling, and I skipped across to the house exhilarated and clean.

Like de Brooke before him, he experienced what might be termed a species of cultural conversion:

> I have now a great respect for the Finlanders' bath: and a respect, too, for their straightforward frankness and primitive absence of reserve, which is the truest delicacy after all.

Near Inari a month or so later – Saturday 6 September 1873 to be exact – an Oxford undergraduate exploring Finnish Lapland with a friend during the long vacation confessed in his journal, posted in instalments to his stepmother, that he had taken a sauna. He spared her no details:

> We have bidden one last & final farewell to every English scruple. We have taken a Finnish bath. There is a wooden hut built on purpose. The water was boiled in a large cauldron on the rocks outside, then it was put into a large wooden bath decorated with crosses at the corners, like Oxford frames. On the other side was a raised kind of hearth on which were placed stones previously heated in a fire. Then water was poured on these until the whole place was like the inside of a boiler, & then you undressed, & then – I can't put off the shocking confession any longer! *She* bade you ascend the platform at the end of the hut & beat you – in the costume of Adam before the Fall – with leafy birch rods steeped in hot water, every now and then almost blowing off the roof of the hut by pouring more water on the hot stones, & then turning you over and whipping you on the other side & having by this time reduced you to a state of abject submission & the consistency of a boiled chicken, she puts you into the bath & scrubs you from top to toe, after which she sealed you with a towel, & must needs dress you and serve you up.

This was Arthur Evans, famous in later life for his achievements as Keeper of the Ashmolean Museum in Oxford, and as the archaeologist who excavated the palace of Knossos in Crete.

It was Mrs. Alec Tweedie who put the Finnish sauna, using its Finnish name, on the map for British readers. 'Finnish Baths', the third chapter of her *Through Finland in Carts* (1897), opens with a litany: 'A Finnish bath once taken by man or woman can never be forgotten!'

> Poets have described the bath in verse, artists have drawn it on canvas, and singers have warbled forth its charms; nevertheless, it is not every traveller who has penetrated the strange mystery. Most strange and most mysterious it is.

The first edition of the book opens 'Finland, or, as the natives call it, Suomi, is a country of lakes and islands'. In the 1913 edition Tweedie's enthusiasm for the sauna has grown rather than diminished, as the opening sentence shows: 'It is worth the journey to Finland to enjoy a bath; then and not till then does one know what it is to be really clean.'

She and her companion were determined to see something of 'the real Finland', but as they were not only English but also *ladies,* getting acquainted with the sauna required a little negotiation if they were to combine it with a proper observation of the social niceties:

> Naturally any institution so purely national as the Finnish bastu was worth investigating – in fact, could not be omitted from our programme. Bathing with the peasants themselves, however, being impossible, we arranged to enjoy the extraordinary pleasure at a friend's house, where we could be washed by one of her own servants.

She describes her experience, a rather genteel one, in detail. The Finnish maid Saima accompanied them to the 'a wee wooden house, like a small Swiss chalet' where they undressed in the outer room. 'The inner room boasted only one small window, through which the departing day did not shine very brilliantly, luckily for our modesty.' As water was thrown on the stones they responded dramatically: 'stifled, we blinked, and gasped, and groaned'. Saima then ascended the steps 'with a pail of hot water in one hand, and a lump of soft soap in the other, on which was a large bundle of white fibre, something like hemp'. She 'scrubbed us hard and long – scrubbed until our skin tingled'. A lot more water 'was thrown onto the steaming bricks, and Saima retired, returning immediately with with a great bundle of birch leaves' with which she 'beat us harder and harder, dipping the leaves into hot water continually'. Finally the ceremony was completed: 'Our bath was taken, the mystery unravelled; we had been washed according to native ideas and customs and understood what the whole thing meant.'

As they travelled around Finland they politely but very firmly declined invitations to join locals in the sauna, but sought out more discreet arrangements. Their modesty was put to the test at Sortavala, on the shore of Lake Ladoga, and elsewhere, where they caused great surprise by insisting always on bathing costumes and caps before entering the water. More than once this led those nearby to believe that they must be drowning. In a strange way the wheel has now come full circle: almost universally today in Britain, where nearly all so-called saunas are in sports centres or gyms, bathers are actually required to wear swimming costumes.

Mrs Tweedie's addiction to baths could not be satisfied by the sauna alone. In Kuopio she heard about the ant bath and insisted on trying that too, while in Kajaani she experienced something even more remarkable, the waterfall bath. (described in *No Particular Hurry* pp.161–2).

Another lady traveller of the period, Rosalind Travers, was rather less inhibited about undressing – she was, after all, a suffragette. At Teerelä, near Suomussalmi, it was the priest who explained the sauna to her:

'Every farm has one,' he said with pride, 'and even the poorest peasant manages to build a sauna. When a man and a girl marry, and, as often happens, they have to make their own homestead, they will first of all set up the sauna, and live in it until the regular house is built. The whole family bathe once a week – oftener still in the winter – and the bath is the chief gratification of life.'

While staying in Pietola, Travers's companion Celia fell ill. She decided to give the local cure-all remedy a try. An old woman led them by lantern light in 'dream-like surroundings' through the snow and supervised their bathing.

The whole thing is curiously pictorial – the dark walls, the straw, the Rembrandt-like shadows and glimpses of bathers in the faint light – no wonder Finnish artists have often painted the sauna.

'[I]t cured Celia's neuralgia for a time, but the pain returned next day.'

Although Finns are proverbially, and actually, silent, Diana Ashcroft*, writing in 1952, noted that in the sauna '[t]he warmth which seeped into every pore seemed to loosen the tongue as well as the joints'. According to John Sykes*, in another post-war account, the sauna 'worked wonders with Pekka', his host and companion, who had always been taciturn: he 'lost his usual deployment of reserve and prejudice and broody involvement to become dryly talkative and smiling.'

The English are proverbial for their sang-froid, rather than for their silence. When they describe being washed by a woman in the sauna, it is often as a curious or interesting experience rather than anything more arousing. William Sansom records the belief that, in the sauna, 'the Frenchman and Italian cannot but react erotically – when a bucket of cold water is the time-honoured remedy.' F. J. North, in *Finland in Summer*

(1938), writes of the sauna with the cool and sensible narration which is the hallmark of his whole book:

> It is a little disconcerting when you first realise that the woman intends to remain, and you, as a foreigner, do not know how to ask her to go away; but it soon becomes apparent that you cannot give yourself a Finnish bath, and long before you leave, invigorated to a degree that surprises you, all sense of embarrassment has gone.

'Invigorated' is as far as North's restrained response will permit him to go. Others have been less inhibited. The Rev Robert Bateman Paul who had been disgusted by the bathing practices of the peasants became a devotee of the public sauna in Moscow, giving details of both the process and the result:

> It is impossible to describe the sensation of lightsomeness which I experienced on my return home, every thing appeared "couleur de rose," the world and all its cares were nothing to me, and I really felt (it is an absurd phrase, but I have no better,) etherialized. Nor was this delightful feeling followed by exhaustion, for when I awoke the next morning, I felt more than usually active and cheerful.

Constance Malleson, writing in 1946, surpasses even this:

> Every foreigner who comes to Finland tries to describe the sauna. Useless, useless, utterly useless! For the sauna is an apotheosis of all experience; purgatory and paradise; earth and air; fire and water; sin and forgiveness. It is lyrical ecstasy. It is resurrection from the dead. It is eternal new birth.

'A sauna is to a Finn what a pub is to a Britisher, what a café is to a Frenchman, what a television set is to an American' wrote Art Buchwald in *I Chose Caviar*. By devoting a whole chapter to the sauna Mrs Tweedie set a trend for books about Finland to include accounts of the sauna, just as books about England describe the British pub. In his description of the 'open-air museum' in Seurasaari V. C. Buckley wrote that 'These baths are a national institution. I saw cottages with their own bath-sheds, or *sauna*, as they are called'.

Sir Walter Citrine was a member of a British delegation of socialists invited to Finland in 1940 to examine at first hand the situation during the Winter War. After a close examination of the workings of an unnamed factory village he and his group 'went to the village bath, the Sauna'.

> When I was baked to the proper stage I was induced to go out into the snow and roll myself in it. I clenched my teeth, squirmed about for a second or so, and then made a dash for the inside again. The snow was clinging to my body, but soon a warm tingling glow suffused my skin.
>
> I was afterwards massaged in an adjoining room by an elderly woman, rather to my embarrassment, but she took it all as a matter of course, and scrubbed and soaped me with as much indifference as though she were laying out a corpse. After this we entered another and cooler chamber, where we then lay resting on a stretcher. I felt beautifully relaxed lying back there and sipping some mineral water. I was reluctant to come out once more into the cold evening air.

The Olympic Games, scheduled for Helsinki in 1940, took place in 1952; Finland was emerging from the hardships of the war settlements, and was open again for visitors. Among them was the Duke of Edinburgh. In his speech at the Anglo-Finnish Society Centenary Dinner at Grocer's Hall in 2012 he revealed that during his visit he had not only taken a sauna, but taken a liking to it. He had been a guest of the Finnish Sauna Society, and afterwards wrote to the Chairman of the society K. F. Hirvisalo:

BUCKINGHAM PALACE

September 1952

Dear Professor,

It was most kind of you to arrange for me to be the guest of the Sauna Club during my visit to Helsinki for the Olympic Games. I had heard beforehand much about the Finnish Sauna, both as a bath and as a National Institution. I was able to satisfy myself by personal experience that the Sauna is indeed as pleasant as it is made out to be.

I was glad to be formally introduced into the companionship of those who have enjoyed the Finnish Sauna and I thank you for sending me the illuminated certificate that I have been duly initiated into its mysteries.

yours sincerely,

Philip

During the Queen's Official Visit to Finland in 1976 the *Daily Telegraph* reported that the Prince Philip 'disrupts the schedule to take a sauna, he explains, "entirely for pleasure".' He would have been able to revive his pleasant experiences in the sauna – a wooden building complete with changing room, and bathroom – given to him and the Queen as a silver wedding present by Finland in 1972.

The Duke's enthusiasm for the sauna was not shared by Francis King, sent a few years later by the British Council as Assistant Representative. In his autobiography *Yesterday Came Suddenly* (1993) he concedes only a few pages to Finland, and the sauna looms large on the list of things he disliked about the country.

I loathed the statutory visit to the sauna. To tell my hosts that I did not enjoy the sauna would have been as insulting as to say that I did not enjoy dancing with the wife of the chairman [of a FinnBrit Society.] Like steamed puddings, the Finns would sweat away in an abstracted but by no means discontented silence, occasionally broken by a few mumbled words. They would then miraculously liven up, whooping and guffawing, as they rushed out to roll in the snow or plunge into an icy lake. I did not join them in either of these activities, despite assurances that it would do wonders for my health.

King's brief account of Finland is given over principally to an assessment of his successful homosexual liaisons; the sauna clearly played no part in them. He was a poet himself, though better known as a novelist, but is unlikely to have read James Bramwell's recently-published *Sauna*, which consists of 38 poems, one of which can be read elsewhere in this volume.

One recent account stands out: Malachy Tallack's *Sixty Degrees North* published in 2015, contains a description of a winter stay in Ekenäs (Tammisaari), and includes a visit to the public sauna (called there by its Swedish name *bastu*), where he went without a companion or guide – feeling his way, as it were.

> I sat back against the wall and looked out of the windows at the ice-covered sea. I was sweating from every pore, and my breath felt laboured on account of the steam. It was relaxing, but not entirely. One could rest, but not sleep. Again I wished for guidance: how long was I supposed to stay in the sauna? Was there something else I should have been doing, other than just sitting?

He accommodates himself more readily to the spiritual aspects of the sauna than to its practicalities:

> A sauna is an ideal place in which to be *omissa oloissaan*, or undisturbed in one's thoughts. Quiet contemplation is something of a national pastime here, instilled from childhood. 'One has to discover everything for oneself,' says Too-ticky, in Tove Jansson's *Moominland Midwinter*, 'and get over it all alone'. Silence and introspection are not just socially acceptable in Finland, they are con-

sidered positive and healthy. They are traits often misinterpreted by those from more talkative cultures as shyness or even bad manners.

The sauna has rarely been neglected as a subject in post-war writing about Finland an but one learns little new or amusing. Wendy Hall in *The Finns and their Country* saw as early as 1967 where things were heading:

> For the Finn, the sauna is a weekly ritual which he often shares with his friends, and one he treats with respect and even reverence. An old proverb runs: 'Two places are holy – church and sauna.' Today it is still considered offensive to talk loudly or move boisterously in the sauna. Mind and body alike are supposed to emerge cleansed and refreshed. In recent years so-called saunas have been built in many countries, but few can catch the feeling and atmosphere of the authentic Finnish bath. Some, unfortunately, are the reverse of authentic, and have given to the name 'sauna' connotations which which the Finns have always determinedly avoided.

'The reverse of authentic' sums it up well. Fifty years later Hall's view of 'so-called saunas', which can now be explored in every country, and on the Internet, would surely have been more strongly expressed. 1967 seems a good date to conclude this little survey.

'They can all read!'

In 1854 Captain Bartholomew Sulivan, in the Åland archipelago during the Crimean War, described in a letter to his wife how he had intercepted a small sloop, crewed by husband, wife, and ten-year-old son. They

> had in the cabin a small Testament and Psalter in one case. It is certainly not creditable to us as a nation that we should be so behind in education those we have previously considered half-barbarous Finns. They can hardly believe that numbers of people in England cannot read.

Other naval officers in the Baltic at the same time recorded with some surprise their discovery that the locals they encountered all seemed able to read.

*

In one of the first serious studies of Finland after World War II, Hugh Shearman wrote 'Education was a special enthusiasm of early Finnish nationalist leaders. They believed that national independence and national culture could spring only from the endeavours of a people who could everywhere read, think, understand, discuss and criticise.' 'No one who knows anything about the Finns will deny that they are the best educated nation in the world' an English educationalist, Ernest Young, had written in a twenty page essay in 1912. This echoes – repeats, almost – the claim made by an English MP, George Renwick, a year earlier that 'They are undoubtedly the best educated nation in the world.' His *Finland Today* was based on two prolonged visits to the country. Every published British account of Finland in the first four decades of the twentieth century shares the sentiment, noting in particular what Sulivan had described. 'Every one in Finland can read to-day' wrote Mrs Tweedie, one of several writers who noted the role of the priest, who 'severely tests their reading capabilities, for no one can be married in Finland unless he be able to read to the satisfaction of his spiritual adviser.' The Church had had such an influence on literacy that, as Harry de Windt put it, 'the most illiterate ploughboy may not marry the girl of his choice until he can read the Bible from end to end to the satisfaction of his pastor, and the same rule applies to the fair sex.'

Captain Sulivan's remarks had been made in passing, and of course were impressionistic. A generation earlier William Allen*, a Quaker philanthropist, visiting Finland and Russia on a fact-finding tour, recorded some of the realities. Education, always central to Quaker beliefs and values, was naturally one of his concerns. In Turku he spent several days in the company of Archbishop Jacob Tengström, Carl Daniel von Haartman, and Johan Jakob Julin. They 'were very earnest to hear from me the history of the School Society, and I gave them a full account of it; they are quite disposed to adopt the system here.' They agreed with Allen that there was much to be done, but he noted that the aspiration of parents formed a firm basis to build on.

> With regard to schools, a more extended system of instruction is obviously needed; the education of girls in general is greatly neglected, and yet the parents are so anxious that their children should learn to read, that they most frequently contrive to teach them, or have them taught. In the country the poor seem to be distributed among the farmers, who are responsible also for their education. The priest makes a periodical visitation, when he regularly examines all the children and gives to each of them a little ticket expressing his opinion of their progress; these tickets are afterwards of use to the children when they are old enough to apply for situations as servants.

In Helsinki he spent several days under the wing of the State Counsellor, Johan Albrecht Ehrenström, who accompanied him for an inspection of the 'poor-house and schools'. 'He is quite alive to the advantages of our system of education for the poor,' Allen recorded 'and engages that a school-room shall be built.' Dining with Count Heydon he recorded that he and his wife 'are, both, earnest to see our school plans adopted, and the Count, who is a benevolent man, desired me to tell Ehrenstrom that, if a society were formed to promote this measure, and other objects connected with the welfare of the poor, he would become the first member of the committee.'

An outward and visible sign of national literacy was the proliferation of bookshops. Rosalind Travers, writing in the 1890s, was one of the first English travellers to remark on this:

> But I must not overlook the three bookshops of Tornea! They exist, mind you, for the primary purpose of selling books, not stationery, nor silver inkstands, nor postcards, and I begin to fear that Finland is very much ahead of Southern England in 'book-learning'.

Finland was still ahead in the 1930s. According to Kay Gilmour:

> One of the most surprising things in Finland is the prevalence of good bookshops and libraries in places where any bookshop at all is a matter of surprise to the stranger. You may find them in the smallest villages far into the Arctic zone and apparently beyond the reach of all ordinary intellectual life. They are not the sort of bookshop one expects in a rural area. Here are no light, cheap novels to while away a dull hour, but good, solid, philosophical, historical, literary and religious works necessitating serious study for their digestion.

The 'Academic Bookshop' at Stockmann's store astonished British visitors. V. C. Buckley was overwhelmed – 'I felt as if I were walking through the book department at Harrods'. Halliday Sutherland wrote that 'the Academy Bookshop, and with its twelve miles of shelving, is the largest in Europe. In proportion to population, the Finns buy more books than any other nation.' 'The Finns,' wrote Agnes Rothery, 'are passionate, omnivorous, and incessant readers'.

Schools were more numerous and usually more visible than bookshops. Henry Nevinson, one of a group of British journalists 'invited by leaders of the Diet to visit Finland' in September 1910, wrote

> Two passions occupy the people's mind – education and patriotism. In every village or small town I could be sure that the most important buildings would be schools. Elementary schools, commercial schools, technical schools, gymnastic schools – a town that would escape notice in our country would have them all. And in no other country was such equal opportunity for every kind of knowledge, livelihood, and work given to women.

Such observations continued after 1917, when some of the visitors went there specifically to see how the new republic was faring. Rothery noted how '[s]chool buildings are conspicuous in every hamlet, town, and city: public schools, private schools, co-educational schools, normal schools, domestic and agricultural schools, schools for adults, vacation schools, Finnish-speaking, Swedish-speaking.' Nursery schools became peepshows for the curious, while particular praise was reserved for the People's High Schools (kansanopisto; folkhögskola). Their object, explained Gilmour

> is to awaken a new spiritual life in the young people, sons and daughters of peasants, between the ages of sixteen and twenty-five who have had an elementary education. To do this, quite as much stress is laid on the intellectual as on the practical courses.

Two commentators, Young and Travers, are of particular significance. Young's career as a teacher led to his appointment as Headmaster of the John Lyon School, Harrow, in

1906, and then of the new Harrow County School in 1911. He was an admired educational innovator, still honoured in the school's history. 'The Lutheran clergy,' he wrote 'still control and, to a large extent, render compulsory some form of religious education.' The 'Reading Examinations' meant that 'it is rare to find a child above the age of ten who cannot read the Bible.' After that age they could put their reading skills to further use – '[t]here surely never was such a people as this for reading the newspaper.'

Young's book was based on two visits to Finland. He does not name any schools, but gives just the sorts of practical detail which one would expect to interest a head teacher:

> In the class-rooms that face to the north, and which require special treatment in view of the severe cold of the winter, the outer wall is panelled on the inside with boards. In these rooms the prevailing tones of the decoration are warm reds, yellows and greens, while in the warmer rooms that face to the south, the colder tones are used. There are no square corners for the accumulation of dust . . .
>
> Overcoats are hung up in cloak-rooms or corridors, and there is not only a separate place for each class, but a separate partition for each pupil. Each of these is provided with a peg, a shelf for caps and bags, a stand for umbrella, and a pigeon-hole . . .

My son, at an acclaimed comprehensive school in England in the 1990s, did not have any of these luxuries. Young notes that co-education is generally accepted as 'the most natural and the most efficient form of training for the young. No one seems to fear the growth of unhealthy sentiment.' He is impressed with, among other things, the requirement for pupils to make a collection of wild flowers 'carefully pressed and mounted', with the provenance and Latin name carefully noted.

Travers's account complements Young's. Unlike many travellers who did not venture far out of Helsinki or out of large towns, she went as far north as Tornio, and from there took the post route across to Kajaani; she could claim to have 'seen the real Finland'. She also had a strong political bias: she was in voluntary exile from her family in England because of her radical excesses, especially as a Suffragette. During the winter of 1908–9, spent in Helsinki, she came under the influence of Helena Tott-Jürgens, one of the leaders of the Woman›s Movement, and a fervent socialist. The schools she visited she compared favourably with their British counterparts: 'It would be difficult to find the equivalent of our uncertified elementary teacher in Finland, or of our under-paid, broken-down schoolmasters and schoolmistresses.' One feature which she particularly admired was was that '[t]he teachers have classes of reasonable size and a great deal of freedom in instructing them, since, though there is Government inspection, no standard examinations have to be worked for.' She praised also the provision of free meals, and sounds envious of 'an excellent system of educational grants, by which the majority of Finnish elementary-school teachers can spend six months abroad, at the State expense, during some period of their working life.' Describing a school she visited in Helsinki, she comments '[b]eing a State establishment, the building and fittings naturally excelled those of the private enterprise, but the pupils were, as an English middle-class parent would say, "dreadfully mixed", for many promising, elementary-school children are sent there.' Using a metaphor popular in the education debate in Britain today, Travers wrote 'The ladder of educational facilities is here a fact, and scholarships are supplemented with grants to parents for the food and clothing of their children while these are attending Secondary schools.' These schools,' she concludes, 'will make the rising generation Socialist, in the finest sense of the word.' Many of the features which she describes are similar to those detailed in articles about Finnish education in the British press a hundred years later.

Travers was echoed in 2012 by a Labour politician, Ed Miliband, Leader of the Opposition: 'If you want the American dream – go to Finland. This isn't surprising. It's harder to climb the ladder when the rungs are further apart.' Sir Paul Lever, speaking in 2017 at a seminar held at the European Bank, noted a recurrent theme of *A Life of Extremes*: the extent to which the homogeneity of society was perceived and admired. It is as if Travers's prediction had come true: as she saw it, the Finnish school system both reflected and reinforced the social equity of the country.

Even during the Winter War education seems not to have been neglected; British observers and journalists remarked on the schools. Sir Walter Citrine, an eminent trade unionist, visited the Alexis Kivi School in Helsinki, where he found everything 'as good in quality as ever I have seen in the schools of any country'. John Langdon-Davies, a war correspondent, agreed: 'the school buildings are palaces compared to the school buildings almost anywhere in Europe.'

Recent enthusiasm in Britain for Finnish education is an interesting echo of these earlier accounts. The revival of British interest came at the turn of the century, with the publication of the first report of PISA, the Programme for International Student Assessment, a worldwide study by the OECD (the Organisation for Economic Co-operation and Development) intended to evaluate educational systems by measuring 15-year-old school pupils' scholastic performance in mathematics, science, and reading. 'Finland,' reported *The Economist* (07/12/2019),

> not previously renowned for its education, topped the table when it came to reading, and excelled in other categories, too . . . [it] appeared to have discovered a way to get brilliant results without the discipline and intense workload of East Asian champions . . . Educationalists descended on Helsinki. They reported back that not only

was education free and comprehensive, but teachers were highly respected, well trained and left to get on with their jobs, which frequently involved enabling children to discover things for themselves.

Finland received several top positions in the first tests, remaining the best performing country overall in Europe in 2012. How this had come about was described by Pasi Sahlberg in his book *Finnish Lessons* (2011) 'In 1950,' he wrote, 'educational opportunities in Finland were unequal in the sense that only those living in towns or larger municipalities had access to grammar or middle schools.' The introduction of the comprehensive school in the 1970s had led to the major reforms of subsequent years which Sahlberg describes.

In the *Guardian* in 2003 John Crace wrote that 'Finland now finds itself a global leader in a brand new niche market: educational tourism.' In Helsinki he was told that among the hundred or so delegations to the Finnish ministry of education there had been 'so far none from the UK'. That soon changed: ever since then British newspapers, magazines and periodicals have regularly sent missionaries to Finland, not to convert the Finns but to be converted: to see how they do it, to report back, and often to ask why we cannot do the same. Becky Barrow returned from Finland in 2004 to write a full-page article in the *Daily Telegraph* titled 'Why Finnish pupils get a better start.' Among many features which which she noted was that 'there is no regulator in Finland – one teacher who had encountered Ofsted on a visit to Britain was horrified': the provision of free hot lunches 'has always been so self-evident to us,' she said, 'that I did not even realise that other countries would not do this.' A full-length article, 'Finishing school' by Richard Vaughan, appeared in the *Times Educational Supplement* in 2011, remarking of Suutarila high school 'It sounds like every teacher's heaven'.

Melissa Benn, a campaigning left-wing journalist and

educationalist, described 'one of the most electric political meetings I have ever attended . . . a lecture on the Finnish educational system given by Pasi Sahlberg, the Finnish educator and author'.

Sahlberg described how Finnish education had evolved, in the postwar period, from a steeply hierarchical one, rather like our own, made up of private, selective and less-well regarded 'local' schools, to become a system in which every child attends the 'common school'. The long march to educational reform was partly initiated to strengthen the Finnish nation after the second world war, and to defend it against Russian incursions in particular.

Finland's politicians and educational figures recognised that a profoundly unequal education system did not simply reproduce inequality down the generations, but weakened the fabric of the nation itself. Following a long period of discussion – which drew in figures from the political right and left, educators and academics – Finland abolished its fee-paying schools and instituted a nationwide comprehensive system from the early 1970s onwards. Not only did such reforms lead to the closing of the attainment gap between the richest and poorest students, it also turned Finland into one of the global educational success stories of the modern era.

. . . Finland teaches us not only that state education will never be considered truly first-rate until we give all our children the same high-quality schooling, but also that a country that educates its children together has a better chance of being at ease with itself than one that segregates different parts of the population from an early age . . . On a more raw political note, the greater the spread of families using a public service, the greater the pressure on politicians to commit sufficient funds to support it. Or as David Kynaston puts it, rather more amusingly: 'One only has to witness pushy private-school parents on the touchline to realise that the state sector will never achieve its full capability without them.'

Dr. Sahlberg's depiction of Finnish education as 'mediocre' before the reforms of the later twentieth century so emphatically contradicted the observations of the British writers I have quoted above, that I wrote to him to ask how this might have come about. He replied courteously and in detail, concluding 'I think we need to be careful in relying on any anecdotal evidence in educational performance.'

Among the dozen or so purveyors of British educational anecdotage there was one dissident, Mrs. Sylvia McDougall (who, as 'Paul Waineman', published *A Summer Tour of Finland* in 1908). 'The Finns, indeed, are *alarmingly* [my italics] well educated,' she wrote. 'In a recent international competition Finland easily won the coveted distinction of having the highest standard of education in the world, even beating the Americans.' Her responses to what she saw of Finnish education were, though, very mixed. 'The board schools of Finland are models of excellence,' she wrote, but added 'I have often wondered what ordinary little peasant children can do with so much knowledge crammed into their brains.' (An answer which I suggested in *No Particular Hurry* was that 'they made modern Finland'.) She is alone among British commentators in not admiring – indeed, in not even mentioning – either social equity, or the equal place which women had in education. What she did note, rather grumpily, was that

> Young girls compete for the honour of wearing the white caps with the gold lyre of a University student, rather than for that of being the toast of a season. Education, it appears, has in a great measure ousted the social gaieties of the capital, and the love of being independent has crept into all ranks.

It must have been a relief for her to return from Finland to Provender*, to the social gaieties of East Kent, and the comforting sight of unspoiled peasant children in the surrounding lanes and villages.

V

BRITISH NOVELS SET IN FINLAND

Sylvia McDougall ('Paul Waineman'),
A Heroine from Finland (1902)

Ingrid Guldhjelm, the heroine of the novel, in a letter to her fiancé, writes 'I have a piece of news for you. Two English ladies are making a tour of the country, and one is going to write a book about her impressions.' Six years later *A Summer Tour in Finland*, was published. This, like the novel, was by Sylvia McDougall, who used the pseudonym Paul Waineman. It was she who made the tour, with her sister-in-law, Edith.

In her memoir *Let's Light the Candles* (1940) McDougall writes 'I was born in Finland, the land of a thousand lakes, where heartstrings are buried deep in the soil.' None of her writings actually get at all close to the soil: she grew up on the upper floor of a mansion in Kaivopuisto (the British Embassy now occupies the site) built by her grandfather Henrik Borgström, who had established the park, and which contained 'a suite of thirty rooms', including a large ballroom. Her father was Emil Borgström, and her mother, Constance Paterson, was of Scottish descent. Sylvia grew up speaking Swedish, French and English.

In 1880, after her father's early death, her mother brought the children to England to be educated, returning to Finland every summer. There the family travelled by steamer to Turholm, their country mansion on Degerö (Tullisaari), where 'Practically nine hours a day . . . seemed occupied with eating and drinking'. As many as forty guests would on chosen days arrive by boat. Ten years later the family moved to England permanently, and lived a leisured and privileged life in Provender*, a historic mansion in Kent. It was here that Sylvia

Borgström turned author. 'I never took writing seriously,' she confessed, but during a visit to Rome she wrote *A Heroine from Finland*, which was published by Methuen in 1902 and went through several editions. She published three further novels set in Finland, *By A Finnish Lake* (1903), *The Song of the Forest* (1904), and *The Bay of Lilacs* (1907).

A Summer Tour is quite unlike any other Finland travel book of the period; Sylvia's tour was based around of country-house visits to wealthy Swedish-speaking families. She stands well apart from the other British woman travellers of the period, deploring all aspects of female emancipation, and writing that 'socialism... in this land where every lake and forest is impregnated with old traditions, is a sin.' This is the world of the novel.

I read *A Summer Tour* carefully in preparing *No Particular Hurry*, but *A Heroine from Finland* had rested unmolested on my shelves for more than forty years: a glance at a few random pages had suggested that this was Edwardian Mills and Boon; even the Finland connection was not enough to attract me actually to read it. My copy is the 'new and cheaper issue' of 1905, costing a shilling; neither this nor any of her other novels are now available. When I dutifully dusted down my copy, I read it with quite unexpected interest. It was most certainly not an undiscovered masterpiece, but the picture of the life of wealthy Finns in the later nineteenth century was an eye-opener, and as extravagant as anything I had read set in Tsarist Russia.

It is in Tsarist Russia in 1894 that the novel opens. Baroness Guldhjelm and her daughter Ebba are staying at the most fashionable hotel in Moscow, the Slavanski Bazaar, during the coronation of Nicholas II. They were clearly privileged guests: 'Not only did I see the Emperor,' Ebba writes to her sister 'but I was so close that I could have touched him as he passed.' I assumed at this point that Ebba was the heroine from Finland, especially when she catches the eye of a handsome Russian nobleman, Count Rostoff. Ebba is

the personification of youth, happy, heedless, and soft
as a puppy . . . A skin fed on Finnish cream and strawberries, which seemed to have taken a shade from each;
clear, rather small, blue eyes which still had over them the
vague and transient haze of childhood.

The Count is a model of courtesy, and 'sans réproche as
far as dressing went'. He is also a romantic, enchanted by the
simple elegance of this unspoilt girl from Finland – 'So fresh,
so young, so innocent. Count Rostoff's eyes softened; there is
always something which appeals to a man's better self in the
young girl – the virgin.' He dances with her at the Grand Ball
where 'all nations were assembled':

> As he placed his arm round her waist it gave him a thrill.
> She wore no corsets, according to the usual custom of
> young Finnish girls, and her body felt deliciously soft and
> pliable. It flashed into his mind that if girls only knew the
> difference it made, a very few would encase themselves
> in that armour of unbending stiff whalebone which they
> wore.

There are several ominous hints here, especially the word
'pliable'. When the Count fishes successfully for an invitation
to Finland and arrives at Fridholm, the Guldhjelms' country
estate, I was not sure that things looked good for Ebba: a familiar situation was beginning to suggest itself. Victorian fiction
is littered with stories of virgins ruined and abandoned by men
of superior class: the 1890s had seen George Moore's *Esther
Waters* and Thomas Hardy's *Tess of the d'Urbervilles; a Pure
Woman*. With Tess, the immediate reaction of her admirer on
first seeing her echoes that of the Count: 'what a fresh and
virginal daughter of Nature that milkmaid is.'

Fridholm, 'the island of peace', is close to Helsinki – the
Russian Cathedral bells can be heard in the distance – and is
closely based on Turholm. Described as 'one of the show places

of the Finnish archipelago', the house overlooks the water with a park bordering the bay on both sides. On the estate 'the ancient gnarled trees' of a large forest contrast with the formal gardens (a nice balance of art and nature), and the farms provide the vast amounts of food, especially cream, needed by the family and guests.

Here we meet Ingrid, 25, Baroness Guldhjelm's adopted daughter and the niece of her late husband. She is engaged to Nils-Olaf, a university professor currently conducting research in Stockholm (and thus leaving his fiancée unprotected). As the days pass, with various idling activities, it becomes clear to the reader, if to no-one else, that the Count's interest is in Ingrid, and not in Ebba, who naively tells him how pleased she is that he likes Ingrid. She is saddened by the thought that had Ingrid not been engaged, 'she might have cared for him'. In fact, responding to his attentions and to 'his deep seductive voice', Ingrid starts to compare him unfavourably with her fiancé, saying to herself 'He understands. Oh, how I wish – how I wish Nils-Olof cared.' 'Go and write – go and write whispered her conscience', which she reluctantly obeyed.

At this stage of the novel Mills and Boon take over briefly. On a Midsummer night boating trip – 'just dark enough to give a poetical glamour to the scene. A night for youth to dream of love', the Count just happens to steer their boat into the rushes. Ingrid feels 'the ardour of his glance'; for him '[t]he hour, the fascination of the scene, seemed all concentrated in those carmine lips. Wholly lovable . . . wholly kissable . . . wholly desirable'. For Ingrid 'the red flames leapt up to the skies and flashed a searchlight into her soul, revealing to her hidden self that she loved the man opposite to her.'

This is how things stand when the novel takes us into another region of aristocratic Finland: everyone from Fridholm sets off for a visit to Countess Barheim at Haflax, 'an old Flemming Castle built in grey stones'. Here we see a formal world which makes Fridholm seem, by comparison relaxed and up-to-date. There is, of course, a ghost, an ancient servant 'dressed in the Barheim, livery . . . of quite an antediluvian cut, faded into an indescribable colour', and even a captive princess, the Countess's granddaughter Valborg: 'I am also a prisoner at Haflax,' she says 'even if I don't sit in the dungeon.' Here all sorts of old customs are observed. A more recent touch is evidence of a bombardment by the British fleet during the Crimean war, 'with an old canon ball firmly embedded in the wall'.

The dungeon is central to this romantic story. Ebba, acting as guide, is in mid-tour when the lantern suddenly goes out. While she and Valborg set off in search of matches the Count's 'pulses rose to fever heat':

> He felt her heart against his own, beating . . . beating . . . as wildly as his.
>
> 'I love you! . . . I love you!' he breathed, and placed his lips on hers in a burning kiss. First they were the lips of a young girl, cold and unresponsive, then they slowly opened. And it was ecstasy.
>
> 'Ingrid!' Ebba's voice sounded far away; 'we have found the matches.'

That night Ingrid 'shut her eyes in hopeless misery, and opened them on the chaos of her soul.' 'Duty and desire' fight it out as she looks at the 'large photograph of Nils-Olof which she had hung upon the wall close to her bed.'

Back at Fridholm Ebba is puzzled because Ingrid is 'always trying to find some excuse for being by herself', leaving the Count to take his long walks alone. Her own life moves briefly towards centre stage when her favourite cousin Erik arrives, and they enjoy mild flirtations which begin while shelling peas.

Chapter 19 opens with a paean to the 'wild, dark, unkempt' Fridholm forest – the abode of Tapio, one feels. There, on 'a small moss-covered height' Ingrid is sitting when

'Ingrid!'

'Andrej!' she whispered.

He came and knelt at her feet, and took her hands in his and kissed them - gently as if in homage.

They are now on first-name terms, but that is not the end of it by any means; they part, eventually, 'intoxicated with happiness'. We are led to believe (at least, I was) that Ingrid will now appeal to her fiancé to release her.

A quiet chapter follows, but the reader knows that a finale is approaching when we hear that 'old Meri', thought locally to be a witch, says ominously to Ebba 'Tell Fröken Ingrid to beware, because her star fell from heaven last night.' Almost immediately a storm approaches and breaks over Fridholm. 'Outside the storm was momentarily gaining in fury' as the Baroness began opening the delayed post: '"Mon Dieu!" she exclaimed, and the hand that held the paper, a letter from Nils-Olaf, trembled as she hastily turned the sheet. "Poor Ingrid, how am I to tell her?"' What she has to impart is told against a Gothic horror background of flashes of lightning 'which revealed her white drawn face', sinister flickering candles, and a storm so powerful that 'The old house of Fridholm seemed to sway' – it is like a scene from *The Fall of the House of Usher*.

SPOILER ALERT: The news which the Baroness has read is not what one expected. Nils-Olaf is not dead, but his heart is 'in a precarious condition, and . . . any shock just at present would kill him.' The Baroness tries to comfort Ingrid with the reassurance that all is not lost: the doctor has 'advised him to marry at once, and go abroad for a complete change and quiet.' At the news that 'he wants the lysning (banns) to be read for the first time next Sunday', Ingrid faints. When she comes to she retires to her room, and it slowly becomes clear to her that she cannot 'stain the honour' of the family; she writes desperately to the Count, begging that he understand: 'I would be a murderess. In this life one can kill one's own heart, but not a fellow-being.' She seals the note and 'furtively' places it in the Count's room:

> Then she turned to go. Her eyes fell on the bed – his bed. She threw herself impetuously on her knees beside it and pulled the pillow under her cheek – his pillow . . . his pillow . . . She lingeringly pressed her lips on it . . . In years to come she would call this her refuge.

The Gothic extravagance gives way to a pathetic scene, centred on the bereft couple. Their private farewell shows the Count at his finest: '"This is not goodbye," he assures Ingrid. "If I have to wait years, I will never give up hope that one day I shall get you, my love – my dear, dear love!".' His voice broke with the intensity of his passion', but 'even as the magic of his caress possessed her body and soul"with a frantic effort she tore herself away. 'Go, go, Andrej, – go!' she panted. 'If you love me, go! – I must be alone!'

The next day the boat which brings Nils-Olaf to Fridholm also takes the Count away:

> He is standing in the stern. The engines snort, and the lit-tle steamer passes on – on – on. Soon one can distinguish nothing but a black speck. Then the waves of the troubled waters broke on the shingle.
>
> Nil-Olaf put his arm around Ingrid's waist, and together they turned towards the old house of Fridholm.

Catherine Gavin, *The Fortress* (1964)

Catherine Gavin, an academic historian, moved on to work as a war correspondent in France and Holland. After the war she made her reputation as a historical novelist, publishing her final novel shortly before her death in 2001. She stands out in this genre as a historian who became a novelist, rather than as a novelist who did some history homework.

Unlike McDougall* and Dunmore* she never lived in Finland; her knowledge of Finland comes from contemporary historical sources. *The Fortress* is set in Finland during the Crimean War, 1854 - 55, when the British Fleet was in the Baltic. This historical reconstruction is the ever-present background, and often the foreground of a complex romance.

As the novel opens in Gothenburg in 1853, John Brand Endicott, a native of Portland, Maine, and captain of a ship of the Tarras Line (owned by his grandmother) has recently arrived from Aberdeen. He is in custody for involvement in a drunken brawl apparently arising from his having brought a young female passenger, calling herself Anna Larsson, from a nearby port. He learns that she is actually an aristocratic Finn called Alexandra Gyllenlöve, who has absconded to avoid an arranged marriage. Released from prison, and removed from command of his ship, Brand immediately asks 'What's the quickest way to Finland?'

In Helsinki Russian troops are gathered for the state visit of Nicholas I. Suomenlinna (Gavin uses the Swedish name,'Sveaborg') 'the Gibraltar of the North', is on full alert; it is 'the key which any invader must turn before he could force the lock of Cronstadt and open the gates of Petersburg.' At a champagne reception, the Czar's 'dull leaden look' turns to a smile when he sees Madame Karamsin, 'as beautiful in her forties as when she first appeared in Moscow society'. She asks permission to present her god-daughter, Alexandra Gyllenlöve; the Emperor

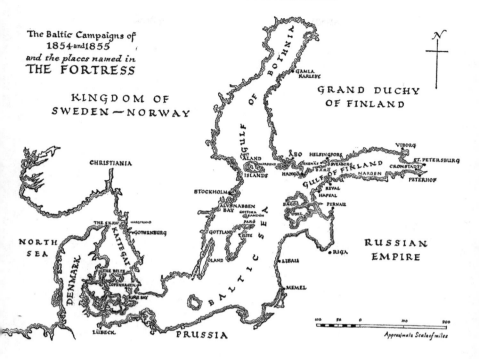

The Baltic Campaigns of 1854 and 1855 and the places named in THE FORTRESS

scolds her as 'the runaway', who ought to return to her father in St. Petersburg 'without delay'.

The two ladies return to the Villa Hagasund, recently built by Senator Walleen, Madame Aurora Karamsin's step-father and 'kind parent', near Hesperia Park. (The villa contains 'the largest private library in Finland' and 'carefully chosen paintings by Ekman and von Wright'). We learn the details of Alix's 'disgrace': she had 'run away to sea under a false name, to escape her enforced engagement to Boris Apraxin', and now refuses to return to her father. Welcoming the news that the British are likely to fight Russia, she blithely exclaims that 'Finland will be free!' – free, of course, 'from the tyranny of Russia'. The Senator tells her to stop 'talking like a fool': 'Finland will be a battlefield. We shall be caught and crushed between two enemies.' He rudely dismisses her talk of Finnish independence as 'that nationalist folly'.

Retiring to the salon, she is, understandably, shocked to find Captain Endicott. They meet by arrangement the next day; he counters her fervent hopes of freedom from a cruel and hated Russia with his impression (after three days) that Finland is prosperous, well-run and peaceable. There is a brief lapse into Mills and Boon ("My darling, you know that I'm in love with you?") but Alix, as he now calls her, spurns the suggestion of marriage and married life: ". . . if you really love me, you will join the war against Russia." As they watch the Czar's procession from the Esplanade into the market place, an innocent protester is kicked to death by the Cossack guards, and the police fire 'over the heads of the crowd'. "Now you know how the Czar rules in Finland!" says a white-faced Alix. Brand is converted.

Prohibited from staying on in Finland, he moves to Stockholm, where he finds a British Navy recruitment drive in progress. He signs up, concealing his nautical experience, and boards the *Lightning*, captained by Bartholomew Sulivan, a master hydrographer: ("'e's like a water diviner with an 'azel twig" says the bo'sun's mate). As they join the British fleet under Sir Charles Napier off the Danish coast, the signal is received: BRITAIN HAS DECLARED WAR ON RUSSIA. From the *Lightning* the seamen join HMS *Arrogant*, where as an 'Ordinary Seaman' Endicott, deemed 'useless as a topman', is moved to gunnery practice.

The *Arrogant* returns to its anchorage in the Stockholm archipelago, where a letter from Alix gives Brand the news that her father will enforce her return to St. Petersburg. The Baltic Fleet heads to Hanko to hinder the building of 'the new Russian fortifications at Hangö Head'. At nearby Tvärminne Captain Yelverton decides on action: "We'll take Ekenäs [near Hanko] and smoke out the Russians.' 'Ekenäs first, then Sveaborg, then Cronstadt [the fortress protecting St. Petersburg].

A tall order for the next five days!' In the event, when marines have destroyed the shore battery and spiked the Russian guns at Vitsand, the captains decide against an assault on the town: they had done what was needed, presumably. Captain Yelverton 'was anxious to be out of Ekenäs and steaming back to the open Gulf'. Ekenäs has a particular resonance for Brand; it was, he had learned, 'the heart of Alexandra's own country, the very place where she was born.' Gavin, in fact, gives the town a much more important role that it actually played in the war.

Right now, though, Alix is travelling in great pomp and circumstance towards St. Petersburg with Madame Karamsin. They arrive at the Demidov palace, where, 'quietly, crushingly, the monotony of the capital's social round once more' fell upon her. She is obliged to accept the invitation of the Czar and Czarina to a fête at the Summer Palace.

During their journey there they call on the Grand Duke and his wife. His young sons are pestering their father to go and look at 'the British ships at sea', which can be seen by telescope in the distance nosing around Cronstadt. Then the Czar – their grandfather – arrives unannounced. After due formalities he sets a trap for Alix, who he pointedly addresses by her Russian name, Alyssa Ivanovna. He orders her to read and translate a poem by Topelius, a famous Finland Swedish poet, *Den första blodsdroppen*. In the poem, he says, the poet "laments, like all of us, the sufferings which the British have inflicted on the the defenceless people of the Grand Duchy". Alix breaks off '"it's hateful – hateful"! she said with a sob, "I won't read more. I can't!" "There are faint hearts in Nyland province," the Czar concludes smugly, "We expect *courage* from our Russian women!"

After this Alix goes with the boys to the roof to view the British ships. When one of them is tentatively identified as the *Arrogant* she has to hide her face. Back indoors 'when she stopped at a hall mirror to tie on her bonnet, it was Brand's ship and not her own reflection which Alex saw in the glass'. Later, as they tour the gardens, Paul Demidov arrives waving a telegram: Madame Karamsin's husband, commanding in the Danube, is dead.

In the misery and turmoil which ensues Alix sees her chance: she sends the major-domo to the police headquarters for the *podorojna*, or exit permit, without which no-one was allowed to leave Russia. She 'was determined to do it well: there must not be another bungled, amateurish runaway like her flight to Gothenburg.' The escape is accomplished professionally: the doorman drugged, Aurora's signature forged, and the carriage ready and waiting.

The next chapter opens in the Åland Islands, at Degerby, where Alix and her maid have been for three weeks, and where she has 'recaptured the simplicity of her country childhood'; it is July, and Napier's fleet is arriving at the nearby Russian fortress of Bomarsund. Gavin gives a hurried account of the Allied Fleet capturing and destroying the fortress. It is really no surprise to the reader when a visitor appears:

'Alix! Darling! My God, I can't believe it!'
'Brand. Brand, are you safe and well?' . . .

Alix is staying with her grandmother's cousin, Miss Agneta Willebrand; she has been charmed by Captain Sulivan, who came ashore to buy provisions, and gave her a Bible. Alix and her maid have work to do, as all able-bodied men have been taken by the Russians as navvies at Bomarsund. A passionate scene between the lovers is broken with Romeo and Juliet trepidation as he hears the bo'sun's whistle 'It isn't time yet, Brand . . .' – but it is.

As the Fleet approaches 'the Finland women milking cows in the island pastures looked up amazed to see the tall British masts towering over the evergreens, and flaxen-haired children came stealthily to the rocky coves to watch.' The day after the fortress is surrendered Alix arrives at Bomarsund, 'the bay full of shipping, . . . the land swarming with men in uniform. Among the frigates she saw several British yachts, whose owners had crossed from England to watch the battle in a spirit of gay adventure'. A battle-weary Brand tells her 'I want you to go away now. There's sickness here, and other things not fit for you to see.' After this untidy parting Alix involves herself with the families of the Finnish battalion, who 'were being marched off to an Allied war prison' along with the Russians.

She goes aboard HMS *Royal William*, one of the troopships taking the prisoners of war to Sheerness – a 'rash action', she later calls it: it certainly was. The surgeon entrusts her with some responsibilities for the mothers and children. She explains to him that these Finns 'never fought the British – never! They were captured by force to do building work'.

The prisoners are discharged into the Hulks (familiar to many readers from the opening of *Great Expectations*) for six weeks in harsh conditions, a chief entertainment being daily fist-fights between Finns and Russians. The Finns are separated out and sent by train to Sussex, to be imprisoned in Lewes. This ingress of 'ten officers and 154 other ranks' includes 'Anna Larsson', masquerading as a Finn. She soon becomes, in the words of the prison chaplain, 'the natural leader of the Finlanders', overseeing childcare, insisting on prisoners' rights, and as an English speaker becoming the intermediary between the prisoners and the local Ladies Benevolent Society. She organises handicraft facilities, and as evening entertainment recites poetry by Runeberg, especially *Ensign Stål*, 'his poetic cycle of the Russian war of 1809'.

Brand, discharged from the Navy and paid off, arrives in London just before Christmas. The naval news is that Napier has been relieved of the Baltic command and replaced by Admiral Dundas; the popular press had accused Napier of 'gross mismanagement', and had been calling for victories at Suomenlinna and Cronstadt. After various adventures in

London, including a night with 'Milly' (who does not reappear), he seeks out Gunnar Falk, Alix's brother-in-law, at the Swedish Legation. Falk knows all about Alix's escapades, and considers that she has been 'hopelessly mismanaged', after 'a childhood running wild in Ekenäs'. It turns out that the Swedish community in London has involved itself with the Lewes prisoners, and the pastor has told Falk about a 'remarkable young woman' who is tending the sick and keeping up the spirits of prisoners. Brand knows at once who this must be, but he does not rush off to Sussex, as a romantic novel would usually require: he goes to Aberdeen, to make his peace with his grandmother. He broaches to her his plan to acquire an American-registered ship, a brig, which could trade and 'move freely in the Baltic', and 'go on fighting Russia' as occasion permitted.

Meanwhile Falk has tweaked diplomatic regulations to have Alix released from prison 'into the guardianship of her family and friends'. She is released also into the arms of Brand, who has travelled to Lewes with Falk; they all briefly pay their respects at the graves of the prisoners who had died of cholera in the prison. Hopes of a romantic reunion are dashed when Falk explains that Alix, as a Russian citizen, must leave the country immediately. Off she goes to the Paris home of 'Princess Mathilde Bonaparte, the sister-in-law of Aurora Karamsin', where she and Aurora are reconciled. There is an informal late-evening visit from the Emperor and Empress 'all completely different from the style of the Czar Nicholas, just as the grey, twitching Czarina was not to be compared with the radiant . . . Empress'. For the second time in her short life Alix defies royalty, refuting Bonapart's assertion "that the British campaign in the Baltic should have been so completely null and void" with her account of what she herself saw: "I was at Bomarsund," she insists.

After due time Brand arrives in Paris with 'Letters of Marque for the American snow brig in one hand and a special marriage licence in the other.' 'Happy and glorious' were the days which followed the wedding 'when the false spring continued, and all Paris was a playground for Brand and Alix'. 'They were as extravagant and gay as two happy folks could possibly be on a Paris honeymoon.' Returned to England, to a modest hotel in Jermyn Street, he takes her to see the brig, which he had registered as *Duchess of Finland*. They put to sea on 5 March; 'he was weeks ahead of the Navy in the Baltic.'

Brand has armed *Duchess of Finland* with a carronade, so he can sail as a privateer, as well as trading. He scuttles one ship which is involved in gun-running, and intercepts a Prussian schooner which is full of material used for mines, handing it over to HMS *Cossack*; Captain Fanshawe invites Brand aboard 'to take wine'.

Near 'Hangö Head' (Hanko) they see a boat from the *Cossack* going ashore with a white flag. As it lands Russian soldiers fire at them; they return the fire, and the *Cossack* guns join in. The *Duchess of Finland* is close enough to be involved, and Mary, the daughter of the mate, drowns. Alix, shaken and unwell, persuades Brand to take her to her house in Ekenäs to recruit, and there she miscarries a three-month child. When she has recovered, about six weeks later, they set sail again, heading east.

Princess of Finland follows Admiral Dundas as he moves the British fleet up the Gulf of Finland for the attack on Suomenlinna, now heavily fortified. The preparation lasts several days, which enables local residents to watch from vantage points in the city. Gavin gives the disposition of the batteries and ships in accurate detail. Despite having superior fire-power, the mortars cannot withstand the heavy demands of continuous firing. The fortifications are heavily damaged, but not destroyed. '[T]he Allies 'could not scale the granite walls of the fortress'; they simply withdraw, with the Russians acclaiming a famous victory. This they plan to celebrate 'at a grand dinner' aboard the *Ezekiel*' (a fictional ship).

This is the place in the novel where fiction parts company completely from history.

It was not for nothing that more than two hundred pages earlier Gavin had given full technical details of Bickford's Improved Water Fuse, an explosive carried by a swimmer, fixed to the hull of a vessel, then set off fifteen minutes later – a predecessor of the limpet mine. Brand had been one of the two swimmers on the *Arrogant* selected for a successful experiment, with a dismasted ship as the target.

Now the mate suggests that the *Ezekiel* should be a real target."It would be suicide," says Brand, in the knowledge that the *Ezekiel* has a powder magazine. Nonetheless, at midnight he and Alix, the best swimmers, arrive 'with their burden of death at the black side of the *Ezekiel*'. Even with a fifteen-minute time gap the explosion rocks their rowboat hopelessly off course, and 'as the flames from the *Ezekiel* light up the fjord' they are fired on and both injured. It is left to the mate, completely disorientated, to row them out of the artillery range, where – miraculously – they find themselves up against the last of the Allied frigates to leave – the *Arrogant*.

*

The reviewer of *The Fortress* in *Kirkus* considered that Alix's story 'is perhaps not equal to the historical background that accompanies it'; this is a tribute to the comprehensiveness of that background. I read extensively about the Crimean War in the Baltic while writing *No Particular Hurry*. I had the help of several modern studies, especially Greenhill and Giffard's *The British Assault on Finland* (1988), as well as the Internet, and the availability on line of nearly all the memoirs and biographies of the participants. With little beyond primary sources, mainly archives and libraries, Gavin is able to state that 'the operations of Her Majesty's Ships and Vessels at sea took place exactly as narrated here.' Her abilities as a naval historian, and her handling of the material, astonished me; she goes far beyond simply coping with numerous naval and navigational details: a particular skill is inserting her fictional characters into existing history. For example, Villa Hagasund, know by its Finnish name *Hakasalmen huvila,* had indeed been 'recently built by Senator Walleen' (it is now part of Helsinki City Museum), and Madame Aurora Karamsin actually was his step-daughter'.

The battle at Vitsand is dramatised in vivid detail: 'The channel leading to Ekenäs was so narrow that he could see meadows running down to the beach on both shores well clear of the tree-line'. 'The British guns roared into action . . . and they silenced the shore battery . . . with two broadsides from the the starboard guns.' To larboard 'the enemy appeared again with a company of horse artillery'. 'A ball tore through the *Arrogant*'s rigging; one of *Hecla*'s masts toppled and fell down'. A '16-lb charge of powder' in a 68-pounder produces 'a fountain of destruction and the delayed clap of the explosion was followed by the screams of the wounded men now dying on the beach.'

One reason that Alix's characterisation is 'not equal to the historical background' is that she has to play a number of different roles, from an elegant and expensive noblewoman mixing with royalty to a brutalised prisoner in the Hulks; from a ballroom dancer to a marine bomber; from a princess to a Degerby dairymaid. Her different names at different times and places underline and perhaps reinforce this scattered character: Alexandra Gyllenlöve, Anna Larsson, Alyssa Ivanovna, Alix.

She is, although technically a Russian citizen, the one character in the novel who is a passionate Fenno-patriot. She cannot accept Russian rule, and nurtures a naive belief that the British are going to liberate Helsinki. Princess Mathilde in Paris gives an astute character reading:

> . . . you're not a modern girl at all. You should have lived seventy years ago, in the Revolution; or there may be girls

like you in your beloved Finland seventy years from now. But you don't belong to the Europe of our time.

Alix is actually only forty years ahead of her time; in the 1890s she would have been at the forefront of the resistance movement against the Russification of Finland under Nicholas II.

*

Eventually, recuperating in Denmark, Brand and Alix come to review. The narrative hardly touches on the rescue by the *Arrogant*, or hospital in Copenhagen. Despite all that they have done, Alix has come to realise that what happened at Sveaborg had not changed the course of history: Finland's independence, she admits, 'will not come in my lifetime'. She throws her lot in entirely with Brand, whether trading again from Aberdeen, as a partner of the firm in London, or, perhaps 'our American home'; 'Finland must wait for its freedom,' wrote the reviewer, 'and the islands of Maine now seem to hold her destiny.'

Helen Dunmore, *House of Orphans* (2006)

Helen Dunmore died in 2017, aged only 64. She did not write a memoir, and, in the words of an obituarist, 'kept journalists at a kindly distance'. With a degree in English, she went as a teacher to Finland for two years (1973–75). She lived in or near Turku, but I have located no-one there who recalls her. She came before the reading public in 1983 when *The Apple Fall*, the first of her twelve volumes of poetry, was published; the first of her fifteen novels came ten years later. There were four collections of short stories and a large number of books for children and 'young adults'. *The Apple Fall* contained 'In a wood near Turku', the first of her poems set in in Finland. In 1997 came *Love of Fat Men*, a collection of short stories, most of which had been previously published in magazines; more than half of these are set in Finland.

House of Orphans, Dunmore's ninth novel, was published in 2006. Set at the turn of the twentieth century in a remote village in central Finland, about a hundred miles north-east of Turku, and distant from the nearest railway town, it opens uncompromisingly: 'Each winter there was an outbreak of fever at the House of Orphans.' The orphanage has an honest matron, and is attended by a kindly and altruistic doctor, who, as the novel opens, is treating a chronically sick child. He leaves an older girl to tend to her during the night. 'What's her name?' he asks the matron. 'Eeva' she tells him.

The doctor, Thomas Eklund, is recently widowed, and lives in a large old-fashioned house in a clearing in the forest, well away from the village. The house itself is a domestic museum, with fine china in a glass case, and embroidered linen in a chest. When Lotta Eriksson, his only close friend, persuades him that he needs a housekeeper he chooses Eeva, who has just turned sixteen. She is markedly different from the other orphans, who will mostly go out to local farms into domestic service (which, we are told, might well be closer to slave labour.) Eeva is not local but from Helsinki, and it soon becomes clear to us that she is out of the ordinary. She has green eyes, is highly intelligent, and speaks Finnish, Swedish and Russian, the latter taught her by her father, now dead, who had been a political activist. We learn later that he had had some part in the murder of a Russian spy.

Thomas prescribes for his patients, advises them, and attends difficult births. At home he nurtures his loneliness, wandering in the uninhabited rooms. His wife Johanna had hated the woodland and insisted on enlarging the clearing to give a prospect, but he has now begun the restore it. The setting, and the slow and archaic way of life at times echo Hardy's *The Woodlanders*. He is rarely at peace as he reflects on his failures as a husband and father – he is estranged from Minna, his daughter, who lives in Turku and rarely visits him. Eeva's challenging, independent, enigmatic presence disturbs him, and a growing fascination begins to dominate his life. He is constantly aware of her, peeping when she rises in the night to read the copy of Pushkin (given to her by her father), and even spying on her bathing naked after sauna. This grows into an obsession which he finds hard to control; in one poignant scene he takes out a quilt, 'made by his great grandmother perhaps', from an ancestral chest. 'He wanted the quilt because Eeva must have it. He wanted those violets and crimsons and flames to lap around her while she slept, and fill her dreams with colour.' He does not dare to take it up to her attic room: 'If that started, where would it end? He wouldn't be able to help himself. He would fall on his knees, and strip back the bedclothes to find the coarse sheets that covered Eeva's body and smelled of her . . .' He constantly teeters between these impulses and his sense of how completely inadmissible any such action would be.

The symptoms of frustrated attraction are not missed by Lotta. She offends the matron, (who is herself possibly in love with Thomas) by voicing her suspicions, and fails entirely to make her husband understand her worries, so she writes to Thomas's daughter. Minna duly arrives, announcing 'Lotta wrote because she knew it was her duty. She wrote to tell me that you were making a fool of yourself over that girl.' The showdown which this unpleasant young woman provokes with her father is the prelude to a semi-comic confrontation with Eeva ('an illiterate girl') which takes place in the woods where she is picking nettles for one of the doctor's tonics. Minna seems to have got her rhetoric from popular fiction: 'You needn't think that I don't know what you are up to. You've got a lot to learn my girl, and you can start by taking that look off your face.' Although Eeva's silent response wins the day when Minna goes almost berserk with rage, it leads her to reveal to her that she is already planning to leave.

While Thomas's thoughts centre more and more around Eeva, she scarcely thinks of him at all. Her mind is full of memories of her life in Helsinki, which she had left several years before, and principally of her father and her close child-hood friend Laurie. 'All the things her father had told her were like jewels which she kept in a box where no one could see them.' He had educated her, especially in politics and lan-guages, and from him she learned about Russification – how Tsar Nicholas and the Russian Governor of Finland, Bobrikov, were ruthlessly dismantling the freedoms which Finland had enjoyed as a Grand Duchy since 1809. 'Her father knew every-one. He was respected. There were meetings in his apartment, and people came and went.' These were revolutionaries; Lau-rie was, she hoped, still furthering the cause since her father's death and her own rustication. So it is that in this remote vil-lage, in 1901–2, we learn enough from Eeva's memories to get the picture of the political situation in Finland. The account of Minna's visit is interrupted by two chapters describing Lauri's radical activities in Helsinki, concluding with the receipt of a letter from Eeva. He persuades her to return.

The two central chapters of the book might have been

entitled 'Eeva's Escape'. Scrupulously careful to take with her no more money than she is entitled to, she steals out at three in the morning, but Thomas appears;

> 'Eeva, where are you going?'
> 'You know where I'm going,' she answered.

For the first time, they have a conversation. He tries to give her money:

> 'What does it matter, Eeva!' he said impatiently, lifting his head. 'Money's not so very important. Take it.'
> 'You only think it's not important because you've always had it,' she said slowly. 'Because having it has made you what you are.'

Unable either to detain her or to let her leave, he decides to walk with her to the station in a distant town. This is the most literary chapter in the book, evoking Hardy on almost every page: *The Woodlanders*, *The Return of the Native*, and *Tess of the D'Urbervilles*. Hardy would surely have agreed with Dunmore's comment that 'Landscape is not a backdrop in my books but a character'.

> There wasn't a breath of air. The trees had trapped it and made it thick with heat. Those trees, everywhere. She couldn't see. She couldn't get beyond them. They marched for ever. He was walking at her side but they weren't talking any more. The track was narrow and overgrown. Brambles caught at her ankles. Birds flew away with screams of warning, and sometimes she heard the crash of a bigger animal moving through the trees. A deer, maybe, or a fox. There were wolves in the forest, she knew that. Bears too, and elk. But they wouldn't hurt you, not in summer with their bellies full.
> And now the trees were growing bigger. Huge pines, dwarfing her and pressing down on her.

She was tired, so tired.

They rest beside a spring where Eeva 'sank on a cushion of moss at the foot of the birches'; Thomas carefully tends her, bringing water, and bathing her feet. As a reviewer of the novel wrote, the 'journey through the forest is sumptuously written, crackling with emotional electricity'. Finally they reach the station. Eeva sleeps in a nearby hut, with Thomas keeping watch. The train comes at midday; he follows it along the platform as it leaves until, finally, he is 'beyond the end of the shallow platform, watching the end of the train sway off down the rails.'

In a note at the end of *The Siege*, Dunmore's highly-acclaimed novel set during the siege of Leningrad, she writes 'It was through living in Finland that I first came to love the brief, astonishingly beautiful Baltic summers, and sombre Baltic winters. This book owes a debt to the Finnish landscape and people.' *House of Orphans* reveals the true size of this debt. Her closeness to the natural world is very evident; those who have not visited Finland can easily visualise her scenes, and those who know Finland will immediately recognise them.

> The crust of snow was a foot thick, but it was softening and it had a greyish tinge. the first melt was ticking off the eaves, drop by drop. It would freeze again by night, but the process had begun.

And

> The boggy patches down by the stream, the smell of water peppermint, the little yellow irises that flowered there in late spring, the wild mallow and stray forget-me-nots and croaking frogs with their slippery billows of spawn.

The Helsinki to which Eeva returns in 1902 could hardly provide a greater contrast:

> Although she'd been away less than three years, plenty

241

had changed. Helsinki was growing so fast. They were tearing down the old wooden houses and putting up stone buildings, they were sweeping away people's little vegetable gardens, straightening roads, putting in gas lamps and enlarging the cemeteries . . . More ships in the harbour, more trains arriving and departing, more people streaming along the streets, new shops, new laundries, and saunas and dairies, a new theatre – new everything.

This listing has a distinctly Dickensian ring to it. Laurie, later in the story, similarly finds himself in a no man's land which which recently 'would have been a village with its own life, separate from the city . . . [T]he expansion of Helsinki had already opened its mouth to swallow up these wooden houses. Soon there would not be a trace left.'

Eeva's reunion with Laurie is more awkward than romantic. He shares a room with Sasha, 'persuasive, manipulative and magnetic', as Dunmore described him in an interview. Laurie's father, like Eeva's, is dead; while he is following in his footsteps as an anarchist, Sasha is an ideologue, and this takes Laurie into new territory. Sasha belongs to a cell which is planning not only resistance to Russian rule but the murder of Bobrikov, the Governor General, who was overseeing the Russification of Finland. (He was actually assassinated in June, 1904.) There are ongoing power games played out between these three. Laurie works long hours, and is dragged by Sasha to anarchist meetings in the evenings, leaving him little time for Eeva, who works in a bookshop and shares a room with a classy young German lady, Magda; their evenings are sometimes spent at concerts or art galleries. Despite these unaccommodating circumstances Eeva and Laurie become lovers.

Eeva, who is a good deal smarter than Laurie, sees through Sasha, tells him so, and tries to warn him off:

'You want a thrill. You get your excitement, and you dress up what you do in words to make yourself sound good. *Comrade*. That's a laugh. Who are you a comrade of? Where do you come from? You're not fit to put the word in your mouth. You leave me alone, and you leave him alone.'

Sasha bullies Laurie into attending a furtive and sinister meeting of Russian revolutionaries where he has set him up as an assassin, asserting that 'His credentials are impeccable'. Laurie 'felt like a bull Sasha had brought to market for them to look over before they decide to buy it.' He ineffectually bluffs his way out, but knows that he has not escaped. All the while Eeva is waiting for him to arrive for the dinner she has cooked for him. He arrives late and distraught. Eeva understands better than he does what has happened: 'They won't let you pull out now. If you try they'll find a way of stopping you.' They find an obvious one: Laurie is arrested by Okhrana, the State Security Police.

Eeva, distraught and helpless, writes to Thomas as 'the only person of importance whom I know'. He travels to Helsinki, a city so changed from his student days that he hardly recognises it:

He felt fuzzy and out of touch, like a man who has been buried in the forest for much too long. Life was moving on fast, but he has hardly moved with it. All those new buildings, all those new people.

He finds Eeva half starved with worry, but all he can achieve is to persuade to eat a little. He is hopelessly at sea in the world which she now inhabits: 'If your friend has done nothing wrong then they'll release him' is all he can say to reassure her. As he begins to glimpse the reality of the situation, his concern is not at all with Laurie, but with Eeva's safety, which he thinks will be best achieved by persuading her to return to the country with him, which could only be done with her as his wife. '"But I have to think of Laurie now", she said carefully, at last, as if she were showing a child how to share a toy.'

He promises to speak to old acquaintances in Helsinki, who might have influence, but back at his hotel he has only the consolation that 'tomorrow would have the great virtue of not being today.' This ends the episode.

The novel ends with four snapshots: Bobrikov, with 'damned prostate trouble', getting himself himself out of bed in the night. Thomas back home delivering a child whose mother he had delivered a generation earlier; "it's just possible that one day I'll deliver [her] grandchild" he muses – Finland is in political ferment, but not there. Laurie, collapsing in the street after being released by the Okhrana. 'They'd released him so they could watch where he would take them'. Sasha, drunk and fantasizing, freezing to death under a bush in Kaivopuisto.

Eeva herself is unaccounted for. After a long meeting with a drunken Sasha, she finally decides that 'she could turn her back on him now. She moved towards the door.' She is perhaps now taking a different attitude to change, one articulated by Magda:

> 'To me, at this stage of history, we are passing through time rather than inhabiting it, if you understand what I mean. We think not about what's here, but about the changes which will come. We put our lives second to that. Things will be better, but perhaps not for us."

*

Dunmore adds *A brief historical context* at the end of the novel, although there is actually enough background material in the body of the book to make this more of a confirmation than a necsssity. The book has an significant place in the corpus of her work, as she explained when speaking to a book club:

> Each one of my historical novels has come from a long-standing interest in the place, people and period, and this was certainly the case with *House of Orphans*.

Looking back, I see a very strong connection between *The Siege* and *House of Orphans*. In *The Siege*, Leningrad is threatened by German invaders, and the Soviet Union – Russia herself – is in danger of losing her identity and freedom. In *House of Orphans* Russia itself is the overwhelming force that has taken control of its neighbours.

'I do believe that a writer has to inhabit the past rather than make use of it, if the book is to work,' she writes elsewhere. The phrase 'inhabit the past' has been used recently by Hilary Mantel and some of the reviewers of her Cromwell trilogy. In *House of Orphans* Helen Dunmore inhabits even more than the political and historical past: she inhabits the spirit of Finland, which on almost every page is presented from the inside. The writing, 'part love-story, part tragedy', is unfailingly intelligent, full of engaging detail, and at different times both astringent and tender.

VI

POEMS IN ENGLISH ABOUT FINLAND

Early in 2003 I received a letter from David Wilson of Jyväskylä University, who had heard that I knew a bit about the British in Finland, asking if I would comment on 'a very rough draft' of an anthology of poems he was compiling of 'poems in English about Finland'. I was able to make some suggestions and add a few poets to his list. The anthology appeared two years later as *Henceforth the Anglo-Saxon is the Brother of the Finn! Poems about Finland 1634–2000*, edited jointly with Anssi Halmesvirta in an edition of 200 copies, published by the university's Studies in General History. This unfortunately necessitated publication in a pocket-book format with few visual attractions. Nonetheless it quickly sold out, and is now virtually unobtainable; there is not even a copy in the British Library.

The reception which this volume received encouraged the editors to plan an enlarged second edition, but unfortunately it was not published. A long (93-page) supplement appeared in 2008, and was then available on line, containing, the editors wrote, 'much of the new material that would have been included in a revised second edition'; I had again been able to provide further poems. It is a great pity that this supplement, with its excellent detailed annotation, is unavailable. I am indebted to these two Jyväskylä anthologies for many of the poems appearing below. I have used an alphabetical rather than a chronological arrangement; that, I felt, would lead to the poems being regarded as an adjunct to Finnish history.

Finlayson in Tammerfors

James Finlayson, Quaker, philanthropist,
engineer. In 1826 building a cotton mill
by Tammer Falls, creating wealth, creating

a working class. The Reds,
crushed in 1918. (Their last stand
was on Pispala Ridge, a mile from here.)

'Finland's Manchester' they say. But I think
of Scotland, a force frothing seawards, an angry
current of memory. Another red river.

Donald Adamson (1999)

Crane Notes

The cranes flew over Ainola
before he died:
the birds of my youth, he said.

He was ninety-one,
barely a note from him these twenty years.

The flame had once been fierce in him.
The young republic gave him honours, wealth,
cosseted him,
demanded another symphony.

He wrote it, burned it.

And now the cranes were returning,
trumpeting their song as hot days faded,
soaring in that first, blessed coolness
of autumn,

breaking the silence.

Donald Adamson (n.d.)

'Finish Off with Finland'

My Finnish Valentine

I send my love a Valentine
From English oak to Finnish pine.

Tell me, for I wish to know
Are you like your winter snow
Or have you depths where I may hide
Like your wooded countryside
So cold around, so warm within
Where all love songs must begin.
Can I ask your serious eyes
Could you count me as a prize
With my flippant, lighter mind
That in Finns is rare to find.
Do your straight eyes brood with fear
Asking, "Is this man sincere;
How can he in jesting fashion
Hide a true, atomic passion?"
Lady, streams that laugh and leap
Have dark waters, wide and deep,
That start in shy timidity
Yet flood in torrents to the sea.
Can Finnish maidens in their turn
Swim where mighty waters churn,
Bringing from their placid lakes
The strength to ride when thunder breaks,
When love advances like a wave
Engulfing all except the brave.
But Finns have "sisu" so they tell
That can such English waters quell.
And you, my Lady, with those eyes
Can quiet the waters, calm the skies
And set my heart upon such flights
More wonderful than Northern Lights.

Today, my Finnish Valentine,
Your ardent 'Yes' shall make divine:
Your magic, born of song and 'sauna',
Shall crown my life – and you the crowner;
And we shall join, hand, heart and soul,
In Love's Eternal Rock and Roll.

Robert Armstrong (1957)

from Sauna

Damp as a fever jungle, steaming hot,
The spirit of the Sauna rushed to sear
My brimming eyes and draw a tight garrotte

With unseen noose spun out of atmosphere.
And spite touched off a fuse of memory:
ALL HOPE ABANDON YE WHO ENTER HERE!

But growing greater I breathed it into me
Till through the mist the dim Inferno stood
In pallid light that flickered fitfully

From a ragged wick: four wavy walls of wood:
A ceiling of rough logs to catch the vapour
And make the cloud of wingless insects brood

Upon the ledge erected for the bather:
A stove, heaped up with stones, heated below:
Four washing tubs and a copper scoop to slake the

Burning ledge and goad the stones to throw
The stings of steam their rising temper bred:
This was Paavo's Purgatorio.

And yet not all. Attendant on our bed
Of sweating planks there sat a speechless crone
By whom the Sauna was inhabited.

She sat beside the stove. Twice she had thrown
Water on the stones, and now she stared
As though at naked sinners who atone

In the presence of a judge for having dared
The luxuries of the bright overworld.
Grilled by her gaze I felt we were compared

With stronger men, while Judgement sat and twirled
A twig from the bundle lying in her lap
Of birch-sprays green with summer, dry leaves curled

Yet yielding the warm savour of the sap . . .
Our sweat ran down in rivulets: but she
Was reptile-cool, inert, as if to trap

Us in some crime she waited watchfully.
But the thought was ludicrous – a worldly gust
That breathed new life into the Comedy –

And I turned to Paavo, grinning as he thrust
His head till it jutted from one bony knee
Like a dripping gargoyle: 'Come, I faint with thirst.

'A traveller on the brink of a deep well.
'My mind is dry and you have tales to tell.'

James Bramwell (1949)

**The restauration; or, a Poem on the return of the most
mighty and ever glorious prince.**

Come then, prepare, prepare for him,
Teach <u>Wichwood</u> Forest how to swim,
The main with canvass periwigg,
Navies of <u>Bucentoro's</u> rigg;
So we shall have a seemly fleet,
A King, a King, a King to meet;

<u>Tritons</u> dance, <u>and Mare-maids</u> sing,
Out of the sea some <u>Venus</u> spring,
And with <u>Cupids</u> trim the boat
In which Great <u>CHARLES</u> himself's afloat;
May we no storms, no tempests have,
No dancing of the air or wave,
No <u>Lapp-land</u> puffs, no <u>Finland</u> weather,
Sent by incarnate Furies hither,
Rather may milder blasts prevail,
And fill the proudly swelling sail.

Arthur Brett (1660)

Finnish

Since you will never master
the details of our tongue – our nouns
encased in place like a twig in ice,
our vowels which well and double
like water under snow, our precise,
declining 'no's – we have
grasped instead your language,
so hard in our white Finnish fists
that when we speak, you laugh.
Listen, Stranger. Our trochees
do not limp. They are the

skis of Lalli chasing Bishop Henry
on the ice, the back-beat
to his muttered litanies, the echo
of his breath. The sky was tight
that night, as a bowl
on the plate of the lake. The Bishop
clasped his Latin texts. Lalli
gripped his axe. Henry had sat,

unbid, by his fire in his elbow chair.
He had patronised his wife.

Kate Clanchy (1999)

Dumping the Christmas Tree

takes both of us, it transpires,
reeling to the park with our irregular
burden, strewing dead spines
like smoke from a censer. Afterwards,
wordless, we bash each other clear
of the needles and tinsel, Punch
and Judy in the freezing air.

What do they know of marriage –
these passers-by staring, these
thin joggers crunching hollow
ice in the puddles? You and I,
we have lived in Helsinki,
we have walked over
the dark rime of the sea.

Kate Clanchy (2004)

To William Godwin, Author of 'Political Justice'

O! form'd t' illume a sunless world forlorn,
As o'er the chill and dusky brow of Night,
In Finland's wintry skies, the Mimic Morn
Electric pours a stream of rosy light,
Pleas'd I have mark'd OPPRESSION, terror-pale,
Since, thro' the windings of her dark machine,
Thy steady eye has shot its glances keen—

Samuel Taylor Coleridge (1795)

The Drunks of Helsinki

Blue sky, a lurching tram makes
headway through the small city.
The quiet company sits shyly,
avoiding its image, else talks

with securing friends. This
passage is through life as if
in dream. We know our routes
and mean to get there. Now

the foetid stink of human excess,
plaintive, and the person beside us
lurches, yet stays stolidly there.
What are the signals? Despair,

loss of determinants – or a world
just out of a bottle? Day
after day they clutter the tram
stops, fall sodden over seats

and take their drunken ease in
the fragile world. I think
they are the poets, the maledictive,
muttering words, fingers pointing,

pointing, jabbed outright across
aisle to blank side of bank or
the company's skittish presence.
I saw a man keep slamming the post

with his fist, solid in impact,
measured blows. His semblable sat
slumped in front of me, a single seat.
They meet across the aisle in ranting voices,

each talking alone. In a place of
so few words, sparely chosen, their

panegyric slabbering whine has human
if unexpected resonance. They

speak for us, their careful friends , the sober
who scuttle from side to side in vacantly
complex isolation, in a company has compact
consensus, minds empty of all conclusion.

Robert Creeley (1995)

[Winter Solstice]

These are the days that Reindeer love
And pranks the Northern star—
This is the Sun's objective,
And Finland of the Year.

Emily Dickinson (poem no. 1696)

In a Wood near Turku

The summer cabins are padlocked.
Their smell of sandshoes
evaporates over the lake water
leaving pine walls to shoulder the ice.

Resin seals them in hard splashes.
The woodman
knocks at their sapless branches.

He gets sweet puffballs
and chanterelles in his jacket,
strips off fungus like yellow leather,
thumbs it, then hacks the tree stump.

Hazy and cold as summer dawn
the day goes on,

wood rustles on wood,
close, as the mist thins
like smoke around the top of the pine trees
and once more the saw whines.

Helen Dunmore (1983)

Ahvenanmaa

Breast to breast against the azaleas
they pitch, father and daughter,

the sun throws itself down
golden, glittering,

pale orange petals clutter their hair
as he catches her shoulders,

braced, they grapple and bruise
among the perfumed azaleas.

The flowers loll out their tongues,
tigers on dark stems

while breast to breast against the azaleas
they pitch, father and daughter.

The ferry slides between islands.
Pale and immediate, the sun rises.

The hull noses white marker-posts
glittering in summer water –

here, now, the channel deepens,
the sky darkens. Too cold in her dress

the girl scutters. Engine vents veil
steam while rain hides Ahvenanmaa.

Helen Dunmore (1992)

Finland

Feet and faces tingle
In that frore land:
Legs wobble and go wingle,
You scarce can stand.

The skies are jewelled all around,
The ploughshare snaps in the iron ground,
The Finn with face like paper
And eyes like a lighted taper
Hurls his rough rune
At the wintry moon
And stamps to mark the tune.

Robert Graves (1918)

Sibelius

It's January. A swan's wing overhead
reminds you of his Fifth
but also of his death, that skein
breaking away to circle him
as if to announce what year it was.

At this age, every instinct shouts
behind you – as it did at the panto
for the ghost – and there's an old man
at a lake still counting wild birds
who hasn't even noticed the time.

January is Janus's month. We should look
both ways. The geese have put their diversion
signs in the sky, but the sun holds up
its lollipop as if a young hero might
cross, find an egg, tie a knot in it.

John Greening (2019)

According to Pritt

(Brief review of a recent book by Mr, D. N. Pritt, K. C., M.P.,
in which Russia's action in Finland is defended)

THE FINNS dislike their Government, by which they are
    oppressed,
And but for British cunning they would like the Russians
    best;
The Russians, on the other hand, have very tender skins,
And greatly feared invasion by the brutal little Finns.

So it was right and proper for the Russians to attack,
And it was very naughty of the Finns to answer back;
The country most responsible, as usual, is Brit.;
And every one is upside down excepting Comrade Pritt.

A. P. Herbert (February 18,1940)

Precambrian Rock

I travelled a long way to Finland,
not really under my own volition.
It's a morose landscape that smiles in summer
and it's friendly to melancholy people, by not
being cheerful, only beautiful.
In winter the Victorian statues turn
abstract with snow, and it's as if
your past doesn't exist. In summer
the light flitters all night long
and changes every second and you realise
this selection of weather's the solution
of all the planet's history of climate
since the beginning, and so are you.
At times you're bigger than the stars,
and then you know you're
a member of the universe like that ant

and not responsible for yourself.
As you watch the high clouds changing
in the lake while you crouch there shaving,
you know you're just what you are,
and then it's gone, you're someone else.

Herbert Lomas (1955)

Kippis

Of all things in this pothouse of a place,
It's this that's simplest. Not as if
We're told to do it. Things just happen.

I can't speak your language. Its bevelled
Vowels, its clicktrack of *Ks* send me
Reaching for my pint. You try your English,

Strictly pidgin, and twist your lips around
What's more or less my name. I venture
Snow, rallying, lakes, reindeer. You nod

Politely and take another cigarette, not
Needing to ask this time. We hit upon
A Swedish film we've both seen, we order

Two more beers. I say cheers. You say kippis.
You say cheers. I say kippis. Simple.
In a week's time, we'll meet again. I'll walk

You to the corner when we're good and drunk,
We'll talk a while and laugh a little,
Then you won't see me again. It's that simple.

Roddy Lumsden (1993)

The Café Kafka, Helsinki

A curving corridor
of vanilla pillars
and pistachio plasterwork.
It's an edible café,
the Café Kafka.

Lampglobes bulge
and overflow
with splashing light.
Even the draughts which flow
along the diamond-patterned floor
are warm in the Café Kafka.

Outside the Café Kafka
the third snow of winter 1992
is slinking through Helsinki
and my charcoal fedora sits proudly
on the black marble table-top.

Only six hours ago,
when I met her
in her magical studio,
her first words were:
'What a beautiful hat!'
Who said that about my hat?
The mother of the Moomins,
Tove Jansson.

Adrian Mitchell (1992)

'Finish Off with Finland'

Helsinki Statue Notes

Cloudberry-juiced to The Senate Square
Poets and Czars were everywhere
Amanda sat among four barking seals
I hope she's not as cold as she feels.

Adrian Mitchell (1992)

Ice Maiden

I walk in my night-dress and slippers
along winter beaches in Finland.
My earrings of polished tin
flash at the Northern Lights.
I shovel up the sea.

But the cold is quick. Quick
as I crack open the rock
of the ocean with my axe,
it freezes behind me.
My task is endless.

Dorothy Molloy (?2004)

On Time: a Reconstruction

I don't know about the snail, it's ok I think,
I don't envy it though. How could I,
having been to Lapland and back in a day,
stamping snowboots on Concorde steps
at tingling Rovanieni with a New Year pack
of reindeer slices in my hand and
five hours of frozen river and pine
inside me, long or short
impossible to say.

Edwin Morgan (1990)

from **The Inquisitor**

1. The Task

What trust would be like they never explained.
The eye of a deer miles away in woodland,
Children running at the edge of a town . . .
But this was not their way of talking.
In a panelled room in an annexe
To the ministry they laid down all the terms.
Knowledge is death. Trust no one, least of all
Friends. Loyalty? There are some secrets here
So terrible we keep them from ourselves.

So they gave you Finland, which was OK
At first but then it got boring. Contacts were scarce
– They had tightened the borders and the Gulf –
One sad Estonian, straight from Le Carré,
Who shared with you ham omelettes, beer and *frites*,
You worked from home, mostly, the cottage
By the kalefields. Rachel, you were sure,
Was having her first affair and you'd return
From Helsinki unannounced, hoping to surprise her.

Blake Morrison (1984)

from **The Seasons: 'Winter'**

Wide o'er the spacious regions of the north,
That see Boötes urge his tardy wain,
A boisterous race, by frosty Caurus pierced,
Who little pleasure know and fear no pain,
Prolific swarm. They once relumed the flame
Of lost mankind in polish'd slavery sunk,
Drove martial horde on horde, with dreadful sweep
Resistless rushing o'er th'enfeebled south,
And gave the vanquish'd world another form.

Not such the sons of Lapland: wisely they
Despise th'insensate barbarous trade of war;
They ask no more than simple Nature gives,
They love their mountains, and enjoy their storms.
No false desires, no pride-created wants,
Disturb the peaceful current of their time;
And through the restless ever tortured maze
Of pleasure, or ambition, bid it rage.
Their reindeer form their riches. These their tents,
Their robes, their beds, and all their homely wealth
Supply, their wholesome fare and cheerful cups.
Obsequious at their call, the docile tribe
Yield to the sled their necks, and whirl them swift
O'er hill and dale, heap'd into one expanse
Of marbled snow, as far as eye can sweep,
With a blue crust of ice unbounded glazed.
By dancing meteors then, that ceaseless shake
A waving blaze refracted o'er the heavens,
And vivid moons, and stars that keener play
With doubled lustre from the glossy waste,
E'en in the depth of polar night they find
A wondrous day: enough to light the chase,
Or guide their daring steps to Finland fairs.
Wish'd Spring returns; and from the hazy south,
While dim Aurora slowly moves before,
The welcome Sun, just verging up at first,
By small degrees, extends the swelling curve!
Till seen at last for gay rejoicing months,
Still round and round, his spiral course he winds,
And as he nearly dips his flaming orb,
Wheels up again, and reascends the sky.
In that glad season, from the lakes and floods,
Where pure Niemi's fairy mountains rise,
And fringed with roses Tenglio rolls his stream,
They draw the copious fry. With these, at eve,

They cheerful loaded to their tents repair,
Where, all day long in useful cares employ'd,
Their kind unblemish'd wives the fire prepare.
Thrice happy race! by poverty secured
From legal plunder and rapacious power:
In whom fell interest never yet has sown
The seeds of vice: whose spotless swains ne'er knew
Injurious deed, nor, blasted by the breath
Of faithless love, their blooming daughter's woe.

James Thomson (1730)

Finland in Winter
The market square in Turku

There is some wisdom here if I could find it –
This market square at four o'clock, the gloaming
Almost a name for night, the final women
Loading the carts with failure for their homing,
The even quietude of Finnish voices,
The blackened forms folded into December,
The corner stand with fiery ranks of flowers –
Three for my hostess, good that I remember –

The wisdom is not here for casual asking,
That much I know, and wisdom of a kind.
The answer is as slow as Finnish granite,
As vocal to the feet as to the mind.
And by the frozen lakes the smoke of saunas
Confers another darkness on the land.
Perhaps, not surely, there I understand.

Chad Walsh (1969)

from **Nuhala**

It seemed the right bend in the dark road. 'Nuhjala?'
I said to the driver; he slowed to a stop.
We clumsily tumbled from the bus, surveyed
By the passive and neutral eyes of the Finns.
To the left, a thin lane; we hoped for the best.
Crossing the highway, we stood at the lane's mouth
In the dark night of Finland asleep
And empty. The sleigh was not there. Always before
It had been day, a horse and sleigh, the old servant and the dog.

The bus hovered like a ship reluctant to leave
Ignorant missionaries on an unmapped island.
A flashlight cut the night. The driver crossed,
Took my arm, pointed up the lane. 'Nuhjala,'
He said, almost as I had said it. 'Kiitos,'
I said, remembering my phrase book. 'Näkemiin,'
He replied; the word hovered like a blessing
Or Eliot's shantih, shantih, shantih. The bus left.
We started up the lane, and after fifty dark yards
The fast complin of sleighbells came racing to meet us.

. . . Next morning we awoke. The porcelain stove
Still radiated its mild benediction in one corner
Of our attic bedroom. From the window
The double line of bewitched trees
Lifted prismatic arms of embroidered ice
Up to the rising sun, on to the frozen sea of crystal.

Chad Walsh (1969)

from In Remembrance of Joseph Sturge

From the locked roadsteads of the Bothniaii peasants,
And harbors of the Finn,
Where war's worn victims saw his gentle presence
Come sailing, Christ-like, in,

To seek the lost, to build the old waste places,
To link the hostile shores
Of severing seas, and sow with England's daisies
The moss of Finland's moors.

John Greenleaf Whittier (1859)

Desire

Arching perfectly-plucked eyebrows
over blue eggshell eyes
she tells me it is possible in her country
to go all the way
from Viipuri on the Gulf of Finland
to Jisalmi, far inland,
on little steamers
which thread through channels in the rocks
and forested islands.
Moving her hand through the air
she describes how certain rivers and lakes
cascade into other lakes
in magnificent waterfalls
which provide all the electricity for Finland.

Hugo Williams (1990)

'Finish Off with Finland'

The Time for Praise is Later

The time for praise is later – and for tears.
There will be room enough for these hereafter,
When in the land of trees and lakes none hears
The bomb's high chuckle and the shell's shrill laughter.

But now the armies, wave on rearing wave,
Beat as in tempest a remorseless tide,
And there's no foot of all they fought to save
But is a landmark where some Finn has died.

This is a saga of the North. Let be your idle eulogy and dim
    applause.
Death they can face, but not the charity of those with only
    words to save the cause,
Which should, in freedom's name, have loosed the blade
Of instant action in the last Crusade.

Humbert Wolfe (1940)

BOOKS ETC. CITED

Adams, Byron, in *Sibelius and his World.* 2011.

Acerbi, Giuseppe. *Travels through Sweden, Finland, and Lapland, to the North Cape, in the Years 1798 and 1799.* 1802.

Agar, Augustus, *Baltic Episode: A Classic of Secret Service in Russian Waters.* 1963.

Alexander, Capt. James Edward, *Travels to the Seat of the War*. . . Vol. II. 1830.

Ashcroft, Diana, *Journey to Finland.* 1952.

Atchley, T. W., *Finland.* 1931.

Bacon, Walter, *Highway to the Wilderness.* 1961.

Bayley, Francis, 'The Travel Diary of Francis Bayley, 1823–1824'. Bodleian Library ms.

Bell, Henry McGrady, *Land of Lakes: Memories keep me Company.* 1950.

Benn, Melissa, *The Guardian.* 24 August 2018.

Borenius, Tancred, *Field-Marshal Mannerheim.* 1940.

Borrow, George. *TARGUM. Or Metrical Translations From Thirty Languages And Dialects.* 1835.

Bosley, Keith. *The Kalevala. Translated with an Introduction from the Finnish.* 1989.

Bowring, John, *Minor Morals for Young People.* 1834.

— *Autobiographical Recollections* . . . 1877.

Brooke, A. de Capell, *Travels* . . . *to the North Cape in the Summer of 1820.* 1823.

Buckley V. C., *Happy Countries.* 1939.

Bullock, Philip Ross (edited & translated), *The Correspondence of Jean Sibelius & Rosa Newmarch, 1906-1939.* 2011.

— in Grimley, *op.cit.*

Carr, John, *A Northern Summer; or Travels through the Baltic* . . . Glasgow. 1806.

Citrine, Sir Walter, *My Finnish Diary.* 1940.

Clark, Sydney A., *Finland on Ten Pounds.* 1938.

Clarke, Edward Daniel, *Travels in Various Countries of Europe, Asia and Africa.* Part III. 1824.

Clements, Jonathan, *Mannerheim. President, Soldier, Spy.* 2009.

Clive-Bayley, A. M., *Vignettes from Finland, or Twelve Months in Strawberry Land.* 1895.

Coxe, William, *Travels in Poland, Russia, Sweden and Denmark*. Fifth Edition, 1802. Vol. IV.

Coxwell, Charles Fillingham, *Through Russia in War-Time*. 1917.

Daintree, Adrian, *I must say*. 1963.

De Windt, Harry. *Finland as It Is*. 1901.

Donner, Patrick. *Crusade: a Life against the Calamitous Twentieth Century*. 1984.

Dorling, Danny and Koljonen, Annika, *Finntopia. What we can learn from the World's happiest Country*. 2020.

Dukes, Paul, *Red Dusk and the Morrow*. 1922

Elliot, Charles Boileau, *Letters from the North of Europe* . . . 1832.

Evans, Arthur J., Journal. ms in the Ashmolean Museum, Oxford.

Evans, Richard J., *The Hitler Conspiracies*. 2020.

Eivind, R., *Finnish Legends for English Children*. 1893.

Fields Marek. *Reinforcing Finland's Attachment to the West*. 2015.

Flieger, Verlyn, *J.R.R.Tolkien, The Story of Kullervo*. 2015.

Fox, Frank, *Finland Today*. 1926.

Franck, Harry A., *A Scandinavian Summer*. 1930.

Frankland, Captain C. Colville, *Narrative of a Visit to the Courts of of Russia and Sweden, in the Years 1830 and 1832*. 1832.

Fry, Helen, *Music & Men: the Life and Loves of Harriet Cohen*. 2008.

Garth, John. Article in *Tolkein Studies XI*. 2004

Gray, Cecil, *A Survey of Contemporary Music*. 1927.

— *Musical Chairs, or, Between two Stools*. 1985.

Gilmour, Kay. *Finland*. 1931.

Green, George, *An Original Journal from London to St. Petersburgh, by Way of Sweden*. 1813.

Greening, John. *The Silence*. 2019.

Grellet, Stephen, *Memoirs*. ed. Benjamin Seebohm. 1860.

Grimley, Daniel M.(ed.). *Jean Sibelius and His World*. 2011.

Gripenberg, Michael, Diary, National Archives, Helsinki.

Grundy, J. B. C., *Life's Five Windows*. 1968.

Hall, Wendy. *The Finns and their Country*. 1967.

Harper-Scott, J. P. E., *The Quilting Points of Musical Modernism*. 1977

Harris, John, *Rudolf Hess: The British Conspiracy*. 1999.

Haynes, E.S.P., *The Lawyer*. 1951.

Henningsen, Charles Frederick. *Eastern Europe and the Emperor Nicholas*. 1846.

Hirn, Yrjö, *Lärt Folk och Landstrykare in det Finska Finlands Kulturliv*. 1939.

Hyne, C. J. Cutcliffe, *Through Arctic Lapland*. 1898.

Ingram, Jim, *I Found Adventure*. 1951.

James, John Thomas, *Journal of a Tour in Germany, Sweden, Russia, Poland during the Years 1813 and 1814*. Vol.1. 1816.

Jones, George Matthew, RN, *Travels in Norway, Finland, Russia and Turkey*. Vol. 1. 1827.

Jägerskiöld. Stig. *Gustaf Mannerheim*, (multi-volume biography).

Kirby, D. G., *Finland in the Twentieth Century*. 1979.

Lambert, Constant, *Music ho! A Study of Music in Decline*. 1934.

Lang, Andrew, *Custom and Myth*. 1884.

Langdon, David, AD Classics: Viipuri Library / Alvar Aalto (online).

Lindman-Strafford, Kerstin, *Tancred Borenius – europé och viborgare*. 1976.

Lindfors, Joanna M., 'Tancred Borenius – our Man in Finland'. *The Shaping of Art History in Finland*. ?2009.

Lurcock, Tony, *Not so Barren or Uncultivated: British travellers in Finland 1760–1830*. 2010.

— *No Particular Hurry: British travellers in Finland 1830–1917*. 2013.

— *A Life of Extremes: The British discover modern Finland 1917–1941*. 2015.

Malleson, Constance, *In the North . . . 1936–1946*. 1946.

MacCarthy, Fiona, *The Guardian*, 17 March 2007.

Macintyre, Ben, *The Spy and the Traitor*. 2018.

Mannerheim, Gustaf, *The Memoirs of Marshal Mannerheim*. 1953.

McDougall, Sylvia, as 'Paul Waineman', *A Summer Tour in Finland*. 1908.

— *Let's Light the Candles*. Memoirs. 1944.

Mead, W. R., *The Anglo-Finnish Society 1911 –2011*. 2011.

— 'Anglo-Finnish Relations'. *The Norseman* VI, 6. 1948.

Milner, Thomas, *The Baltic, its Gates, Shores, and Cities*. 1854.

Nevinson, H. W., *Fire of Life*. [1935].

Newman, Bernard, *Baltic Roundabout*. 1939.

Newmarch, Rosa, *Jean Sibelius: a Finnish Composer*. 1906.

— *Jean Sibelius*. 1944.

North, F. J., *Finland in Summer*. 1938.

Paul, Rev. Robert Bateman, *Journal of a Tour to Moscow in the Summer of 1836*. 1836.

Pinkerton, Robert, *Russia: or Miscellaneous Observations . . .* 1833.

Porter, Robert Ker, *Travelling Sketches in Russia and Sweden in the Years 1805, 1806, 1807, 1808*. Vol. 2. 1813.

Rae, Edward, *Land of the North Wind*. 1875.

Ransome, Arthur, *Six Weeks in Russia in 1919*. 1919

Renwick, George, *Finland Today*. 1911.

Richards, J. M., *Memoirs of an Unjust Fella*. 1980.

Rothenstein, John, *Summer's Lease: Autobiography, 1901–1938*. 1965.

Rothery, Agnes, *Finland, the New Nation*. 1936.

Sahlberg, Pasi, *Finnish Lessons*. 2011

Sansom, William, *The Icicle and the Sun*. 1958.

Scott, Richenda C., *Quakers in Russia*. [1964].

Screen, J. E. O., *Mannerheim: the Finnish Years*. 2000.

Shearman, Hugh, *Finland. The Adventures of a Small Power*. 1950.

Stevens, Lewis, *An Unforgettable Woman: The Life and Times of Rosa Newmarch*. 2011.

Sutherland, Halliday, *Lapland Journey*. 1938.

Sulivan, Bartholomew. (Henry Norton (ed.). *Life and Letters of the late Admiral Sir James Bartholomew Sulivan*. 1896.

Sykes, John, *Direction North: a View of Finland*. 1968.

Tallack, Malachy, *Sixty Degrees North*. 2015,

Tawaststjerna Erik, *Sibelius*, edited and translated by Robert Layton. 2008.

Travers, Rosalind, *Letters from Finland August, 1908 – March 1909*. 1911.

Tweedie, Mrs. Alec, *Through Finland in Carts*. 1897.

Warner, Oliver, *Marshal Mannerheim and the Finns*. 1967.

Webster, Diana, *Finland Forever*. 2013.

Whitehorn, Katherine, *Selective Memory*. 2007.

Wilson, John Dover, *Milestones on the Dover Road*. 1969.

Wilson, William Rae, *Travels in Russia*. 1828.

Wraxall, Sir Nathaniel Willliam, Bart., *Cursory Remarks made on a Tour through some of the Northern Parts of Europe . . .* 1775.

Whatley, Thomas Denman, *Murray's Handbook for Travellers in Denmark, Sweden, Norway and Russia*. 1839.

Wood, Sir Henry, *My Life of Music*. 1938.

Wraxall, Sir William Nathaniel William, Bart., *A Tour round the Baltic . . .* Fourth Edition, 1807.

Young, Ernest, *Finland: Land of a Thousand Lakes*. 1912.